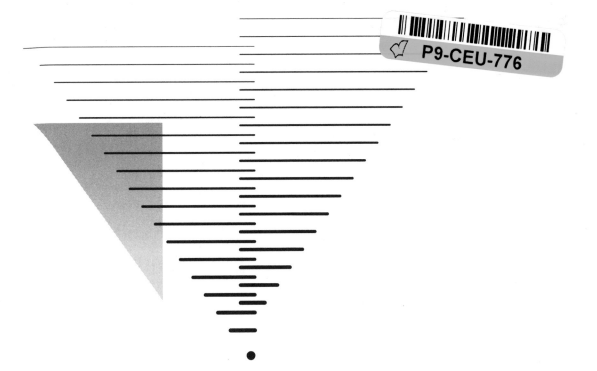

P9-CEU-776

Intranet Document Management

A Guide for Webmasters and Content Providers

Joan Bannan

Addison-Wesley Developers Press
An Imprint of Addison Wesley Longman, Inc.

Reading, Massachusetts • Harlow, England • Menlo Park, California
Berkeley, California • Don Mills, Ontario • Sydney
Bonn • Amsterdam • Tokyo • Mexico City

Many of the designations used by manufacturers and sellers to distinguish their products are claimed as trademarks. Where those designations appear in this book, and Addison-Wesley was aware of a trademark claim, the designations have been printed in initial capital letters or all capital letters.

The author and publisher have taken care in preparation of this book, but make no expressed or implied warranty of any kind and assume no responsibility for errors or omissions. No liability is assumed for incidental or consequential damages in connection with or arising out of the use of the information or programs contained herein.

Screenshot number two on the cover was provided by Netscape Communications Corporation. Netscape has not authorized, sponsored, endorsed, or approved this publication and is not responsible for its content. Netscape and the Netscape Communications Corporate Logos are trademarks and trade names of Netscape Communications Corporation. All other product names and/or logos are trademarks of their respective owners. Copyright 1996 Netscape Communication Corp. Used with permission. All Rights Reserved.

Screenshot number three on the cover was provided by INTRANET Technologies. Copyright © 1997 by INTRANET Technologies. INTRANET Technologies can be found at http://home.intranet.ca/

Screenshot number four on the cover was provided by Hummingbird Communications Limited. Copyright © 1997 by Hummingbird Communications Limited. Hummingbird Communications can be found at http://www.hummingbird.com/

Library of Congress Cataloging-in-Publication Data

Bannan, Joan.
    Intranet document management / Joan Bannan.
        p. cm.
    Includes index.
    ISBN 0-201-87379-6
      1. Intranets (Computer networks)—Management.   2. Web sites—
Management.   3. Records—Management—Data processing.
    4. Information storage and retrieval systems.   I.   Title.
    TK5105.875.I6B36   1997
    651.7'9—dc21   96-53496
                                                             CIP

Copyright © 1997 by Joan Bannan
A-W Developers Press is a division of Addison Wesley Longman, Inc.

All rights reserved. No part of this publication may be reproduced, stored in a retrieval system, or transmitted, in any form or by any means, electronic, mechanical, photocopying, recording, or otherwise, without the prior written permission of the publisher. Printed in the United States of America. Published simultaneously in Canada.

Sponsoring Editor: Kathleen Tibbetts
Project Manager: John Fuller
Production Coordinator: Melissa Lima
Cover design: Dietz Design
Text design: David Kelley Design
Set in 11-point Minion by NK Graphics

1 2 3 4 5 6 7 8 9 -MA- 01 00 99 98 97
First printing, March 1997

Addison-Wesley books are available for bulk purchases by corporations, institutions, and other organizations. For more information please contact the Corporate, Government, and Special Sales Department at (800) 238-9682.

Find A-W Developers Press on the World Wide Web at:
http://www.aw.com/devpress/

To David Robert Lewis,

My Mentor, Inspiration,
and Friend

About the Author

Joan Bannan is a writer, Web developer and conference speaker who lives in a towering grove of Redwood trees in the mountains above Silicon Valley. As the Assistant Webmaster for Pacific Telesis Shared Services Web Services, she manages documents for the PTSS Intranet, Internet, and Extranet. She is a member of the Northern California SGML Users Group.

Her previous books include *PERFECT GIFTS for (nearly) PERFECT MEN, Teach yourself . . . Word 6 for DOS*, and *Excel 5.0 Slick Tricks*. She has also written numerous in-house technical manuals for major corporations.

When Joan is not writing, orchestrating Web navigation, or coding HTML she loves to travel and, like many others, loves to take walks on the beach. She spends most of her free time, however, with her kindergartener son Peter, or with her three grown children and five grandchildren.

Each time she signs a contract for a technical book, she says that it's the last and that her next book will be a novel.

She would love to hear from you at her web site http://www.bannan.com.

Contents

Acknowledgments

I did not write this book by myself. Each of the people in this list deserves credit and has my gratitude:

Dave Lewis, Pacific Telesis Webmaster
Kim Fryer, editor, now at Microsoft Press
Mark Brotherton, chief geek at Logic by Design, Walnut
    Creek, California
Michael Peterson
Pamela Ganzberger
Chris Reavis, Silicon Graphics Computer Systems
Ann K. Smith
Michael Leventhal, founder, Text Science, Inc.
Mark Richardson
Robert Silverberg
Lora Banks

I also would especially like to thank my Addison-Wesley editor, *Kathleen Tibbitts,* her assistant, *Elizabeth Spainhour,* and the wonderful Addison-Wesley production staff.

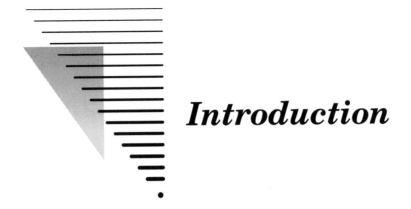

Introduction

What You Can Do with This Book

This book is like the friend who helped you set up your first computer. He or she did not hold your hand each step of the way but she (this time, I promise to use *he* next time) got you started. She set you in the right direction, familiarized you with the environment, gave you places to go for information, and offered candid advice about products and applications. She probably didn't know everything, but she took you where you needed to go to accomplish the task at hand. You probably found after a while that you could teach her a few things you learned after your skills increased. If you find that you have knowledge about Intranet Document Management surpassing what is contained in this book, and you would like to contribute to the next edition, please contact me at joan@bannan.com.

I have been "crash coursing" in Internet technology for the last couple of years. Because the pace of growth in this field is so accelerated, making total mastery difficult, I focused my energy in one area of expertise rather than on all Internet technology. In order to excel as a Web site manager, I focus on document management. I team with others who focus on the server/programming side of running a Web site, and I count on them to be expert geeks. They count on me to write well, program HTML well, orchestrate the presentation of documents on the Internal Web for greatest relevance and usability, and consider users' and contributors' needs.

Who This Book Is For

If you are a Web site manager or author, this book is for you. It is about the documents, resources, applications, and databases that run on servers and networks. If you will entertain this metaphor, Document Management is the rider and the Intranet is the horse. Or to be more contemporary, let's call it a Ferrari.

Resource List

If you want to set up server hardware and software or networks, this is not your book. But here are some resources to complement this book (I'm sure there are many more):

- Your server and server software vendors are probably the best source of help in this area. See Table I.1 for a short list of well-known vendors.

URL	What You Will Find There
http://www.sun.com/	Sun hardware
http://www.sgi.com/	SGI hardware
http://www.hp.com/	HP hardware
http://www.ncsa.uiuc.edu/SDG/SDGFlier/ SDGHowToObtain.html	NCSA software
http://home.netscape.com/	Netscape software
http://www.apache.org/	Apache software

Table I.1
Server Hardware and Software Vendors

- *Web Weaving* by Tilton, Steadman, and Jones; published by Addison Wesley Longman, Inc.
- *Running a Perfect Web Site* by Chandler; published by Que

What You Will Find in This Book

Definition of an Intranet and why you may want to invest in Intranet document management.	*Chapter 1, "Why Use an Intranet for Business Communications?"*
An overview of the Intranet document management security measures you need to consider.	*Chapter 2, "Intranet Security"*
An overview of Intranet basic messaging requirements.	*Chapter 3, "Basic Messaging Requirements"*
Some vital information about using e-mail to manage the bulk of unformatted documents on your Intranet including some information about attachments, distribution lists, setting up workflow, and threaded discussions on public forums.	*Chapter 4, "E-mail, Workflow, and Online Meetings"*
Discussion of • Web authoring, including preparing HTML files, text files, and alternative viewing possibilities. • Authoring tools (such as HTML editors), conversion utilities, and testing your HTML code. • Legacy document considerations including a discussion of styles.	*Chapter 5, "Authoring Intranet Documents"*
Help in designing and managing a Web site: understanding your user audience; creating predictable paths; uploading files to your Web servers; creating home pages, what's new pages, and symbolic links; managing changes in Web site design; and creating a strategy for managing user help.	*Chapter 6, "Effective Web Design" and Chapter 7, "Web Site Management"*
How to incorporate scripts and databases into your Intranet using CGI variables, HTML forms, appropriate development languages, and how to build advanced Web applications.	*Chapter 8, "Using Scripts and Databases"*

How to use online document management retention to improve how information is shared throughout your Intranet, collaborate better by reusing existing work, and improve your systems for creating and maintaining documents.	*Chapter 9, "Managing Large Collections of Documents"*
How to manage documents too large to download to client workstations using SGML to create self-describing documents.	*Chapter 10, "Managing Large Documents"*
How to control the inevitable evolution of your Intranet using information modeling, deconstructing your environment, managing personnel and services, and keeping an eye on the future.	*Chapter 11, "Controlling the Chaos"*

Some Conventions Used in This Book

I often call the World Wide Web, "the Web" with an uppercase *W*. I use a few other capitals that you might not find in the dictionary—"Intranet," "Intranet Document Management," "Document Management Systems," and "Internal Web"—I like the emphasis. I tried to switch back and forth between using "he" and "she" without counting. I hope I didn't use one more than the other. I call it "e-mail" with a hyphen though I'm sure it's just as proper without. Other than that, I also use a lot of slang words, like "geek," which is a name I reserve for the most intelligent, capable, resourceful, honored computer engineers and technicians. I use other slang words as well that you will not find in the dictionary. If you can't figure out what they mean, please e-mail me at joan@bannan.com. I would love to hear from you.

1 Why Use an Intranet for Business Communications?

What You Can Do

You can use an Intranet as an effective, economical infrastructure for business communication—doing so can revolutionize the way you do business. Most companies are somewhere between where they need to be and where they want to go with online document distribution. It might be easier (but not less expensive) to start from scratch rather than reengineer existing systems and legacy documents to accommodate Intranet technology. This chapter lays the groundwork to help you understand why you may want to reengineer your company's document management to become an interactive Intranet. The goal is to help clarify your vision of what it means to manage documents on an Intranet. With luck, it will also help you share your vision with others in your company.

What You Will Need

There are three principal reasons to put your document management online via an Intranet:

- information transfer
- knowledge transfer
- storage and distribution costs

The savings potential in information and knowledge transfer are possibly immeasurable. Everyone who uses a calculator and is concerned about the bottom line will understand the impact of storage and distribution costs.

1

In addition to understanding these three issues, you'll also want to have a clear definition of an Intranet and Intranet documents.

I know you'd rather start saving money immediately, but we will start with the Intranet definitions.

How to Use an Intranet for Business Communications

What Is an Intranet?

An Intranet is a mini-Internet within your company. It is similar to the Internet because you are all connected by wires and servers to access e-mail, more servers, databases, and software programs. It is different because you can control the environment. On the big "I" everyone has different ways to access the Information Super Highway and different ideas of what should or should not be viewed. On your own personal little "I" you can build a *firewall,* (discussed in Chapter 2), build a homogeneous e-mail system (discussed in Chapter 3), use standard software applications, including a standard Internet browser, and set standards for structure, design, and content of an Internal Web (discussed in Chapters 6 and 7). You can dictate how to manage large collections of documents (discussed in Chapter 9), and you can determine which format you will use to distribute large documents, such as engineering manuals (discussed in Chapter 10).

Definition   Firewalls *are software- and/or hardware-based systems that allow for a high degree of access control and logging of network activity.*

What Are Intranet Documents?

Before you begin revolutionizing, reengineering, and reducing paper in your company, you need to understand what kinds of documents you produce now and how they will travel on the Intranet mini-highway.

There are four components associated with any Intranet document:

- the author's words and use of other symbols such as whitespace and punctuation
- notation applied to the document, which tells a document processing program what to do with that particular document
- a container for packaging the document so that it may be stored, retrieved, and transported
- document processing programs

Three Kinds of Documents

Consider three categories of Intranet documents:

- unformatted
- formatted
- self-describing

Unformatted documents are sort of disposable. Examples are e-mail, bulletin board messages, dated memos, and annotations. They often carry formatted documents as attachments, but by themselves they are simple and readable in almost any program. This simplicity leads to the greatest advantage of unformatted documents: they are highly portable and can be effectively processed by lightweight programs. In fact, usually the only thing that hinders the processing of unformatted documents is when a formatted document is attached, causing the computerized hiccups between programs.

Formatted documents represent the lion's share of Intranet documents. Examples are word processing, desktop publishing, and HTML documents. There is a wide range of formatting requirements for formatted documents, and they are specific to each type of media and application. For example, desktop publishing demands a rich notation to support complex page layout. The downside of this is that desktop publishing

applications are extremely complex, require lots of computer processing power, and have a very high notation to text ratio, resulting in very
large documents (in bytes). Word processing demands less on the
page layout side. Therefore, capabilities are less; the applications are
simpler; the computer resources required are less; and the documents,
although still possessing a high notation to actual text ratio, are
smaller.

Self describing documents have the ability to define the type of notation they will use independent of any processing program that may
be applied to them. Their metamorphic quality can therefore be
processed in many ways including formatting for print on paper or online, and the content becomes a searchable database of information.
For instance, a huge airplane engineering manual may have all chemi-
cal safety warnings tagged in SGML (the subject of Chapter 10).

Intranets are challenging our very notion of what a document is as
we look to the capabilities of the computer and networks to deliver just
the information we need in the particular format that we need it. We
expect to be able to take the same piece of information and print it on
paper, display it online, retrieve it through a search engine, store it in a
database, send it to a colleague working in a completely different kind
of environment, make it interactive, add it to a video presentation, and
so on. Self-describing application-neutral documents are able to be
used and reused with this kind of flexibility. Neither do self-describing
documents become dated as document applications evolve and new
types of applications are added.

Structure can also be used to address problems with network traffic,
that is, by *chunking* information so the server and client are not over-
burdened downloading large documents in which only one small piece
of information is really needed. Both the self-description of self-
describing and the formatting of formatted documents can be used to
determine what sized grain of information to deliver to the user out of
a larger pool of information.

Definition   Chunking *a document means breaking it into smaller documents. This is a bandwidth-friendly way to present information. Usually you can just link each section to the next and
create a hyperlinked table of contents to retain the document's
unity. (Chapters 5 and 10 discuss chunking large documents.)*

Information Transfer

Consider the following scenario: A company has a corporate travel program with discounts at major hotels, two of the major car rental agencies, and of course with the airlines. The one caveat is that the company must use the authorized travel agent. Each employee who travels needs to complete the employee profile form, review travel policies, see which hotels offer prenegotiated preferred rates, fill out a form that details travel preferences for a specific trip, and when the trip is completed, fill out the customer satisfaction survey. The procurement department makes sure that each of its 13,000 management employees gets a new copy of the travel program each year, which entails five or six printed pages that need to be copied, put in envelopes, addressed, and distributed. Quite often throughout the year, there are changes to one or two of the pages. At that time, rather than send out a whole new package, the procurement travel manager sends only a page or two that needs to be copied, put in envelopes, addressed, and distributed. When employees receive their travel program document, they need to file it somewhere where they can find it. When they get the update, they need to file it in the same place. When they want to plan a business trip, they need to first of all remember where they filed the document and then review and compare both documents (possibly more depending upon how many updates have been sent). Next, they need to fill out the employee profile, the travel preferences form, and fax or mail these to the travel agent. There will probably be subsequent phone conversations, which most likely means the employee and the travel agent might also get to play a little phone tag and voice mail transcribing. If you have ever used the Web and e-mail, you know where this is going.

This scenario is fun for me because it's a true story with a happy ending, and I got to be part of it. The transformation of this document when it became a document on the Internal Web not only obviously improved the efficiency of Information Transfer; it also greatly reduced Storage and Distribution costs. The procurement travel manager in this scenario, with the help of a Web site manager, first formatted the word processing version of the document with styles, then converted it to HTML using HTML Transit. It would have converted without the styles, but with them HTML Transit was able to automatically create a hyperlinked table of contents. The advantage of using conversion software in this case is that some people will still need a printed document version of the entire document. When updates are made, they are made to the printed version and then run through the conversion software to update the HTML version. For more about converting printed documents to HTML, see Chapter 5. The corporate travel document is now stored on the Internal Web. No one needs to copy it, put it in an envelope, address it, manually distribute it, or file it. Employees know where to find it, and they know it's the latest version. When they want to make travel arrangements, they fill out the forms on the Web and e-mail them to the travel agent. The travel agent e-mails back information that the employee can print out rather than transcribe. An added advantage of bypassing the transcription is that when the travel arrangement details arrive in the e-mail message, the employee does not have to take a lot of time with it, other than briefly check it over for accuracy—unlike a voice mail message, which he must listen to in its entirety to see if some detail needs immediate attention. If an employee would like to have a printed copy of all or part of the corporate travel plan document, he can print out part from the Web or access a link to a word processing version. When the tired traveler returns, he can find the customer satisfaction survey on the Web the next day and click to send it off to the procurement travel manager. I don't need to tell you how this revolutionizes corporate productivity and efficiency.

Definition   WWW (World Wide Web).

Supercharging the Sales Force

This same transformation of Intranet document distribution can supercharge your sales force in two ways: (1) offer easy access to up-to-date information about your company, personnel, and products; and (2) leverage WWW information to keep apprised of competitor information. Consider another scenario: A sales manager needs to make a presentation to a customer in a few hours, and she is mostly prepared, but three things have changed in the last day:

1. Her staff. A new representative was hired for this customer's region.

2. Her main product line released a new product yesterday that was beta tested for the last few months.

3. She just heard something on the radio about her competitor (who she's sure is making a presentation to the same customer in the next few days), but she didn't exactly catch all of the news flash.

With a competently constructed and managed Intranet, this manager uses the next hour to

1. Open her Internet browser and click on "Employee Personal Home Pages" to pull up the bio on her new representative. Next she pulls up the pages for the other two reps in that district just to familiarize herself with their backgrounds. She finds out that one of them, David, has just won a community service award. Good stuff to share. She quickly switches to her e-mail program and takes a few minutes to send off a note of congratulations to David.

2. She switches back to her Internet browser, clicks on "Home" and "Important Announcements." She finds the announcement about the new product and reads a full description of all features. She decides to read it again in her cab on the way to the meeting and selects "Print." She then clicks on the product information forecast page and checks all the updated information about the other products she wants to tout to this customer. Hmmm. This product of ours is outselling that competitor's version three to one, according to the latest database information that updated this page last night (more on this in Chapter 8).

3. Oh yeah, what is going on over at ole Mynemesis, Inc., anyway? She clicks on the "Internet Search" button and types in "mynemesis," and then reads the latest press release off their home page.

4. One more thing. She clicks on her bookmark for the "Infoseek" Internet search engine. (She completed a personal profile page with them a while back which helps them filter information specific to her interests.) She wants to see what has been automatically updated from the WWW overnight. She wants to make sure she knows what all her competitors are up to this morning, not just Mynemesis, and she wants to see if anything new has popped up regarding a possible merger of her two biggest suppliers.

In this scenario, you can see that your competitors and customers who use Intranet technology can be more informed than your sales force if you are not equipped with equivalent tools.

Knowledge Transfer

Here is another example that has apparent information transfer ramifications and focuses on another important aspect of business communication. Mike, a valued employee who started out in the mail room in 1966, is about to retire after thirty years of service. Nobody knows how much he knows. Even he doesn't know how much he knows. And where are all the files, programs, drawings, and spreadsheets he has created or edited in the last two years? Well, some of them are on his hard disk at work. Some of them are on his hard disk at home. Some are on shared drives because other people are working with them as well. Oh, some of them have been saved under different names on the shared drives, but they are the same document, or nearly the same document. Of course there might be some of these files on those 100 floppies in Mike's top desk drawer. Hmmm, Mike, when did you say you were leaving?

One of the biggest reasons your company should invest in a sophisticated document management and distribution system is because knowledge is hard to trace. Companies who are heading for the twenty-first century have a few Mikes. But a bigger knowledge transfer challenge is the transient contractor or consultant who comes in to get a project on its feet and then moves on. Most permanent employees are expecting to change jobs every five or six years. A sophisticated document management system protects workflow, information transfer, and knowledge transfer.

Organizations that produce a lot of documents typically seek to maintain high quality standards and consistency while reducing production costs. A simple form of automation is to impose standards for formatting and organization of information on authors to reduce the amount of work required to go from raw input to a finished product. But authors resist rules and often resent having to learn one more software application. You may need to sell benefits to users, which includes letting them know you value the work they produce for you. You value it enough to safeguard it and format it for the future.

Accessing Legacy Documents

One of the challenges you will face is providing access to legacy documents. It's also one of the most frequently asked questions of document management consultants. There are two aspects to the legacy angst. The first, of course, is "What is it going to take to get the volumes of existing company information online?" And the second is "How can I create documents today that will help make them reusable on the Intranet of the future?"

Existing Documents. Take comfort, it's getting a little more possible all the time to port existing documents in archaic formats to online distribution and viewing environments. Reuse of these documents is a little more of a challenge, but stay tuned to modern technology; I think there will soon be answers way beyond OCR scanning. Document Management Systems are designed to give your users viewing capability from a Web browser. They often allow you to view formats that cannot be opened in other ways. Universal viewing software, which plugs into Web browsers, is evolving rapidly to read almost any format with different levels of success. Many of the alternative viewing possibilities discussed in Chapter 5 allow you to quickly view snapshots of documents. In the near future, you may need only a browser and e-mail software, which are often combined (see Chapter 3).

Creating the Legacy Documents of the Future. Boy, hindsight is great, isn't it? If only you'd known you might want to put all those single-page tariff documents on the Web when you created the template for them five years ago! Speaking of templates, modern templates are the ingredient that will give your documents a future and continued reusability. The more structure you put into a document, the easier it is to translate it into multiple formats. For example, a simple keystroke or mouse click that changes each heading from a normal style to a heading style makes it possible to control all the formatting of headings for printing as well as online translation. It also enables HTML conversion programs to automatically create a hyperlinked table of contents to each of those headings. A sophisticated style sheet can even be mapped to SGML, though that level of sophistication would require expert SGML planning. One thing that you can do right now is teach your authors to use *styles* and templates (discussed in Chapter 5). Regardless of the Intranet strategy you adopt, you will be one step ahead in the right direction. Using a predefined set of templates for documents such as contracts, reports, and service agreements can produce consistency in other ways besides setting up a smoother conversion to delivery in multiple formats. Authoring with "style" frees your authors to

- Create documents with a common look and feel.
- Take advantage of group authoring techniques.

- Identify document components and content for search and retrieval (for example, query for all styles with the name "warnings").
- Reuse information more easily. Documents, or components of several documents, created with one structure can be easily merged into larger documents.
- Increase their productivity as they focus on content instead of structure.

Definition   Styles *are a saved set of formatting characteristics for a paragraph or characters that have a name. Styles not only help with conversion; they also make the author's job easier. For example, making a title big, bold, and blue will take only one step when applying the style as opposed to three steps without the style.*

Electronic Filing and Storage

As the volume and complexity of documents rise, you need a standard procedure to capture business knowledge as people leave. You also need an adequate document management retention system to manage, control, and selectively publish workgroup document information. Because licensing, support, implementation, and training for a stellar Document Management System can be expensive, you need to carefully consider your requirements. You should look for the following capabilities:

- version control and version history
- check-in/check-out
- tracking lists
- variable security
- customized document properties
- authorized retention management
- compound document relationships
- a search engine that allows search by content or by document properties
- integrated viewers
- automated renditions
- automated Web publishing

- e-mail links
- application integration with other programs selected for your Intranet

The realm of document management vendors can be confusing because over a hundred of them say they do document management, but many of them are coming at it from different histories, angles, and designs. If you send out an *RFP (Request for Proposal)* looking for document management vendors, you may get numerous responses varying in spectrum from engineering, to imaging, to workflow-oriented software, to forms processing, and so on.

There are general purpose Document Management Systems and specific purpose document management systems. An example of a specific purpose system is one that tracks resumes. It has unalterable fields to track specific resume properties such as skill sets, education, and so forth, but you couldn't take that same product and use it for general purposes in your legal or engineering groups.

So, as you look for a Document Management System you need to determine whether you have a specific need for a specific department or if you need a general purpose document management tool. Some of these have more powerful search engines, which may or may not be necessary depending on the size of your company. You may be interested in a system that has a no-brainer check-in/check-out system that is hard to misunderstand and requires little training. That type of system, however, may also hinder efficiency because it does not have as many features as you need to track multiple kinds of Information Systems documents and protect them with various levels of security. A general purpose document management tool that is programmable and scaleable is more suited for Information Systems. There are fewer of these. Chapter 9 will help you assess your business requirements and vendor solutions.

Once you sort out the business problem you are trying to solve, you will be less vulnerable to really cool new technology that may suck you in but not meet your needs. What you really need is to integrate and enable information consumers and information producers.

Definition   RFP (Request for Proposal). *Companies often write up desired specifications and requirements for a particular service or product and then submit it to vendors. Vendors who wish to compete for the contract write a proposal detailing how they can meet those specifications and requirements.*

Storage and Distribution Costs

Paper is not going away—it may always be the best way to read some material. However, the cost of storing and distributing paper is huge. By storing and distributing documents electronically, you can cut costs and save time. Most companies that have already spent years investing in personal computers, network servers, and training are on the threshold of reaping high returns on their investment by plugging into Intranet technology. Even if significant investment in the technology is ahead of you, it will not take long to get a return on your investment as your Intranet Web replaces paper, printing, and storage costs. You will also reap the benefit of potential savings from postage and shipping costs as you use your e-mail system not only to distribute information within your Intranet but also to transfer significant amounts of communication between your company and its suppliers, vendors, and consumers.

The first scenario in this chapter, regarding the corporate travel plan document, portrayed how one change can significantly impact your bottom line. Traditional, paper-based publishing is costly, slow, wasteful and requires extensive maintenance to keep content up-to-date. Multiply this one document distribution scenario by the number of documents your company produces each year. Consider also that e-mailing one little announcement throughout your company—instead of copying it, putting it in an envelope, addressing it, and delivering it to your employees—not only saves paper and distribution costs but also greatly speeds up access to information.

Summary

Although all companies like the immediate gratification of a more profitable bottom line, I believe the biggest payback over the next few years will come to companies who use their Intranet to become more effective in information and knowledge transfer. Your Intranet can serve information on your Internal Web and house it on Web servers, document warehouses, or in databases connected to your Intranet. The rest of this book discusses how to manage your company document distribution on a common network and messaging environment.

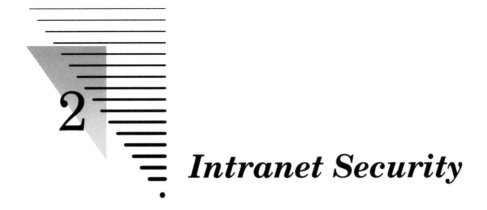

Intranet Security

What You Can Do

Security should be a primary concern in planning and implementing your Intranet. If your system contains information that is useful to your employees, then it most certainly contains information useful to your competition. Beyond the issue of commercial spying there may be intrusions by the overly curious—and sometimes malicious— hacker. Finally, almost any organization employs individuals who might, due to either ignorance or ill will, compromise the integrity of your data and systems.

What You Will Need

In this chapter we discuss the design and implementation of an effective security policy based on

- user behavior
- user access needs
- passwords
- network vulnerabilities
- security advisory organizations
- development considerations

We then discuss how to build a secure firewall based on Internet and World Wide Web security mechanisms such as

- routing and protocols
- secure protocols
- encryption
- digital certification

The Case for a Security Policy

A comprehensive security policy is essential. Intranet systems offer tremendous potential for cost-effective management and communications solutions. Yet there be dragons in the world, and the technology to open windows tends to outpace that of latch and key. Careful preparation will maximize opportunity for growth, as you protect your data against intruders and set policies to guide the firewall design of your system.

User Behavior

The best starting point in securing your Intranet is to consider your users. Many of your employees will have had little or no experience with Internet technologies, and the medium, while very empowering, is rife with pitfalls and dangers. The most obvious dangers are *viruses* and *Trojan horses,* with the latter of particular concern given the interconnected and open nature of the Internet.

Definition   Viruses *are computer programs designed to destroy data on a computer, so named because they tend to replicate in the host system.*

Definition   Trojan horses *are even more insidious programs designed to give outside users access to data, individual computers, and, by extension, whole systems.*

Another potential security loophole users often introduce is the selection of poor passwords. Many users select passwords based on common names or words found in the dictionary (for example, Bigboy, HeelAchilles, or geek4life). Such selections are easily breakable by freely available password-cracking programs. Even the most simple cracking program will attempt to match dictionaries against more sophisticated word and letter usage, mixing cases and juxtaposing letters, cracking combinations like "Eohstfos" and "bellyjean." Good passwords contain a mixture of numbers and letters, upper- and lowercase characters, and replacement patterns made more than a little complex (for example, sT@RwarZ, bS90210).

User Access Needs

One major security problem results from the attractions of the Web and the insatiable curiosity it elicits in some people. This inquisitive-ness causes some to peek at information that you might not want them to see. Such curious types may be hackers who stumble across your address, or unfortunately, your own employees. Consider the following: Does every employee need to have access to the personnel database?

- If not, how are you going to reap the rewards of having a distrib-uted and truly open-enrollment program?
- If so, which elements represent too much access?

For example, there may be some reports that would be valuable to a distributed sales staff and a distraction to others. Furthermore, com-plete access to all information will hamper performance for those who really do need it. A good security policy has a positive effect on general system performance.

You have to concern yourself not only with logical blocks of content, but also with the variety of services made available to system users. Just as an employee might misuse the e-mail system, unauthorized access to a file-transfer (*FTP*) directory can cause your organization a great deal of trouble. For example, inappropriate graphics can damage morale and careers and take up valuable system disk space and CPU clock time. At the same time, properly managed and secure common file space can dramatically improve workflow.

Definition   File Transfer Protocol (FTP) *allows users to send and receive certain files from one computer to another on the Internet. See also* TCP/IP.

In addition to these user considerations, hackers have more sophisti-cated means of attacking your systems.

The Need for a
Secure Firewall

Definition   Firewalls *are software- and/or hardware-based systems that allow for a high degree of access control and logging of network activity.*

Computers in a networked environment base their communications on certain protocols, or electronic exchange patterns. These protocols transfer data across the Internet in units called *packets.*

Definition   Packets *are small blocks of information that contain requests for network services, computer addresses, and data.*

Packets are organized in particular formats and give the Internet its great efficiency and flexibility. They are transferred independently through network *protocols* and then linked up in the proper way at their destination. Figure 2.1 shows the basic organizational layers used by network protocols.

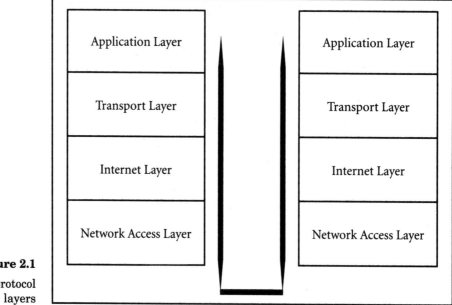

Figure 2.1

Network protocol
layers

The most common of these protocols is the *Transmission Control Protocol/Internet Protocol (TCP/IP)*.

Definition   A protocol *is a communications convention or standard.*

Definition   *The* Internet Protocol (IP) *is a standard numbering convention for computers attached to the Internet. See also* TCP/IP.

Definition   *The* Transmission Control Protocol (TCP) *is a standard that dictates how computers connect to the Internet. See also* TCP/IP.

Definition   TCP/IP *is the combined protocol standard that generally determines how computers send and receive data over the Internet.*

The Application Layer is where Internet applications such as Telnet and FTP are handled. The Transport Layer is handled by TCP, and the Internet Layer by IP. The Network Access Layer is where technologies such as *Ethernet* and *Asynchronous Transfer Mode* (ATM) take over across your Local Area Network (LAN) or Wide Area Network (WAN).

Definition   Telnet *is a network service that allows users to connect to a shell or command-line interface on a host machine.*

Definition   Ethernet *is a particular physical network system that combines high-bandwidth fiber optics (from 1.45 to 100 megabytes per second) with special send and receive hardware. Ethernet is used in a variety of network topologies.*

Definition   Asynchronous Transfer Mode (ATM) *is another high-performance network system approach that allows packets to be sent via disparate lines at disparate times. Each packet can then attempt to find the most efficient route at any given moment in time.*

The TCP/IP protocols organize each packet with header information that labels it with the protocol type, origin, and destination address. If any data is transferred improperly, or lost on the way, TCP/IP mechanisms at the destination address re-request the information from the host system. Other protocols utilize this basic mechanism to accomplish more sophisticated handling of the data upon arrival at the destination. The Web, and thereby your Intranet, utilizes a method known as *HyperText Transfer Protocol* (HTTP) built on top of TCP/IP.

Definition   HyperText Transfer Protocol (HTTP) *is a network protocol built on top of TCP/IP that allows for the transfer of data formatted for the Web.*

Each of these protocols is associated, or bound to, a specific channel on your server. These channels are known as *ports.*

Definition   Ports *are defined locations in memory that dictate the path of information transfer between a CPU and its peripherals.*

Incoming electronic mail (a TCP/IP system) is usually sent to port 25, while regular Web HTTP requests come in on port 80. While these network layers may seem complex, they represent a system dramatically more simple than those controlling your desktop computer. Hackers extremely proficient with these protocols and conventions can exploit them, because most network operating systems have security holes not easily protected against. Vulnerabilities in e-mail servers, file-copying facilities, and other Internet services are manifold and vary greatly from O/S to O/S.

So why aren't the patches to these holes built into your system? One answer is that different organizations offer different services, and often they vary those services from server to server, and from client to client. Because the manufacturers of these systems offer the most commonly used programs, it is up to your organization to determine which programs should be used in which circumstances. Another answer to this question is that a great deal of computer software is sent to market as rapidly as possible, sometimes with holes: Even seemingly robust and secure tools can have holes identified after the fact. No basic networked O/S or program is immune to this problem. For example, Solaris, the UNIX O/S developed by Sun Microsystems, has had problems with the basic Sendmail facility for almost as long as Solaris has been in existence. And Java, a supposedly secure language, was found to have security problems; Netscape's implementation of the Java interpreter had still more holes. Even *Pretty Good Privacy* (PGP), which allows for military-level *encryption,* is only very, very good. It is not 100 percent effective.

Definition   Encryption *is the masking of information, usually through sophisticated mathematical algorithms.*

Definition   Pretty Good Privacy (PGP) *is a publicly available program developed by Phil Zimmerman that encrypts data via an electronic key. This freeware is so good that the U.S. government attempted to ban its use.*

How to Secure
Your Intranet

While all of the dangers noted here are real, a simple and well-supported plan will protect your data, your investment, and your peace of mind. The vast majority of these protective elements are both client- and server-based.

A Basic Policy

The Internet is known for encouraging new thinking and new operational approaches from its users. Consider that the best defense against user-based attacks is an educated staff. Write your security policy into your operations manuals. Make all system users aware that abusing the technology is just as inexcusable as abusing any other company property. Finally, prepare for the worst—any computer connected to the Internet is inherently open and insecure to some degree.

Virus and Trojan horse programs, for example, do not just materialize on an individual's computer. They tend to be introduced by unwitting users who install executable binary programs (for example, games, utilities, or software tools) on their desktop. Provide your users with scanning utilities that detect and remove destructive programs. Make sure that these tools are understood by each user with access privileges, and support them with your IS staff. Table 2.1 notes some of the more commonly used scanning programs, compiled from the USENET alt.comp.virus newsgroup.

Operating System	Program	URL
Mac O/S	Virex	http://www.datawatch.com
	Disinfectant	widely distributed freeware
Windows 3.11/95/NT	Microsoft AntiVirus	http://www.microsoft.com
	Norton AntiVirus	http://www.symantec.com
OS/2	Virus Scan	widely distributed freeware
	Dr. Solomon's ToolKit	http://www.drsolomon.com
UNIX (most variants)	Vfind	http://www.cyber.com

Table 2.1

Common Virus Scanning Programs

Passwords

One defense against external password cracking is to crack your employees' passwords internally first, using the same programs the hackers use. Some password utilities can be set up to check passwords as they are first entered by users, while others check entire files that contain passwords from all system users. Any passwords cracked by these mechanisms should be changed immediately. Some organizations have decided to preempt this problem by assigning users passwords that are more secure to begin with. Instead of "mickeymouse," a user's password might be "34fRw4b." Unfortunately, this policy tends to cause users to write down their passwords or keep them in plain-text files on their systems. The risk here is that a visitor, or even a coworker, might learn the password and use it for unauthorized or damaging purposes. A sound security policy discourages such notation of passwords, or at least guides users to store their written passwords in physically secure areas (that is, locked away from prying eyes).

The next level of security is that of user access. Just as you don't give every employee access to your corporate checkbook, you usually do not need to give every employee access to each page of information. Most network operating systems offer security on multiple levels. The most basic security is at the file or directory level. Each file can be assigned read/write/execute privileges. Some operating systems, UNIX and NT for example, will allow for even more finely granulated levels of control per file: Privileges can be assigned by both user and group. For example, the accounting and marketing departments might be given access to certain Web pages containing financial data, while access would be denied to unauthorized users in other departments. This same kind of access control is also generally available at the directory level, allowing for rapid classification of whole sections of information. This approach has its limitations, however, especially in light of dynamic page-generation (see Chapter 8 for examples of this concept) where information is output on the fly, rather than in static files.

A more comprehensive security policy includes password control to certain systems. This approach further restricts access to entire classes of information. User passwords for the Intranet should, if at all possible, be independent from e-mail passwords. This policy, while more demanding, helps to minimize potential damage when either system is compromised. Once again, users can be grouped by department or other organizational unit for read/write/execute privileges.

Network Vulnerabilities

Having considered internal matters, you should expand your policy to include the suite of services generally available in network operating systems. As mentioned earlier, any number of vulnerabilities exist within your networked computers. To learn more about these vulnerabilities, start with your system vendor. Generally this means the manufacturer of your operating system, rather than your hardware manufacturer. It is not in the interest of the manufacturer to have you invest time and money in a custom Intranet system if the out-of-the-box facilities fail you. Sun Microsystems, for example, makes readily available the patch that removes the basic Sendmail vulnerability mentioned previously.

Security Advisory Organizations

Beyond the security problems identified by the vendor directly, many organizations publish data about new vulnerabilities as soon as they are clearly identified. One of the most well known of these organizations is the Computer Emergency Response Team (CERT) hosted by Carnegie-Mellon University. For a rather hefty fee, CERT will provide direct intervention when the security of your systems has been compromised. On the other hand, for absolutely no charge whatsoever, individuals can subscribe to the CERT advisory mail group. This group publishes reports about vulnerabilities in all major networking systems, and quite a few minor ones as well. CERT also maintains an archive of these reports and openly publishes them at their Web site (`http://www.cert.org`).

Another solid source for security updates is the National Computer Security Association (NCSA, not to be confused with the National Center for Supercomputing Applications, the maker of Mosaic, and NCSA httpd, a popular Web server).

Definition   HyperText Transfer Protocol Daemon (httpd) *is a type of information server that uses HTTP.*

NCSA (`http://www.ncsa.com`) is more of a white-paper organization, looking at theories behind computer security and practice, although it too documents specific vulnerabilities and has more recently started a security certification process.

These are not the only sources, to be sure. Because systems are configured differently from one organization to another, a good approach is to find organizations that seem to have similar systems and learn from them. For example, when one particular department of Pacific Bell needed additional information to round out its approach to securing their Intranet, they found extremely useful information hosted by the genome project at the Massachusetts Institute of Technology (`http://www.genome.wi.mit.edu/WWW/faqs/www-security-`

`faq.html`). This MIT resource contains a strong body of content regarding O/S-specific security issues. Be sure to include a statement in your security policy regarding frequent research of both vendor and nonvendor repositories.

Development Considerations

The final element of your policy defines the way Common Gateway Interface (CGI) programs are developed (see Chapter 8 for more information regarding CGI scripts and programs). If your O/S is a UNIX variant, you or your developers might be tempted to use shell scripting to accomplish simple tasks (for example, forwarding inputs from a form via e-mail). Do this and you might lose the farm! Shell scripts are run as a real user on your system and can easily be compromised. Using a language such as C or PERL is infinitely preferable to shell scripting, although each of these languages has potential danger areas. PERL is an interpreted language, and your system must contain the binary that interprets the PERL code at runtime. Never place this binary file in a directory where your Intranet users might find Web pages because the interpreter can be compromised. C, on the other hand, is a compiled language, so there are fewer worries about an attack. However, certain C language commands actually open shells and are just as vulnerable as simple shell scripts. For more information on specific language vulnerabilities, please consult `http://www.cerf.net/ ~paulp/cgi-security`.

Now you are well on your way to having a secure Intranet and have, at this point, protected yourself in some of the most basic and fundamental ways possible. However, the more advanced hacker might still be able to access your system via sophisticated tricks on your server's protocols and conventions. To defend yourself from more powerful and dangerous attacks, your policy should include the construction and maintenance of a firewall.

Building a Secure Firewall

Firewalls are computers, software, or hardware–software combinations that help control access to your system via protocols and ports. Firewalls are fairly complex systems that require proper planning in order to be effective. Improperly constructed firewalls not only hamper system performance; they can even introduce security problems because their existence may cause a false sense of organizational security. The guidelines mentioned here simply scratch the surface of this complex issue. One tried-and-true resource for a more thorough treatment of the matter is *Building Internet Firewalls,* by D. Brent Chapman and Elizabeth Zwicky, published by O'Reilly & Associates, Inc.

The simplest firewall packages are strictly software-based. They give you additional controls over password authentication and access, while logging both user activity and movement. Table 2.2 documents a few of the more commonly used firewall software packages.

Operating System	Program	URL
Mac O/S	Catapult Proxy Server	http://www.microsoft.com
Windows 95/NT	Catapult Proxy Server	http://www.microsoft.com
	Eagle	http://www.raptor.com
BSD Unix	Eagle	http://www.raptor.com
Solaris	Firewall 1	http://www.checkpoint.com
	SunScreen SPF-100	http://www.sun.com
HP-UX	Eagle	http://www.raptor.com

Table 2.2
Some Basic Firewall Programs

A detailed summary of available packages can be found at `http://www.zeuros.co.uk/firewall`. Software-only firewall packages really do not cover the bases as securely as a full-fledged hardware–software solution. A dedicated software/hardware firewall system allows for easier administrative control, helps in the physical routing of information and requests, and allows for faster transfer of information relative to simple software controls.

Secure Protocols

One of the simplest of the protocols mentioned earlier is the Internet Protocol (IP). Each networked computer has an IP address associated with it. Specialized computers such as *routers* are assigned IP addresses, as are networked desktop systems and printers.

Definition A router *is a system acting as the traffic light for network traffic.*

An IP address consists of four sets of numerical values from 0 to 255, separated by periods. The lowest and highest of these values are generally reserved for special aspects of routing, so this generally leaves 254 possible values per set. One computer's address might be 210.193.7.38, while its router might be 207.193.7.30, and both might be considered part of the network known as 210.193.7.0 (the lowest value "0" designates the network as a whole). The IP address dictates the source and destination of packets as they travel across the Internet. A few large organizations have what are known as class-A networks (whereby the first value is static and the other three are open to local control) while most organizations have control over two values (class-B), one value (class-C), or less. The Internet protocol helps divide up authority for the Internet. Your organization controls a small number of these addresses.

If your organization controls at least a class-C network (one value with a range of 255 possible addresses), it has the opportunity to sub-network itself into various divisions. Subnetting allows your organization to have different controls for each division. For example, you might allow one division to provide FTP services, and another not to.

A Very Simple Firewall

A good network firewall consists of at least five hardware elements: the device that connects your network to the Internet (that is, ISDN or a CSU/DSU modem), an external router, a computer for unsecured Web serving and other services, an internal router, and an internal computer for secure Web serving. Figure 2.2 illustrates this firewall architecture.

The basic approach outlined here is to create a "Demilitarized Zone" where security is a nonissue. No critical services, except the serving of pages and the redirecting of requests, are controlled from the computer in this zone. The external router in this zone examines each packet of data as it arrives in your system. Packets that seem to fit the general norm for information requests are passed along, while those that seem suspect are denied or rerouted. This process is known as *packet filtering.*

The router knows which packets are acceptable and which are not by virtue of rules that are programmed into its internal operating system.

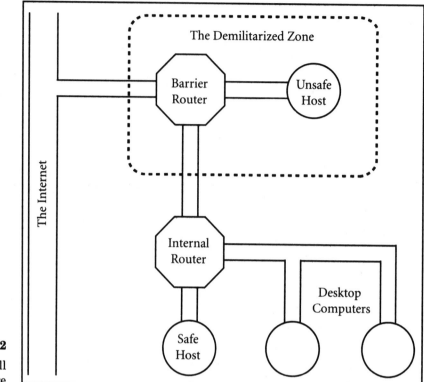

Figure 2.2

Sample firewall
architecture

These rules do not come preprogrammed, however, and programming
them is the real challenge of setting up a packet-filtering firewall. In
essence, the rules examine the protocol of each packet (TCP/IP, UDP,
and others), the requesting host, the destination host, and the destination port. If, for example, a packet claiming to be an HTTP request is
coming in for port 23980, more than likely it's bad news; you would establish a rule to reject such a request. The most sophisticated attacks
attempt to fool your router by claiming to be an internal request. You
can write rules to reject such requests because if the IP address of the
requesting host were really coming from within, it wouldn't be coming
from the outside world. The rule sets you establish will need to address
all of the major protocol/port combinations.

   The two routers in our example work in tandem, know each other
well, and trust each other by virtue of their rule sets. Information is ex-

amined not once, but twice, meaning that if one system is compromised, the other should still hold. Services such as e-mail, FTP, and basic HTTP are safely handled by the external computer, while more proprietary data is safely tucked away inside.

One other significant advantage in this architecture is that it allows for server-*caching*, whereby the more commonly requested pages are sent to the external computer on a regular basis. This technique uses what is commonly known as a proxy server. Proxy servers keep a copy of your Web site on the unsecure server and retrieve updates to your Web site. The firewall then allows pages to be transferred from the secure server to the unsecure server—and only the unsecure server. Even if the proxy server is compromised, the firewall will only allow for connections to the specific Web port on your secure server, thus minimizing any potential damage.

The proxy server is also the choke-point for outgoing requests. You will be required to do some additional configuration of your users' browsers if you allow them to surf external seas. Proxy servers enable you to establish your firewall without hampering Intranet performance.

Definition   A cache *is a designated area of hard disk or memory that holds commonly referenced information.*

Firewalls are a very sophisticated defense mechanism for very sophisticated attacks. A good firewall will encompass both hardware and software, enabling you to examine traffic, log activity, and control access in a variety of ways.

Additional Web Security Facilities and Techniques

You now have a plan, a policy, access control, and a firewall. Are you done? Not yet. While the remaining facilities are not absolutely necessary for basic Web serving, each has its own merits and should be used to round out the defenses on your growing fortress.

Before we discuss these defense facilities, mention should be made about Web servers themselves. Most Web server software packages are generally secure. However, new users of these packages sometimes make the mistake of running their servers as root, the UNIX superuser. This is asking for trouble because if someone tricks your CGI scripts while the server is running as root, it is quite possible that they can seize or corrupt any file anywhere in the system. Run your Web server as a user dedicated to that task alone and you'll minimize the potential for damage.

Encryption

As more and more people began thinking about the possibility for electronic commerce via the Internet, companies who are connected to the Web began considering how best to protect their systems. This led to the development of two primary Web-specific security facilities, *Secure HyperText Transfer Protocol* (S-HTTP) and *Secure Sockets Layer* (SSL). These two facilities operate in a similar fashion, but they accomplish their goals differently. The basic idea for both S-HTTP and SSL is to provide encryption and *digital certification* services.

Definition   Digital certification *is the process of trusted third-party electronic verification of an organization's identity.*

Definition   Secure Sockets Layer (SSL) *is a system of WWW information encryption that occurs between the Application and Transport Layers in the network hierarchy.*

Definition   Secure HyperText Transfer Protocol (S-HTTP) *encrypts the transmission of WWW information in the Application Layer of the network hierarchy.*

Contemporary encryption is based on sophisticated mathematical algorithms that lock your data into a thoroughly inscrutable mishmash of characters. These mechanisms tend to rely on a digital key. One problem with older forms of key cryptography was that both the sender and the receiver had the same key, thus doubling the possibility that the key would be compromised. A few years back a new mechanism, Public Key Cryptography, was developed. Many Internet services such as PGP, S-HTTP, and SSL rely on this technique. Here's how it works: each user has two keys—one public, one private—that are created at the same time. You publish the public key, which anyone can then use to encrypt a message to you, and, in theory, only your private key can decrypt this message. Current domestic keys use 128-character keys and provide military-level secure encryption, which incidentally makes this technology illegal to export outside of the United States.

Digital Certification

Digital certification works hand in hand with encryption techniques. Certification involves a trusted third party to vouch for the identity of your organization. Certificates exist to support a concept known as nonrepudiation, whereby you can't claim not to be you if something has gone awry. At the same time it makes it difficult, if not impossible, for others to digitally claim they are you.

VeriSign (`http://www.verisign.com`) and RSA Data Security (`http://www.rsa.com`) are two of the largest and most trusted certification authorities in the United States. Generally, when acquiring a digital ID or certificate you must first generate an encrypted key and provide this to the certification authority. These authorities will then associate your domain name, contact name, and their own imprimatur to create the certificate. Once the authority has verified your organization's legal status and the contact names associated with the original key, you will be issued the certificate. This will then be installed on your Web server. The digital certificate will simply tell other computers who you are, that you are legitimate as far as the certification authority goes, and that a secure connection can now ensue.

Another solution is to acquire a certificate server of your own. As certificate managers allow you to trust other clients and servers, you can establish certificates for clients, having your server explicitly trust them. Thus only those users defined as trustworthy will be allowed secure connections.

S-HTTP was developed by Enterprise Integration Technologies (EIT). S-HTTP handles the encrypted exchange of data in the Application Layer mentioned earlier. It is a modified version of the basic HTTP and supports authentication, encrypted messaging, and message integrity.

SSL, developed by Netscape Communications Corporation, supports authentication, encrypted messaging, and message integrity. It handles encryption a bit differently in that it wedges itself between the Application Layer and the Transport/Internet Layers and consequently is a somewhat more portable facility.

One last defense mechanism at your disposal is your server log files. These files will, at minimum, show you who is accessing which of your files and pages and where errors are occurring in your Intranet site. Some Web servers will have additional logs for the various browser types, as well as the referring agents to each page (more on this in Chapter 8). Monitoring these access log files along with system log files can help you identify when someone might be attempting to hack at your system. For example, Telnet activity just after an HTTP access message at 3 A.M. from the same host just might be an attempt at unauthorized access. Similarly, UUCP activity just after a CGI script has been accessed might be a danger sign.

Definition   UNIX-to-UNIX copy protocol (UUCP) *is a file, directory, and disk copy mechanism particular to the UNIX Operating System.*

Your error log files will also show you who failed to properly authenticate themselves when trying to view information behind password access points.

Summary

As you can see, a little paranoia can go a long way. Security requires a sound organizational foundation, solid planning, robust software and hardware systems, and a security-conscious system administrator. These policies and preparations will save you time and energy later and will allow you to reap the rewards of Intranet Document Management.

3 Basic Messaging Requirements

What You Can Do

This chapter will help you understand the basic messaging requirements of an Intranet. The purpose is not to teach you how to install your Intranet but rather to help you understand what you need to install it, then point you to resources that can provide further implementation assistance.

What You Will Need

To understand what your basic messaging requirements are, you will need to know

- what the Internet is
- how an Intranet differs from the Internet
- how the Internet works
- something about client/server environments

How to Use Internet Protocols

What Is the Internet?

The Internet began about thirty years ago as a U.S. government project called ARPANET (Advanced Research Projects Agency Network). Before work on the ARPANET began, it was envisioned as an intergalactic network. First a few computers were connected in the southwestern United States as an experiment to enhance research capability. Then more computers were connected across other states. Next universities were connected to this network. In those early years, David Clark, senior research scientist at MIT's laboratory for computer science, said, "It is not proper to think of networks as connecting computers. Rather, they connect people using computers to mediate." This perspective of "people communicating with people" soon caught the attention of commercial organizations who created more internal networks. Eventually these links crossed the ocean to form a global network. It didn't quite attain intergalactic status, but the age of interactive computing was born. It is both interesting and important to note that the Internet was not created but rather evolved and matured into what exists and is still evolving today. If the history of the Internet interests you, you might enjoy visiting the URLs in Table 3.1.

Definition   TCP/IP *is the combined protocol standard that generally determines how computers send and receive data over the Internet.*

The Internet is basically the interconnection of many independent networks of various organizations all across the world. It is important to understand that no one really owns the Internet. It is merely a worldwide cooperative effort of innumerable people and organizations who want their computers connected. The Internet is one of the largest and most excellent communication mediums ever conceived. It enables people all over the world to have discussions on any subject and, more incredibly, find others who are experts or who are just as interested in those subjects. You can get advice about making beer from Germans or

URL	What You Will Find There
http://www.cs.columbia.edu/~hauben/papers/nwg.txt	Behind the Net: The untold history of the ARPANET, Michael Hauben
http://www.columbia.edu/~rh120/ch106.x07	Behind the Net: The Untold History of the ARPANET and Computer Science, another chapter by Michael Hauben on the same subject (but these are not linked)
http://www.columbia.edu/~rh120/ch106.x03	The Social Forces Behind the Development of Usenet, another chapter by Michael Hauben
http://www.cs.unca.edu/~davidson/history.html	History of the Internet, by Bruce Sterling

Table 3.1
History of the
Internet

discuss scuba diving with someone from Australia. Officers and founders of large companies, inventors, and famous innovators often willingly interface directly with anyone who wants audience with them through e-mail. The development of the World Wide Web has made it even easier to find information. The only problem now is that there is so much to find; sifting the useless information from what you are looking for can be a daunting process.

How Does an Intranet Differ from the Internet?

As stated in Chapter 1, an Intranet is a mini-Internet within your organization, whether your organization is commercial, academic, or governmental. An Intranet is similar to the Internet because you are all connected by wires and servers using computers to access e-mail, more servers, databases, and software programs. It is different because you control the environment. As you set up the basic messaging requirements, you need a homogeneous e-mail system for traffic within your company and also a robust interface with the big "I" in order to leverage global WWW information.

How Does the Internet Work?

A broad range of services are provided on a network. Some of these are apparent and some are behind the scenes. All of the services described here are built on the TCP/IP protocols. TCP/IP, along with UDP (mentioned later in this chapter), is the language and backbone of the Internet. TCP/IP has provisions for describing where your computer is, where the computer you are talking to is, and how to actually talk to the other computer. TCP/IP stands for Transmission Control Protocol/Internet Protocol. It is actually two different protocols, one layered on top of the other, that allow computers to communicate with each other over a complex interconnection of networks. TCP/IP are not the only protocols for interactive connectivity, but they are what the Internet and the Web are based upon. I will explain how they work in simple terms and give you a basic understanding of the physical parts of the Internet and what their functions are.

Definition   Protocols *are sets of rules, conventions, or standards that enable everyone to understand how something is supposed to work.*

Internet Protocol (IP)

The Internet Protocol is a set of rules for sending information between computers on the Internet. If you want to send information to a computer, the first thing you need to do is find it. If you wanted to send a note to a friend today, you could send it by *snail mail.* For this you would need an address.

Definition   Snail mail *is the jargon among e-mail users to describe the usual ole way to send mail on p-p-paper by post or one of the numerous, competing couriers.*

IP Address. The *Internet Protocol* defines addresses for computers in the form of an IP address. Each and every computer on the Internet has a unique IP address. IP addresses are made up of four parts, separated by periods, or in Silicon Valley lingo, a "dot." For example, my computer's IP address is 129.245.87.42. Each section of an IP address has a range from 0 to 255. An IP address is similar to your street address. There is only one house that has your exact address. Each computer at any given time has a unique IP address. Anyone in the world can send mail to your house if they have your address. Likewise, any computer connected to the Internet can send e-mail to your computer if it knows your IP address, unless, of course, a firewall exists to prevent delivery.

Definition   *The* Internet Protocol (IP) *is a standard convention for computers attached to the Internet. It is a best-effort delivery system that takes data and tries to get it from one computer to another over a network. No promises are given that the data will arrive error-free or even arrive at all. See also* TCP/IP.

To extend the snail mail metaphor, consider what else is needed besides a destination address. One requirement is a return address. The address of the sending computer is called the source IP address. Just as you could reply to your friend by using the return address on the envelope, connected computers can read each other's IP addresses to send e-mail back and forth. The combination of the source IP address, the destination IP address, and the data itself is called an *IP packet.*

Definition   *An* IP packet *is the collection of necessary information needed to move a chunk of data from one computer to another using the IP protocol. This information includes the data itself, the source computer's IP address, and the destination computer's IP address.*

IP Routing. An IP packet going from one computer to another needs to find a path through the maze of wires that connects these computers together. To deliver snail mail the post office determines the path (plane, train, truck, or automobile) for each leg of a letter's journey. The chosen path depends upon where the letter needs to go, how many paths there are to get there, and how busy each of these paths are. Each post office has a certain number of paths to choose from depending upon the destination address, and the reliability and capacity of the different paths. Eventually the post office gets your letter to someone who delivers it to your mailbox. Similarly, an IP packet gets its directions from *routers*. Routers are like post offices in that they take your IP packet and send it via a path determined by the destination IP address, network reliability, and network load balancing algorithms.

Unfortunately, e-mail can resemble snail mail in another way as well. Have you ever sent a letter that never arrived at its destination? Or have you received a letter that looks more like it has been run over by a plane, train, and truck than carried by one of them? Finally, have you ever mailed two letters to the same person on the same day and had them arrive on different days? All these scenarios are possible as well using the Internet Protocol. You might ask, why are we using something that has so many weaknesses? The answer is that the main purpose of IP is to navigate its packets though the network. Making sure it gets there on time, undamaged, or at all are left to the higher level protocols such as TCP. The Internet Protocol is known as a best-effort delivery system. It makes its best try but makes no promises to fulfill requirements, just like the postal system.

Definition   A router *connects two or more independent networks and chooses which one to forward the IP packet to based on the destination IP address, network bandwidth, and network load balancing algorithms.*

Finding the IP Address. You may now be wondering why you don't see IP addresses when you are surfing the Web. All you've ever seen is the *URL* (Uniform Resource Locator) that you've typed in or that appeared in the "Location" or "Address" box at the top of your browser screen. A URL actually has the IP address encoded in itself. A normal URL looks something like this:

```
http://www.computer.com/some/file/some/where.html
```

The part before the colon tells a Web browser which protocol to use. This one says `http`, the Web protocol discussed in greater detail later in this chapter. Here's another common URL:

```
ftp://ftp.computer.com/some/other/file.exe
```

Here the Web browser first sees `ftp` (File Transfer Protocol), another of those protocols that we will discuss later. So where is the IP address? The IP addresses are actually the underpinnings for `www.computer.com` and `ftp.computer.com`. Because humans are generally bad at numbers and good at words, the computer's IP address is referenced either by the number or by a name that gets translated into a number by the computer. These names are called *hostnames.* The translation is covered later in this chapter in the DNS section, but for now we can say that the computer "reads" the hostname `www.computer.com` and "thinks" the IP address `123.123.123.123`. Although you are normally not concerned with IP addresses, they are still good to know about. Another good thing to know is that a single computer is not limited to a single hostname. This means that just because two links have different hostnames doesn't mean that they are two separate computers. For all we know the hostname `ftp.computer.com` could translate to IP address `123.123.123.123`. All computers have one hostname that is its primary name. All other names are known as *aliases* to that computer.

Definition   A URL (Uniform Resource Locator). *It's that sometimes very long string of characters at the top of your browser that starts with* `http://` *and often includes* `www`. *If you put an address there then press Enter, it "tells" the browser what page to open in the World Wide Web or once your browser opens the address you entered, the URL indicates what page is already open. For more about URLs, particularly about "Relative URLs," see Chapter 5.*

Definition   *The* hostname *of a computer is an alphanumeric representation of a computer's IP address that can be converted by the DNS protocol.*

Definition   *An* alias *is a duplicate hostname for a computer.*

Transmission Control Protocol (TCP)

Some of the weaknesses in the Internet Protocol were mentioned in the previous section:

- not being able to tell if an IP packet has arrived undamaged or at all to the destination computer
- no guarantee that IP packets will arrive in the same sequence as they are sent

TCP is designed to ensure a guaranteed, error-free, on-order delivery of information between computers. It still relies on the Internet Protocol to get the packets routed through the network, but it adds other information to make sure that data sent by one computer is the same data received by the destination computer. This overhead enables TCP to resolve the IP weaknesses.

There is another IP weakness to be mentioned. There may be many programs running on a networked computer. How can you tell which process gets which data that comes from the network? This is where port numbers enter the scene.

Port Numbers. Continuing with the snail mail metaphor, another important item required to send mail to someone is her name. There may be many people living at the same address. Using her name on the mail will ensure that the mail goes to her, instead of someone else. The corresponding portion of the Internet is the *port number*. The port number is a number that describes which service on a computer is the right one to use. For example, consider the three URLs from our earlier discussion:

```
http://www.computer.com/some/file/some/where.html
http://www.computer.com:90/some/file/some/where.html
ftp://ftp.computer.com/some/other/file.exe
```

You may recognize which part is the alias for the IP address, but now we are looking for port numbers. Every service on the Internet has a default port number. Table 3.2 shows some of these. This takes the mystery out of looking for a specific service on an unknown computer. In these URLs, the first entries before the // identify what kind of service is requested. The browser sees this and knows the default port number to look for. The first URL starts with http. If you look at Table 3.2, you see that http has a default port number of 80. The third URL starts with ftp, which has a default port number of 21. The second URL also starts with http, so we would expect it to use port 80 again. However, this URL also has a :90 behind the hostname, and this instructs the computer to use 90 instead of the default port number 80.

Port Number		Service Offered
25		SMTP
21		FTP
119		NNTP
80		HTTP or Web

Table 3.2
Common Port
Numbers

Definition   A port number *helps a computer refine its search to the right service after it finds the right computer using the IP address.*

Guaranteed Delivery. TCP, unlike IP, will guarantee the delivery of a message over the network. It does this using a process that is like having a little conversation about each and every packet that travels over the network. If you really need to deliver something in the mail, you have the option to send it by registered mail, which notifies you when the package is received. The same thing happens on the network with TCP. First the message gets sent to the destination computer. If the destination computer receives the packet, then it sends a confirmation to the source computer. The source computer will wait awhile for the response, which is called an *ACK* packet (acknowledgment packet, which is actually a TCP/IP with a bit switched on). If the ACK does not show up, then it resends the packet and waits again. This continues until the source computer receives the ACK or the maximum number of retries has occurred, in which case the computer gives up and notifies the user that the connection to the destination computer has been lost. Usually this happens only if something on the network is broken or the destination computer went down. However, with the growing demand for the Internet and the less rapidly growing network capacity, this will probably start happening more and more as the packets cannot get through the increasingly congested network.

Definition   An ACK (acknowledgment packet) *tells the source computer that the destination computer has received the message packet.*

Error-Free Data. TCP is also an error-free data transport protocol. This means that TCP can detect errors by computing a *checksum,* which is a complex way of adding all the data of a message and getting a result. This checksum is then appended to the message before it is sent on the network. When the receiving computer gets the message it also computes a checksum of the data of the message and then compares the checksum it found with the one calculated by the source computer. If the two checksums are the same, then the message should be undamaged; if, however, the two checksums are different, then something was damaged or changed somewhere in transmission and the packet is discarded. Then a message is sent to the source computer requesting another copy of the packet to replace the damaged one.

Definition   A checksum *is a mathematical method to ensure that data has not been changed during transmission.*

Correct Sequence of Data. One last feature of *TCP* is that messages are presented to the destination computer in the same order as they left the source computer. This is done by attaching a sequence number to each packet leaving the source and checking as each packet is received by the destination. In this way, the destination computer can see if there are any gaps in the packets. If the destination computer has received packets 4, 5, and 7, but 6 is nowhere to be found, it can request a new copy of 6 and wait for it. The sequence number also lets the computer know to hang on to packet 7 (and any later packets) until packet 6 has shown up.

Definition   TCP (Transmission Control Protocol) *allows computers to have error-free bidirectional communication over a network. TCP utilizes IP for routing and delivery with sequencing, error detection, recovery, demultiplexing of services, and guaranteed delivery added to allow error-free communication.*

User Datagram Protocol

Sometimes the overhead associated with using TCP is not justified for the information that is being sent over the network. If the data integrity of what you are sending is important, then you probably need

TCP. For example, downloading the newest version of the Netscape browser requires that the data contained in the package arrives at your computer in the same condition as when it left Netscape's server. Otherwise, the program will not function correctly. However, if the data you are sending is more time critical or you don't wish to use TCP error correction, then it's better to use another protocol called User Datagram Protocol.

Why Use UDP? Imagine that you are watching a live video broadcast over the network. Then imagine that there is a problem with some of the data that is received on the network due to a transitory problem. If you are using TCP/IP, your computer will have to contact the video server and get it to resend the corrupted data so it can continue the video feed. This process takes time. You might wonder what your computer is doing while it is waiting for a replacement copy of that data. Let us return to the snail mail metaphor. Suppose you have a friend who is building a house for you. Every day he takes pictures of the progress and then mails them to you. The envelopes he sends are numbered and come by registered mail so he knows when you've seen each one. Also, you are not allowed to open the envelopes out of order. This is basically what TCP/IP does. Now, if one piece of mail gets lost, you have to wait until a replacement copy of that envelope is sent before looking at the progress of your house. Once you get the replacement, you can view a whole bunch of the backed-up envelopes and pictures and then proceed with viewing them one at a time as they are delivered daily.

If this were systematic delivery of computer video pictures, the video would temporarily lurch forward once the missing data was redelivered. Now, would you rather see all the frames of the video even if it means delay and lurches? Or would you just forget about the missing or damaged frame and continue on with the video you are still getting? Most people prefer the second option. This is where *UDP* comes in. UDP uses the same additional data as TCP, but reacts differently to it. Simply stated, it uses the error checking and sequencing data to determine if the data it is currently receiving is valid for delivery or should be discarded for more recent data.

UDP Ports. UDP also has the port number concept like TCP. They are so similar that some services have been implemented in both TCP and UDP and use the same port number for both protocols. It is not a requirement, simply a convenience.

Definition   UDP (User Datagram Protocol) *allows computers to have error-detection and unidirectional communication over a network. UDP uses IP for routing and delivery with sequencing, error detection, recovery, and demultiplexing of services.*

Multicast Protocol

Because Multicast Protocol is still fairly young and not very widespread, many computers and routers do not understand it yet, but they are learning. Multicast is an extension of IP that can be used to greatly reduce the use of network bandwidth for certain specific high-bandwidth applications. These applications involve a large number of users receiving the exact same data over the Internet. This can be most useful for Internet-wide live broadcast, or on a smaller scale, perhaps a corporate broadcast to all computers in a company.

Once again we use the snail mail metaphor to understand how the Multicast Protocol works. Imagine that you need to mail something, say a catalog, to a large number of people. In the traditional world you would have to print one copy for each recipient. This is currently how many live broadcasts are delivered on the Internet, which eats up a great deal of *bandwidth* with identical copies of data going out, each addressed to a different computer. Suppose that we can send out a single copy addressed to everyone that needs or wants it, similar to mailing a single catalog with an address label that lists everyone who gets a copy. When this copy gets to the post office, they make copies of it and send one down each path, maybe one with each local mail carrier and one by each plane and truck. When each plane and truck arrives at its destination, they once again duplicate a copy for each necessary path. Obviously, the post office cannot be expected to do this, but if it could, there would be much less duplicate mail to haul around. While the postal service cannot do this, the Internet, if properly equipped, can. The routers on the network need to be a little smarter to recognize a Multicast packet and then send it to every necessary interface. If there are fifty people watching the broadcast on one network, only one copy, instead of fifty, will be on the network. This also relieves a huge burden from servers. Currently if a few thousand people are watching a broadcast the server has to make a few thousand copies of the broadcast. If the network could be relied upon to make its own copies, then the server would only have to make a single copy.

Definition Bandwidth *measures the amount of data that is moving on a network. As the current bandwidth increases to the theoretical maximum bandwidth, effective bandwidth decreases.*

Definition Multicast Protocol *drastically reduces the amount of bandwidth needed for certain specific types of applications such as live audio and video broadcasts.*

The Physical Stuff

In addition to all of these protocols, there is a lot of hardware that makes networks work.

Wires. The most basic part of a network is wires. Wires carry data between computers and take many forms. The most common type of wire looks like a thick phone cord. It can be used in both 10BaseT networks and 100BaseT networks. A 10BaseT network has a maximum capacity of 10 MBS while a 100BaseT network has a maximum capacity of 100 MBS. The 10BaseT and 100BaseT networks are star configuration networks that require a hub or switch that is the central point of the network. Each computer has a wire that runs from itself to the star. (If you were to draw out the networks, the central connection looks like a star, thus the name.)

Another common type of network is the 2BaseT network. This network runs through a wire identical to that which runs into your television cable box at your home. It has a lower maximum bandwidth but has an advantage of not needing a hub or switch in its most basic configuration. Several computers can connect on a single line of cable. Network lines need Network Interface Cards (NIC) to plug into computers. The NIC must match the type of network you have. Some network cards allow you to connect multiple types of networks into them, but they still allow only one connection at a time. With 10BaseT and 100BaseT some of the newer NICs will sense which type of network it is and run at the correct speed.

Routers. The next basic part of a network is the router. Routers connect two or more networks and enable these networks to communicate with each other to form a larger network or an Intranet. Routers that link Intranets to the Internet are called gateways.

A Client/Server World

Now that you have an understanding of what makes the Internet work we can start looking at the parts that make it interesting. First though, a bit about what client/server is and why we use it. The original computing paradigm was *mainframe* computers. These computers were large, powerful machines that everyone logged on to directly to access information. Most people had something called a *dumb terminal* interface that was a monitor, displaying only text and numbers. Dumb terminals have no local storage, processing power, or memory. This meant that all the processing power was in one box (the mainframe). These computers were large and ungainly, and if they happened to go down, all work stopped.

When desktop computers became relatively inexpensive, individual systems moved to people's desks. This had the effect of distributing the processing power throughout the organization. Users were no long dependent upon the mainframe to get work done. Unfortunately the need for mainframes did not completely go away. Some large applications still need more power than the average desktop machines can muster.

Today, most of these large applications have moved into the client/server world. A client/server application is one where the entire application is broken into two parts. One part, the *client*, runs the interface and requests information on your desktop computer. The *server* is reserved for pure processing of data and responding to the clients' requests. This allows applications to take advantage of the distributed computing base of the desktop systems while the larger systems concentrate on data processing without interface issues. It also has the advantage of making these large-scale applications easier to create and use. For example, the Netscape browser is a client, and the Web servers are servers.

Definition   Mainframes *are the large monolithic computers that dominated the computing industry in the recent past. These systems were accessed via dumb terminals and were often warehouses of an organization's computing power.*

Definition   *The* dumb terminal *interface consisted of a monitor and keyboard only, without any local storage or processing power.*

Definition A client *is a software application that runs on a desktop computer and accesses a server process for information.*

Definition A server *is a system that responds to clients' requests with information.*

Open Protocols versus Proprietary Protocols

All of the protocols mentioned in this chapter are open protocols. This means they were developed in an open forum, and everyone is allowed access to how they work without paying royalties or other fees. In a profit-driven world this may seem a little strange, but it has many advantages that proprietary protocols lack and may be one of the reasons for the Web's success. Open protocols allow anyone to create either a client or a server and have it work with everyone else's clients and servers. If there is some feature you want in a mail reader that doesn't exist, you can create one without having to re-create the entire mail infrastructure or paying money to some bloated corporation for private protocols. Open protocols allow for creative growth and a marketplace that is much more level than one where information is hidden and inaccessible.

Request for Comments (RFC). I have described some of the protocols for the Internet and will describe more in the pages to come. But just in case you want more detailed information, there are places you can look for the official descriptions of all the open protocols that exist on the network. These documents are called *Requests for Comments.* Originally they were for people developing protocols who wanted input from others about the design. Eventually RFCs acquired an official demeanor to them, and now they are the way this type of information is distributed. To acquire a copy of an RFC you need to FTP to ds.internic.net. If you are really interested in the latest version, be sure to check back often because these documents are constantly updated. Table 3.3 lists some of the RFCs that relate to several of the protocols discussed in this chapter.

RFC Number	Title
768	User Datagram Protocol
791	Internet Protocol
793	Transmission Control Protocol
821	Simple Mail Transport Protocol
959	File Transfer Protocol
1460	Post Office Protocol, Version 3

Table 3.3
Some RFCs for
Protocols

Domain Name Service (DNS)

DNS is a service that allows computers to find or look up the IP address of a computer from a hostname. Originally computers just kept a file, usually called `hosts`, that held a list of hostnames and IP addresses. Many computers still have this file, although today it is normally fairly small. Back when you accessed only a few computers, these lookup files worked fine. As the number of computers "talking" to each other increased, these files became unmanageable. This inspired the creation of DNS, a client/server process that allows a computer to ask a local server for the IP address of a hostname. Instead of all the different computers having lookup files, all the computers can look to one source for the data. This is a good first step, but it still requires that your DNS server know every IP address. Since there are over 4 billion possible IP addresses, this does not work very well. Therefore each DNS server also knows about DNS servers from other organizations. When your computer asks your DNS server about some.computer.com, if your DNS server does not know the IP address, it can ask other DNS servers. There are higher level DNS servers that do not know IP addresses, but can look at a hostname and determine which DNS server does know the answer. Hostnames are changed to IP addresses on the Internet by a cooperative effort of many DNS servers across the world. This may not seem efficient but it works. One enhancement that can speed things up is to enable your local DNS server to remember the IP address for any hostname that it has asked for recently, thus avoiding redundant requests.

Definition   DNS (Domain Name Service) *is a client/server process for acquiring the IP address that belongs to a hostname.*

Simple Mail Transfer Protocol (SMTP or E-Mail)

Throughout this chapter I have made comparisons between the postal service and the Internet. Of course you can also send mail over the Internet. This is similar to mailing a normal letter except that it is electronic, thus the name electronic mail, better known by its nickname, *e-mail.* There are two main reasons why e-mail is so popular. One is that it is free. You can send e-mail to anyone on the Internet and it does not cost you more than your in-place Internet connection, even if the recipient is halfway across the world. The other reason is that e-mail is fast. It is hard to predict how soon someone will receive an e-mail, but it will always be faster than sending snail mail. Usually e-mail arrives in a matter of minutes.

Definition   E-mail (electronic mail) *is a method of sending mail to someone over the Internet.*

In order to send e-mail you need the correct e-mail address. E-mail addresses look like joan@bannan.com. The portion of the address before the @ is the user name of the person you are sending mail to, and the part after the @ is the hostname of that person's mail server. In this example, joan is my userID. But it could just as well be a random mixture of far less meaningful numbers and letters. Normally there is just one or perhaps a few mail servers for an organization, but there are often hundreds of e-mail accounts on one mail server. Mail servers operate on the basis of SMTP (Simple Mail Transfer Protocol), a simple way to move e-mail around the world from place to place.

To send e-mail, first a connection to a mail server is made. Next the TO and FROM addresses must be specified. Optionally you can add CC, BCC, and a SUBJECT. All of these are entered in the top of the message window. Everything else is the body of the message. From this point on the mail server will examine the TO address and determine in a method similar to the IP routing description where to send the e-mail next. This will continue from mail server to mail server until it either arrives at the final destination, or it gets *bounced* back. When the e-mail finally arrives at the destination, it gets appended to the end of the *mailbox* for the specified user. When the user next logs on to the mail server, it will inform him of the waiting mail.

Definition *An e-mail message is* bounced *(returned to you) if it cannot be delivered for some reason. This is one reason why having a correct return address is important.*

Definition *A* mailbox *is a temporary storage place for e-mail until the user gets around to reading it.*

Post Office Protocol (POP3). You may get your e-mail on a PC and not actively log on to a mail server. The process that delivers mail to your computer is not covered under SMTP. If you access the mail server directly, for example, on a UNIX system, your e-mail will be waiting for you there, but many users prefer that e-mail show up when they log on to a mail client on their desktop. This heralds the introduction of POP3, which allows mail clients to access the mail server and move mail to your PC on demand. This may sound a little redundant. Why not use SMTP? There are a few reasons, but most importantly, SMTP is designed to be run on a system that is always up. This is fine for server machines since the only reason one of these machines goes down is because of a problem, but desktop machines are different. People are always turning them on and off, and for SMTP that would mean that if an e-mail arrived while it was off, that e-mail might be lost. Therefore, running SMTP on your PC doesn't really work. POP3 is a protocol that does not wait around for e-mail to arrive like SMTP but instead goes out and asks the POP server for it. It just has to be on when you are accessing e-mail. SMTP and POP3 complement each other nicely. Outgoing messages go to the SMTP mail server for delivery, while incoming messages go the POP server to wait around for your PC to ask for them.

Mailing Lists. Mailing lists are more or less exactly what they sound like. Instead of typing in a whole bunch of e-mail addresses, you can just enter the name of the mailing list, often called an *alias.* Mailing lists come in two flavors, one that is kept with your local mail program and the other that is maintained by the network administrator for your organization. Perhaps everyone in your HR department is supposed to get a weekly e-mail concerning all open job requisitions or some such thing. Depending upon the size of your company, a company-wide alias for HR could make life a lot easier.

List Servers. A list server is similar to a mailing list but with an added twist. List servers are a way of creating a discussion group where any number of people can participate. List servers have their own e-mail account on the network. When someone sends e-mail to this account, the list server also sends a copy of that e-mail to everyone who participates in the discussion. You can subscribe or unsubscribe to a list server by sending a correctly formatted e-mail message. While they can be interesting to join, often this type of server initiates a flood of time-consuming, personal e-mail messages.

E-Mail Clients. There are a number of clients available for e-mail. Two common open standards clients are Eudora and Netscape Navigator available at `http://www.qualcomm.com/` and `http://home.netscape.com/`, respectively. Due to the open architecture of POP3, there are many programs that can access e-mail and more coming out all the time. Eudora and Netscape Navigator are available for both the Macintosh and Windows and provide a full suite of e-mail features. Often one of these applications is given out by Internet Service Providers to their clients for e-mail access.

Proprietary Options. There are also a number of proprietary options for e-mail. The most common are the Microsoft suite of office tools. Microsoft Exchange is a nice tool that provides both e-mail and scheduling that are closely tied together. These types of tools work extremely well when you are using them in a homogeneous environment, but can be limited in a more heterogeneous environment. The Exchange e-mail and calendar server are proprietary, so you must be in the Exchange environment to use them.

File Transfer Protocol (FTP)

The File Transfer Protocol (FTP) is a method of sending and retrieving files. Using FTP for file transfer is preferable to e-mail for two primary reasons. One is that e-mail must be initiated by someone on the sending side, and two, there are limitations on the file size of an e-mailed document. This limitation is hard to predict and often not under your control. The only real way to find out the limitation is to send the file and see if it makes it. Usually if the e-mail is too large, you will receive a bounced message telling you that the maximum e-mail size for mail server X is Y size. The smallest size I've seen is 100 kilobytes, which is pretty small when you are trying to e-mail files. You can get around this by breaking the e-mail into many parts, each of which must be smaller than the maximum size, but what a hassle for users on both sides and it's error prone.

Assuming your user ID has permissions to access a particular server or files on a server, FTP allows you to connect to the destination machine with a user ID and password and then browse the system's files until you find what you need. You may then retrieve files in a binary or ASCII format, binary for non-text files and ASCII for text files. If the retrieved file does not open correctly, you probably need to try the other format. FTP also lets you put files on the remote system.

So far FTP sounds a lot like mounting a remote file server volume, but there are differences, and one does not replace the other. File servers allow you to connect network drives to your computer and view them as if they were directly connected to your computer. Although there is an Internet standard that is used for this purpose called *Networked File System* (NFS), it is not heavily used by desktop Macintoshes and Microsoft Windows, both of which have their own standards for connecting network drives to them. I suppose that it is possible to connect a network drive over the Internet, but the overhead created would make it difficult to use, while FTP has very little overhead.

Anonymous FTP. Anonymous FTP is just a special case of a regular FTP server that allows anyone to connect and retrieve files from it. Normally anonymous FTP servers do not allow visitors to leave files, or at least allow them to leave files only in a special directory. Sometimes as a security measure, anonymous FTP servers are set up such that you cannot see the filenames directly, but instead must know what the filenames are before retrieving them. Anonymous FTP servers are most commonly used by computer software and hardware companies that want to allow customers to get updates, tech notes, and the like. Another use for an anonymous FTP server is archiving public domain and shareware software. You can find a list of anonymous FTP sites at

```
http://www.roma2.infn.it/infn/ftp-interface.html
```

Personal Servers. It used to be that the only computers that could have an FTP server running on them were UNIX servers. Today there are FTP servers that run also on Macintosh and Windows, allowing you access to files on your own computer from anywhere over the Internet. Most FTP servers are easy to set up and allow you to create user names and passwords for log-in purposes. This does mean that the computer running the service must remain connected to the network and be on all the time, but for those who want this ability, it is not too much of a sacrifice.

FTP Mail Server. When I mentioned before that e-mails had to be initialized on the sending side, that was not 100 percent correct. There are things called FTP mail servers out there that allow people without FTP access to get at an FTP server in a roundabout way. You can send files to an FTP mail server as you would to an individual e-mail address, but you need to embed special commands in the e-mail message. These commands can also tell the FTP server to send a uuencoded file back to you via e-mail. This is a slower, ungainly method for retrieving files, but it does provide an FTP server to those without any other access.

FTP Clients. The normal client access to an FTP server is command-line based and not especially user friendly. It uses commands such as `open ftp.apple.com`, `put data.zip`, `get netscape.exe`, and `prompt` to tell the server what to do. For someone who is not familiar with the client, it can be difficult to use correctly. Luckily there are GUI tools that perform the same function but with a more intuitive interface. Again, these clients work equally well on both Macintosh and Windows. On the Windows side the best program that I've found for this is WS_FTP. It has a wide range of features that most people will not use, but can make life much easier than it would be if you didn't have them. On the Macintosh there is a program called Fetch that is also very nice and easy to use. Both of these are commercial software products that are well worth the money if you will be using FTP to any extent. Netscape Navigator also has an FTP client built into it, but this client is mostly specialized for accessing anonymous FTP servers and can be difficult or impossible to use correctly in other circumstances. The URLs for these FTP clients are listed in Chapter 7.

Network News Transfer Protocol (NNTP or Newsnet)

The *Network News Transfer Protocol* (NNTP or more commonly known as Newsnet) is a collection of thousands of discussion groups that span the world. The discussion groups are much like a list server. Each discussion group talks about a specific subject that all the subscribers share an interest in. There are many Newsnet servers all over the world. They all communicate so that when someone posts an article on one server, that server forwards it to others until it reaches all the Newsnet servers everywhere. The individual newsgroups have names such as `misc.job.offered`. The newsgroups are divided into seven main categories shown in Table 3.4.

Category	Topic
comp	computers and computer science
sci	sciences other than computer science
news	the Newsnet itself or general interest
rec	recreation activities
soc	social topics
talk	subjects that promote debate (politics and religion)
misc	subjects that do not fit into other categories

Table 3.4

Newsnet Categories and Topics

Beyond these seven categories are other newsgroups such as the `alt` group, which talks about more controversial subjects or subjects that were added to `alt` because it was easy to do. Local servers may add newsgroups that are of specific interest to the organization, and block newsgroups that are of questionable content such as `alt.sex`. If some of the newsgroups you are interested in are not available on your local server, there are also commercial Newsnet servers out there that can be accessed for a minimum fee.

Newsgroup Clients. There are many newsgroup clients available for all platforms. They all offer a wide range of features that make reading news very easy. Some of the older news readers are rn and nn, both of which started life as command-line programs.

Both Netscape Navigator and Microsoft Explorer offer newsgroup readers within the browser environment.

HyperText Transfer Protocol (HTTP)

The HyperText Transfer Protocol (HTTP) receives a lot of attention today because it is the heart and soul of the Web. HTTP allows the transmission of HyperText Markup Language (HTML) files to the client browser. HTML files are text files that describe how to display text, graphics, colors, and links on the client machine. This protocol allows the end user to easily jump from page to page simply by clicking on the hypertext or links that tell the browser which page on which server to use next. Multiple links can exist on a single document.

Web Servers. The server is the software that sends out HTML pages (or whatever pages are called by the HTML code) to the clients. There are a number of servers on the market, some free and others quite expensive (see Table 3.5). Each server has different capabilities and capacity. Some are designed to run on larger expensive computers that can provide the serving capability for a good-sized company, while others can run on your Windows 95 machine. The major players in the Web server field are Microsoft, Oracle, and Netscape. Each product has pluses and minuses. The Microsoft Internet Information Server 2.0 is included in the price of Windows NT 4.0, which makes it attractive to people who like that platform. However, it does not offer a solution to those who are running UNIX machines, which many of the Web servers in the world today are. Since currently Sun's line of Ultra servers seems to give the greatest capacity for the dollar by a strong margin, UNIX machines probably won't be removed from the playing field anytime soon. The Oracle and Netscape servers have versions that

URL	What You Will Find There
http://www.apache.org	Apache
http://www.oracle.com/	Oracle WebServer
http://home.netscape.com/	Netscape Enterprise Server
http://home.netscape.com/	Netscape Fast Track Server
http://www.microsoft.com/	Microsoft Internet Information Server
http://java.sun.com/	Jeeves

Table 3.5
Web Servers

can be run on both Windows NT and many flavors of UNIX. This makes them more desirable since you can have the software regardless of the hardware platform. Both these systems have strong database support, which makes it easier to build dynamic Web pages. My personal favorite is the Netscape Enterprise Server because it's easy to administer and comes bundled with tools such as the verity search engine. Sun will soon be releasing Jeeves, the first Web server written in Java. (For those who wonder what Java is, just wait a few paragraphs.)

Web Clients. There are also a number of browsers available on the market today (see Table 3.6). The two most popular are Netscape Navigator and Microsoft Internet Explorer. Both browsers have similar features, but there are some differences that can cause problems if you're creating Web pages that will be viewed by both. One major difference is that Netscape's browser currently incorporates an e-mail reader, while Microsoft offers its Exchange e-mail software as a separate product.

URL	What You Will Find There
http://home.netscape.com/	Netscape Navigator 3.0
http://home.netscape.com/	Netscape Navigator Gold 3.0
http://www.microsoft.com/	Microsoft Internet Explorer
http://www.sun.com/	HotJava

Table 3.6
Web Browsers

Databases

While this is outside the realm of Internet protocols, it is important to understand the importance of database servers on the Internet. Databases allow the creation of dynamic Web pages and the ability to access important data across the Web. Static Web pages are only able to present static information, seriously limiting the effectiveness of the Web. Imagine these two scenarios: You just moved and you need to submit a new IRS W-2 form. Since you work at a company that has a strong Web presence, you access the Intranet and search for W-2. If your company has a static Web page system, then you might find out where to get and send the new forms. If, however, your company has dynamic Web pages with databases connected to the Web, it is very possible that you could modify your W-2 online using an electronic form and never touch a piece of paper. This would also mean that whoever has to deal with payroll would never need to touch your records. Employees could take full responsibility to update this type of information. This is some of the real power behind the Web on an Intranet environment. It does not really matter which database system you use, so long as the data is in there someplace and accessible via the network so that a Web server can use and modify it when appropriate. For more about databases, see Chapter 8.

JAVA (Welcome to a New World)

One of the new and exciting aspects of the Internet is the introduction of the Java programming language from Sun Microsystems. Java is a platform-independent programming language that is gaining great support in the Internet world. Currently the programs being written in Java are simple things, but just over the horizon great things are brewing. For example, Corel is developing a product that allows word processing, spreadsheet, presentation design, and more, all over the Internet or Intranet. What this means is that through your Web browser you can start to access the same types of applications that today must be run on your desktop. In fact Sun Microsystems is developing whole computer systems based on Java that will have extremely low maintenance. These systems will have no hard drives or local software to cause problems. They will be networked computers in the truest sense. Even their basic operating system will be loaded over the network and, as such, will have many advantages in the correct arena. Hmmm. Does this sound familiar? The "mainframes" of tomorrow will be a lot smaller and more powerful, and the new "dumb" terminals won't be so dumb.

Summary

This chapter just gives a feel for some of the basic parts of the Internet, but leaves much unsaid. For further information on many topics about the Internet check out the resources in Table 3.7. Another source of information is the Web itself. There is more information out there than you can digest in a lifetime, but finding what you need could take a good portion of that lifetime. Start your quest with a visit to one of these search engines:

```
http://www.altavista.com
http://www.yahoo.com
```

Book	Topic
Douglas E. Comer and David L. Steven, *Internetworking with TCP/IP*, vols. 1–3, Prentice Hall	TCP/IP
W. Richard Stevens and Gary R. Wright, *TCP/IP Illustrated*, vol. 1 and 2, Addison-Wesley	TCP/IP
Craig Hunt, *TCP/IP Network Administration*, O'Reilly & Associates, Inc.	TCP/IP
Cricket Liu and Paul Albitz, *DNS and BIND*, O'Reilly & Associates, Inc.	DNS
Bryan Costales, with Eric Allman and Neil Rickert, *sendmail*, O'Reilly & Associates, Inc.	SMTP
Cricket Liu, Jerry Peek, Russ Jones, Bryan Buus, and Adrian Nye, *Managing Information Services*, O'Reilly & Associates, Inc.	HTTP, FTP, list servers, Gopher
Susan Estrada, *Connecting to the Internet*, O'Reilly & Associates, Inc.	Internet connections
Peter van der Linden, *Just Java*, Prentice Hall	Java

Table 3.7
Internet Books

While the Internet is certainly a powerful tool, it can be overshadowed by the usefulness of a properly deployed Intranet. I believe that the Intranet is the way to make a truly paperless office. Much of the support structure that is currently maintained in the workplace could be moved to Intranet applications. With the advent of Java and other similar tools I believe we are on the verge of a new revolution in computer science.

4 E-Mail, Workflow, and Online Meetings

What You Can Do

Let's assume that your company has site-wide electronic mail that allows users to send messages (unformatted documents) with attached files (formatted documents). This chapter offers some pointers on how to manage the information that travels through this vital component of your Intranet. We discuss different ways you can use *e-mail* to organize correspondence, "workflow" business processes, and set up an environment with less paper and less voice mail (yippee!).

What You Will Need

Electronic mail has a lot of possibilities, and you will definitely need to know something about the following features:

- using e-mail to "push information"
- distribution lists
- e-mail etiquette
- e-mail security
- attaching formatted documents
- setting up workflow and public forums
- workflow
- shareware and information examples

- online meetings
- levels of security
- user e-mail management and retention tips

How to Share Information on an Intranet

Definition   E-mail, *short for electronic mail, is simply the process by which messages are routed from one individual to another or several, using an electronic messaging system. E-mail has been around for quite some time, but, in the past, users were limited to sending and receiving messages from others on the same computer network. With the growth of the Internet and Intranets, companies have begun communicating via e-mail, person-to-person and company-to-company around the globe.*

Using E-Mail to Push Information

Electronic mail systems can be used to route messages traditionally sent in paper form, including

- internal company distributions: memos, company announcements, and flyers
- work group documents: proposals, project plans, and status reports
- employee information: resumes, evaluations, timesheets, and travel reports
- externally distributed documents: letters, requests for proposals, and vendor communications

In traditional e-mail environments, the e-mail system is used to "push" information to others. The originator of the e-mail determines what information she wants to send, to whom she wants to send it, and then "pushes" the information out to the recipients via e-mail. In this manner it is fairly straightforward to use an e-mail system for one-to-one and one-to-many communications.

Distribution Lists

A *distribution list* is simply a list of names and associated electronic addresses grouped together for group mailings. The reason the names are associated are varied; perhaps the members belong to the same department, project, classification of employee, or are persons interested in a particular subject. In company-wide e-mail environments, the system administrators often set up distribution lists to meet company-defined groupings of employees. Additionally, individuals may set up personal distribution lists to facilitate individual mailings to personally defined groups of people. Individual distribution lists are often housed in an electronic *personal address book.*

Definition   Distribution lists *are the electronic version of traditional mailing lists.*

Definition   *An individual user's* personal address book *is housed within the e-mail system where she may set up individual entries or distribution lists to facilitate mailing information quickly and efficiently. It is essentially an on-line "Rolodex," with additional options.*

By using distribution lists, e-mail can become a robust platform for individuals, groups, and entire companies to easily disseminate information to multiple recipients. Instead of printing and mailing information via the standard paper process, companies can reduce the cost, inherent delays, and waste created by traditional paper routing. Suddenly the process of sending out a company newsletter can be streamlined and done in a matter of days; preparing and sending out a company announcement can be done in a matter of hours;

and sending out an emergency bulletin can be done virtually immediately.

E-Mail Etiquette

Upon receipt of a direct e-mail, a user may reply to the sender. Most systems allow for REPLY and REPLY TO ALL functions. Use REPLY to reply to only the sender of the message. Use REPLY TO ALL to reply to the sender and all other recipients. A word of caution, make certain that you understand the default setting of the reply option within the e-mail system you use. Many a user has inadvertently replied to all with not-for-public consumption information when his intent was to merely reply to the sender. For instance, I had a friend who was considering taking a job in a different department. His boss had no idea he was considering the switch. He replied to a person who sent a message via a distribution list. The way this distribution list is set up, REPLY goes to the whole distribution list not just the person who sends the original message. You already know, of course, that his boss was one of the "oops" recipients.

In addition, some systems allow the flexibility of directing messages not only in a TO field, but include a CC (courtesy copy) and, some, a BCC (blind courtesy copy) field. Typically, a recipient listed in the TO field is receiving information that the sender believes the recipient needs to know or is expected to act on. The CC is for someone to whom the information is sent as an FYI (for your information), but no action is expected. The third field, BCC, routes the e-mail to others without revealing the identity of persons and e-mails listed in the BCC field to the recipients listed in the TO and CC fields. The BCC field may be used for many reasons, including simply not wanting to divulge the e-mail addresses of the persons listed there to the other recipients. A person receiving an e-mail via a BCC address is not expected to act on the message unless the nature of the message suggests otherwise. Additionally, you can use the BCC field to anonymously send yourself a copy as a reminder that something in the e-mail requires your attention.

E-Mail Security

A word of caution regarding the security of electronic mail: E-mail systems are extremely easy to use and, because of this, the information captured in an e-mail is vulnerable to security threats, unless protected. While many systems offer security to mark e-mail as private, or even to encrypt e-mail, most systems and users do not go to this extreme, so you should use caution when mailing sensitive information via an e-mail system. Not only can e-mail systems be vulnerable to standard security threats, but the recipient could choose to forward your e-mail to others. A safe rule of thumb is to ask yourself three questions before hitting the Send on any e-mail:

- How would I feel if everyone on my team read this e-mail?
- How would I feel if everyone in my company read this e-mail?
- How would I feel if everyone on the Internet read this e-mail?

If you feel okay with all of these, then go ahead and send it. If you have any hesitation, make sure that you secure the message appropriately. In extreme cases (shudder) don't send information via e-mail if you have concerns about the security or privacy of the information contained within.

Attaching Formatted Documents

In addition to the unformatted document contained within the content of the electronic message, most e-mail systems allow for the attachment of electronic files, or formatted documents, that are then routed with the message. It is important to know the computing environment of the intended recipients so that any attachments are decipherable by them. Once assured that this is the case, many types of information can be attached and sent via e-mail. Typically attachments are

- attached word processing documents, spreadsheets, and presentations.
- pointers or links to information housed on a shared resource such as a shared drive address, Web address, URL, or a document housed in a Document Management Retention System. (For more about Document Management Systems, see Chapter 9.)

Sending information to a user located on a different system typically involves actually attaching copies of documents or files you have generated on your system. For example, when a recipient is located at another company, this is the desired method for transferring documents. If, however, the recipient has access to shared computer resources (shared network drives, servers, and so forth), often a pointer or link to the referenced information is sent in lieu of a copy. The reasons for this are numerous. Primarily, it is to limit the number of copies of the information in order to preserve the integrity of the original document. Secondly, referencing the document, instead of sending a copy, ensures that the recipient views the most current version. Perhaps the document has been updated between the time the original message was sent and when the recipient reads it. A pointer to the location of the document ensures that the recipient views the most current version. This also allows users to take advantage of the check-in/check-out and version control of a Document Management System. Finally, sending a pointer or link limits the amount of information sent over the network to the recipient until (and unless) the recipient requests that the information be sent, thus conserving bandwidth.

Speaking of bandwidth, which is a recurring theme throughout this book, there are several recommendations which, if you educate your users, will be kinder to recipients as well as avoid a potential e-mail "clogged artery." When sending attachments, if you know what platform your recipient is using, it's always preferable to `zip`, `stuff`, or `tar` files. Sometimes, however, they cannot open them at the other end; for example, if you create a self-extracting zip file which is actually a Windows application and the recipient is a MacUser. Another recommendation is if you don't need to send an attachment as a formatted document or even worse, as an image, don't. For instance, say you just want someone to read the contents of a word processing file, to see if they concur, have comments, or suggestions. Unless they need the formatting, it's a lot nicer to cut and paste the information. I have sat wondering why a message is taking soooo looonggg to come in only to find out someone sent me a captured image of a "404 Not Found" message on one of my Web pages to let me see what it said. If you encounter one, it is a lot more bandwidth friendly to just tell the Webmaster what the alert box said than to include a 275K bitmap file.

Another consideration is how your messaging system encodes files. As an avid MS Exchange user I have often had to go into my personal address book and tell MS Exchange not to send to particular people in Exchange in Rich Text Format. You may find that you will need to choose to send messages coded in MIME or UUEncode depending on how your recipient's messaging system is set up. Often, unfortunately, it's a trial-and-error scenario, but it can be worked out with communication.

Information referenced in e-mail can be housed on shared drives, in Document Management Systems, in database systems, or on the Web (Intranet or Internet). An e-mail message can then directly link to this information. Direct linking allows the recipient to select the referenced item and immediately access it. This enables e-mail to suddenly facilitate a "pull" system of distribution instead of merely a "push." The pull method enables you to pull the information to your computer when you decide to look at it, instead of having the actual information pushed to you in e-mail. The reference to the information is still pushed, but the actual distribution of the information is pulled when needed.

Workflow

Traditionally, *workflow* is associated with highly sophisticated, rule-based computer software engines that, following analysis of a business process, model the process electronically. This involves routing information via an electronic messaging backbone, typically an e-mail system, and setting up decision points so that the information "knows" what to do next. Entire processes can be modeled in this manner and when integrated with electronic signature capability can completely replace standard paper-based processes. This clearly is the goal for many organizations and processes. Companies and individuals, however, can achieve significant return on investment via simple electronic mail–based workflow that merely routes documents electronically based on decisions made by users. E-mail, alone, may be used to automate workflow routing. Simply routing information electronically can provide a significant improvement in overall processing time and provide tools for tracking and managing the information.

Definition   Workflow *uses computer networking technology to route work processes in a manner that models the path taken to carry the process from start to finish.*

One of the easiest workflow systems to set up and understand is a traditional electronic mail–based system that employs folders or directories to organize the items contained within. Most users start with single IN and OUT boxes. Projects can further be classified by topic matter and moved into individual folders to model the business process. For example, a project involving an engineering change to a system might include the following project phases, each with a unique folder grouped hierarchically under the project in the e-mail system:

- specification
- awaiting approval
- released to engineering
- released to quality assurance
- awaiting final approval
- approved for release

The user moves the message containing the current version of the project document to the appropriate folder and routes copies, or grants access to, others as they become involved in the process.

In mail systems that use public folders, additional users with varying levels of viewing, reviewing, and approving, can be granted access to the documents at different points in the cycle and, when appropriate, move the document to the next level of the process, by moving it to the next relevant folder. Typically an e-mail message is sent signifying that the project has passed a milestone and is ready for the next reviewer. The e-mail highlights the document's current location in the workflow hierarchy. Some e-mail systems with public folders serve as discussion databases, where comments about the items contained within the public folders can be captured and associated with the item referenced. The actual location and virtual location of the e-mail are typically separate as most systems merely pass references to the e-mails associated with the folders or directories that reference it. In this manner it is easy to virtually associate multiple copies of the e-mail in multiple folders, while in fact there is only one e-mail with multiple references to it.

Combining e-mail with document management provides a platform to effectively reengineer many business processes using simple workflow. Adding messaging backbones, forms, decision-based workflow routing, and electronic signatures, provides a platform to replace many traditional paper business processes with electronic processes. Check out the first URL in Table 4.1 regarding Collaboration Strategies, a groupware research firm that has analyzed this growing trend toward electronic workflow.

URL	What You Will Find There
www.collaborate.com/intranet.html	Analysis by Collaboration Strategies of how major corporations are leveraging networks and collaborative software for competitive advantage
http://www.internetdatabase.com	Internet Resources Database guide to information, including shareware, available on the Internet

Table 4.1

Shareware and Information on E-mail, Workflow, and Online Meetings

Numerous shareware tools exist for e-mail. The best place to look for them is, of course, on the Web. Running a search for "shareware e-mail" will turn up numerous possibilities. But a good place to get started is to visit the second URL in Table 4.1, the Internet Resources Database.

Shareware and Information Examples

Searching for your particular platform will narrow the options. Peruse the features offered, and in addition to the ones referenced in Table 4.1, look for an e-mail package that allows you to send MIME-compliant attachments. Additionally, most Internet browsers let you send and receive messages without leaving the browser environment. Check out the one you have, be it Netscape, Internet Explorer, or another. See what functions the embedded e-mail option offers; perhaps it already meets your needs. Browsers are not stopping there, however. The Netscape browser and Internet Explorer are now offering groupware functionality by integrating their other product lines that include sharing information, threaded discussions, and calendar programs. In the past most of these groupware features were associated with products, such as Lotus Notes, which now offers an Internet option. Be sure to find out what your vendor of choice offers. Many companies work licensing deals with software vendors that allow users to have multiple copies of the software, one for the office and one for the home office, because the intent is that only one copy be in use at any time. Be sure that using a copy at home conforms to the guidelines set forth by your company; some companies allow for incidental use, and others prohibit it.

Online Meetings

Meetings traditionally involve several people taking time to get together to discuss and resolve issues. Online meetings merely offer an alternative virtual space in which to conduct a meeting. These meetings can be facilitated in many ways including electronic mail, discussion forums, even video teleconferencing. Depending on the media, online meetings can be facilitated in such a manner that all members are participating at the same time, or each party participates at his or her convenience.

With the computing and networking technology available today, we have become the empowered electronic workforce. With employees able to work anywhere anytime, time and location become less and less of a barrier to conducting business. Meetings, the final frontier, pose opportunities for fully exploiting available technology to eliminate the need for groups of people to gather together in person to hash out issues. Communicating electronically provides a platform to resolve issues that traditionally required calling a meeting. Using e-mail, teams can communicate and, in many cases, effectively conduct business previously conducted in person. But, depending on the mail system, threads to original information can be lost. Another risk is that required or desired participants can be inadvertently left out or brought in at a point where they missed valuable background information.

This is where discussion databases can facilitate efficiency. A discussion database is a platform where users can throw out issues, questions, and information. It is a vehicle that captures comments, answers, and related information and then relates it back to the original item, threading associated information along the way. Discussion databases are often housed within sophisticated e-mail systems. A participant can join a discussion database thread long after it starts and can immediately gain access to the entire discussion.

A couple of basic guidelines should be established when using discussion databases to do business. One of the benefits of a meeting is that all parties are in attendance, tasks can be assigned, dates and milestones decided and agreed upon, and issues resolved. Typically discussion forums are more open ended, and vigilance is required to ensure that items are acted on and issues resolved. This can be managed in numerous ways. The easiest is to have the originator of the item assign dates at which the discussion will cease and a decision will be made to go forth. Participants are sent e-mail linked to the items that require action, input, and so forth, and are informed of appropriate deadlines. Comments from the participants, including requests to change deadlines, are captured in the discussion, and the originator of the item drives it to completion. Much of this management can be programmed into e-mail–based discussion database systems, but users must learn to participate in order for their "e-voices" to be heard.

Levels of Security

Mail systems, as mentioned before, are not known to be exceptionally secure. The greatest saving grace, however, is that most systems used in corporations are reasonably secure within the company's own Intranet, and unless a user explicitly includes an external Internet address, the mail will not be routed outside the company. Even so, make certain that you understand the security features, limitations, and loopholes of any e-mail–based messaging system that you are using for e-mail, workflow, or online meetings. Use the same caution recommended for e-mail to secure any information that you provide so that you won't be embarrassed by your input making its way to the wrong person. E-mail security is improving, but in most systems, it is still the responsibility of the user to take appropriate security measures; for example, marking items as private, using encryption, not sending secure information in the body of the message, (but referencing it in a secure repository), or in extreme cases not posting or sending sensitive information in the first place.

E-Mail Management and Retention Tips

One of the best features of e-mail is the simple fact that you can save an online version of whatever you get and whatever you send. Most server-based systems limit how much e-mail you are allowed to save on the server. The user, however, can always save other copies elsewhere: on a server, in a document database, on local hard drives, or even (cringe) on floppy disks. Any data that is entered into e-mail–based systems for workflow or online meetings can be saved in a similar manner, but typically these systems are covered by some retention and backup policies and procedures. Be sure you understand who can delete information and when or why that might happen on any system where you save your e-mail or enter data in workflow or online meeting systems, so that you don't encounter any surprises if an administrator deletes the stuff you haven't backed up.

Saving backups of your e-mail is usually your own responsibility. Shared resources, such as workflow systems and online meeting systems, may be covered by company backup and recovery procedures, as we mentioned, but make sure you know what they are and how to retrieve any data stored there in the event it disappears online. Also, if the data is due to be archived, store a copy someplace where you can retrieve it.

Organization of your e-mail can help significantly when you are trying to retrieve things. In addition, most mail systems offer tools that assist with retrieval. Some are better than others, but up-front organization can do more than any e-mail retrieval system I've ever encountered. For example, take me, a writer, assistant Webmaster, independent contractor, colleague, and friend. What do you think my e-mail organization looks like? Figure 4.1 is a snapshot of how it looks on a good day, with most of the incoming mail sorted into logical folders for future use. To give you an idea of how to sort your mail, here's a breakdown of how I use mail folders.

My e-mail system alphabetizes rather than prioritizes so I am going to take these out of order. First I want to talk about the *TODO* folder, which contains all the hot items on my list for my current job as a Web site manager/assistant Webmaster. In the standard time management terminology, these would be my "A" items that need to be done soon

Figure 4.1

One way to organize incoming e-mail

and have a high level of importance. This is where I often hold messages to myself or blind courtesy copies that I sent to myself when I replied to a message, that reference other TODOs further down in the hierarchy. At any point in the day when I look in this folder, typically first thing in the morning and last thing before I log off in the evening, I can quickly prioritize these items and then move my focus to the next task.

Next is *Keepers*. This is where I store e-mail that I've received from others that contains information I want close at hand; for example, my current boss's new pager number, a hot lead's company name and phone number. You get the idea: stuff I might need immediately and don't want to have to search for. Nor do I want these hanging out and crowding my in-box. As soon as they come in, I move them into Keepers. I sometimes snag items from my sent mail folder to add to this folder's collection.

Third on my list, but first in my heart, is my book. Here's where I keep organized all the e-mail related data that you are reading right now. The folders in this category are fairly self-explanatory:

- *Contacts* contains messages with e-mail addresses and phone numbers of all the fantastic folks who helped me pull together this information in an incredibly short amount of time. This includes my editor and other contacts at Addison-Wesley, except for the publicist, whom I filed in the next folder.
- *PR* contains the notes I exchanged with the Addison-Wesley publicist and e-mail from my wonderful editor, who found conventions where Addison-Wesley may send me to speak about topics in this book.
- *Reviews* contains the messages I received from peer reviewers of this book's proposal. It had comments from each of them to which I refer as I am writing. This is where I will logically file any e-mail regarding reviews of this book.
- *Sent* is where I file all the mail I send out to experts whom I interviewed to complete this project. I can check up on the status of each of these items or resend if my experts haven't gotten back to me yet.
- *TODO* is where I file all book-related e-mail that comes in requiring action. This allows me to put it off until I'm through working for the day at my regular job, or until the weekend. (Boy am I looking forward to weekends when this folder is emptied!)

Fourth on my list is the category *Webmaster.* This is where I collect all the e-mail that I reuse in my capacity as assistant Webmaster. The folders under this category contain

- *Hosting.* I keep reusable e-mails that I send to new clients and point them to important help pages regarding setting up an organizational site and detail what the requirements are to host a site on our Intranet server. I have other template messages that manage their expectations for how long it will take them to get write privileges and a message in which I "fill in the blanks" about the initial password they have received and how to change that password. I also keep e-mail from users who have requested services but have not been fully set up yet.

- *Newsgroups.* We kept getting feedback from the Internal Web regarding difficulty in accessing newsgroups. As the technical mysteries were solved, I kept a record of each one. Now when I receive a note from a user describing an error message, I pull out the appropriate scenario from the past and forward it on.

- *Search.* We have several kinds of servers and several search engines. The process of harvesting search information has been a challenge, so I created this folder to keep all our messages that resolved search engine problems and issues.

- *Stats.* As I was learning the UNIX commands to run our stats program, I filed all the e-mail correspondence between the Webmaster and me. I have a complete "how-to" record and great examples of how the stats program worked (and didn't work).

- *TODO.* When Webmaster action items come in, I usually do them right away, but if I have some reason to put them in abeyance, I file them here.

Finally, *Fun Stuff* is where I keep all the stuff that my colleagues and friends send me that makes me smile: jokes, amusing news clips, shared stories, and inspirational items. Without fun stuff, life would be too dreary for us all!

Okay, that's the organized approach. Now what if you forget to file a couple items and your in-box is overflowing, or you filed an e-mail, but can't remember where? What other options do you have for finding stuff? Most e-mail systems are set up with some simple sorting functionality. Typically you can sort by any of the fields captured in the properties of the message such as date, to, from, and subject. Some systems provide additional sorting options, enabling you to compose sophisticated searches; for example, "Give me all items sent to Joan from Dave in 1997, where the subject included the word Web." My experience has been, however, that none of these searches can compete with spending some time organizing your e-mail as you send and receive it. Searching and retrieving via queries is typically not quick, but when all else fails, you can use them to find what you're looking for. As e-mail systems become more database-like, sophisticated queries will become more user friendly, flexible, and robust.

Summary

In addition to the topics we've discussed to help you organize information, streamline processes, save time, and gain access to information you need when and where you need it—don't forget that one of the biggest rewards for moving from paper to online is wasting less paper. The time, cost, and overhead associated with managing paper and paper waste is enormous, and the environmental benefits associated with reducing paper waste and saving trees, water, and the wildlife in the forest cannot be measured. This transformation to the electronic medium for what have traditionally been paper processes will not only make you a more efficient performer, but you'll be able to take your great grandchildren to visit the forest in the next century and tell them that you helped to save the trees.

5 *Authoring Intranet Documents*

What You Can Do

You are creating documents and you have a Web server. Your users have a Web browser. This chapter addresses different ways you can create, test, and convert formatted (legacy) documents to be viewed on an Internal Web.

What You Will Need

The online authoring process has a lot of possibilities, but for sure you will need to know something about

- HyperText Markup Language (HTML)
- how to prepare text files for Web browsers
- authoring tools, such as HTML editors, *WYSIWYG* editors, or how to use Notepad or a word processing application as an HTML editor
- how to test your HTML code regardless of the editing tool you use
- utilities that convert word processing documents, graphics, and spreadsheets into HTML
- styles for multipurpose mapping, that is, maintaining a word processing and online version of the same document or converting legacy documents to *HTML* or *SGML*
- alternative viewing possibilities

Definition   HTML (HyperText Markup Language) *is the document coding language of the Web. It's a bandwidth friendly way to hyperlink. Its formatting capability is evolving rapidly. HTML is a SGML language. To most who have used WYSIWYG word processing for several years, it will seem like a giant step backward to the era of WordStar. Surely someone remembers WordStar?*

Definition   SGML (Standard Generalized Markup Language) *is an international standard for defining markup languages used for document encoding. SGML is typically used to create markup languages that describe the content of document objects. For example, within a document you can identify all places where the content is, say, a warning or perhaps programming code. This information could be used to apply a certain formatting style to the document object, or it could equally be used as a search criteria or as a basis for extracting information into a database.*

Definition   A WYSIWYG (What You See Is What You Get) *view of documents gives you a very good idea of how the printed page will look while you are viewing it on the screen.*

How to Create Web Documents

HTML

HyperText Markup Language (HTML) is the language of the Web, but browsers can view files in many other formats. The simplest form to view is text files, but there are several other options that launch helper or plug-in applications. HTML, however, is the lightest-bandwidth information vehicle with the greatest hypertext capability.

HTML is a set of tags placed around the text of a document that is then interpreted and displayed by browser software. It enables you, the author, to "tell" the browser to

- format documents,
- hyperlink to other documents, images, or resources (such as a database), or
- launch other "helper" applications (if the browser is configured for this).

Thanks to HTML editors (some are even WYSIWYG) and conversion utilities, and the ease with which HTML can be copied, a neophyte Web content provider does not need to master HTML to get a totally cool hypertext document ready for the Web.

In spite of all these utilities and possibilities, however, at least one of your content providers will need to understand HTML. You will want someone who can tweak the inevitable anomalies produced by WYSIWYG editors or conversion utilities or merely do some "postprocessing" when these editors and utilities do not produce precisely what you have in mind. And, alternative viewing possibilities can never replace a hot hyperlinked home page that navigates to other documents stored in whatever formats you choose to offer on your Internal Web. Otherwise, why bother with the Web? You could just have shared drives where users can find their documents (usually) and view them with native applications. For online HTML instruction, check out the URLs in Table 5.1:

URL	What You Will Find There
http://www.ncsa.uiuc.edu/General/Internet /WWW/HTMLPrimer.html	A Beginner's Guide to HTML
http://www.pcweek.com/eamonn/crash course.html	Crash course on writing documents for the Web
http://werbach.com/barebones/	The Barebones Guide to HTML

Table 5.1
HTML Resources on the Web

Another resource is existing Web-head authors like me. All the resources in this book and new resources destined for reprints will be kept up-to-date on my home page at `http://www.bannan.com` or you can e-mail me and ask me questions at joan@bannan.com. One of the many newsgroups where authors find each other and help each other with this ever evolving technology is the HTML Writers Guild. Their home page (at `http://www.hwg.org/`) states, "The HTML Writers Guild is the premiere international organization of World Wide Web page authors and Internet Publishing professionals. Guild members have access to resources including: HTML and Web business mailing lists, information repositories, as well as interaction with their peers."

There are also numerous books that cover HTML authoring in depth such as

- *Teach Yourself Web Publishing with HTML 3.0 in a Week,* by Laura Lemay (SAMS)
- *The HTML Source Book,* by Ian Graham (Wiley)
- *Webmaster in a Nutshell,* by Stephen Spainhour (O'Reilly Nutshell Handbook)

Creating Hyperlinks

The most common hyperlink uses HTTP, but several other protocols or tags can also be coded into your HTML:

- HTTP
- FTP
- MAILTO
- GOPHER
- NEWS
- TELNET

The three tags you will use most often when authoring for an Internal Web are HTTP, MAILTO, and FTP.

HTTP is the one you will use most as you author Web documents. It's the reason the Web is a web. You can use relative URLs (discussed later in this chapter) to establish links between documents within your server or full URLs to establish links to any Web server in the world.

MAILTO is sooo handy. If you've surfed the Web at all, you've seen one. This protocol lets your users send e-mail directly from the Web page to a feedback e-mail address, to the author of the page, or to anyone on e-mail. For instance, on my home page at `http://www.bannan.com` I have my e-mail address hyperlinked with the MAILTO protocol. The HTML looks like this:

```
<A HREF="MAILTO:joan@bannan.com">JoanBannan</A>
```

FTP is another of my favorites because it can fetch documents stored on computers that do not have Web servers installed on them and therefore do not support HTTP. When users click on this kind of hyperlink, they are prompted to download the file using FTP. An example of a good use for an FTP hyperlink is making available the printed copy of a huge electronic document delivery whitepaper that you have *chunked* into small HTML pages for Web consumption. You want to offer the whitepaper in its original, printable form on the first page of the Web version. You have a server and a "public" drive behind your firewall where you keep these sorts of papers so you'd rather store it there where everyone expects to find it, rather than place it on your Web server. Your FTP hyperlink might look like this:

```
<A HREF="FTP://coserv/public/doc-mgt/edd/
eddwhite.zip">EDD White Paper (zipped version)</a>
```

Definition   Chunking *means breaking a document into smaller pieces. This is a bandwidth-friendly, not to mention a user-friendly, way to present information. Usually you can just link each section to the next and create a hyperlinked Table of Contents to retain the document's unity. (See Chapter 10 for information about chunking huge documents.)*

For more about offering differently formatted versions of documents at your Web site, see Chapter 7.

There are four factors to consider when creating hyperlinks:

- relative URLs
- relevance
- reasons
- recommendations

Definition   A hyperlink *is a text or graphic that jumps to a new location when you click on it. On the Web the click may jump you to a document or resource on a server somewhere else in the world. In an online help application, the click only jumps you to somewhere else in the document or opens a little window displaying, say, a definition. On the Web, a common practice is to use an image in place of the text for the hyperlink.*

Using Relative URLs

Relative URLs are particularly useful if you are creating a multipage document with dependent links. For instance, you may have a large whitepaper that you would like to publish on your Internal Web, but you don't want your Web users to have to wait for 25 pages to download all at once. You therefore create an HTML version of the document that breaks at each point where a Heading 1 style starts a new topic. This is known as chunking. You then add navigational aids that link to each "next page" of the document, to each "previous page," to the hypertext table of contents, possibly to a hypertext index, and to the home page or title page of the document. As you are coding this document with HTML, you assume that all the pages of the document will be loaded into the same subdirectory on the Web server. Relative URLs make it easy to test the navigation of the document while you are still holding it on your local drive, and they still work when you move the whole set to another directory on the server.

Definition   A URL (Uniform Resource Locator) *is the string of characters at the top of your browser that starts with* `http://` *and often includes* www. *If you put an address there and then press* Enter, *it "tells" the browser which Web page to open.*

Definition   A relative URL *is a Web address that "tells" the computers to "start where you are and use* `http://` *to find the address you are looking for as opposed to an "absolute" or "full" URL, which gives the full protocol and path of the item you want to hyperlink. For instance, if you want to point to an HTML document named d-duck.htm from within a document named m-mouse.htm and they are both located within the Disney subdirectory of your*

Web server, you only need to put `<A HREF="d-duck.htm">` `Donald's Home Page</A>`. *You do not need to put the full address, which might be* `<A HREF="http://Amusement/Disney/` `d-duck.htm">Donald's Home Page</A>`. *Or if you want to use a relative address to point to an image file on the same server but in a different subdirectory, you need to "tell" the computers, using slashes and dots in front of the filename, to start here, and go back or forward through the directories. Using the previous example, to go back to the* `Amusement` *directory (back one directory) then into another called* `images` *(at the same level as the* `Disney` *directory), the relative URL might be* `<IMG` `SRC="../images/mickey.gif" ALT="Mickey Mouse">`.

The easiest way to explain a relative URL is by example. For instance, you may have a contact list containing everyone's home/work phone numbers, e-mail address, home address, birthday, and emergency contact. You, of course, would have this residing in the Personnel Department of the Human Resources Department. (I know it's the Department of Redundancy Department, but this is *only* an example.) Your company Web server has a subdirectory named `Personnel` under another subdirectory called `Human-Resources` within the `Orgs` (for Organizations) subdirectory off the company home page.

The full URL within the hyperlinked reference HTML tag might look something like this:

```
<A HREF="http://home.mycompany.com/Orgs/
Human-Resources/Personnel/contact.htm"> Contact
Information</A>
```

If you place other documents in the `Personnel` subdirectory you can use a relative URL to point to this list, and it would look like this:

```
<A HREF="contact.htm">Contact Information</A>
```

The advantage of using relative URLs is the mobility of a set of related documents. For example, you might author twelve related Human Resources documents in a local directory of your office computer and then move all of them to the server. You might not even know the server subdirectory on which they will reside. It doesn't matter. You can complete your documents, link them to each other, and test without knowing what the full (*absolute*) URLs will eventually be.

In this case, if you used full URLs you would have to know the full path on the server where you would be placing the documents, and if you move them, you would have to edit each document within the set. Note that you can also include full URLs to other locations within these documents that point to places elsewhere on the Web. You do not need to exclusively use relative URLs. For more about uploading files, testing links, and finding "broken links" see Chapter 7.

You can also *anchor* a spot in an HTML file using a relative address and jump to that spot from within the same document or from another document. This makes it easy to set up a hyperlinked table of contents at the beginning of a larger document. For instance, in `contact.htm` you could put an anchor using the HTML `name` tag within the contact information document at someone's name like this:

```
<A NAME="bannan">Joan Bannan</A>
```

A relative link to this anchor from within the same document would look like this:

```
<A HREF="#bannan">Joan Bannan</A>
```

A relative link from another document within the same subdirectory would look like this:

```
<A HREF="contact.htm#bannan">Joan Bannan</A>
```

A full URL reference to this anchor would look something like this:

```
<A HREF="http://home.mycompany.com/Orgs/
Human-Resources/Personnel/contact.htm#bannan">
```

You could also use a relative URL to another subdirectory within the Human Resources subdirectory, which could look something like this:

```
<A HREF="../Benefits-Forms/">Health and Dental
Forms</A>
```

The HTML coding in the previous example tells the browser to go back one subdirectory from where this HTML document is loaded, then forward into the `Benefits-Forms` subdirectory. Since there is no file listed after the slash (`/`) this URL will bring up an index of the files in this subdirectory or a page that has been associated with the index to replace it. Table 5.2 is a cheat sheet for coding relative links and anchors. For more about linking a page to the index of a subdirectory, see Symbolic Links in Chapter 7.

Link	Tells the Web Server to Use HTTP and ...
/DirectoryName-or-FileName	Start at the root
DirectoryName-or-FileName	Stay in the directory you are in (or document—see #AnchorName below)
../DirectoryName-or-FileName	Go up one directory toward the root then into a directory at the same level you are in
ThisDirectory/NextDirectory WithinThisOne	Start in this directory and go into a deeper directory
#AnchorName	Stay in this document and find the spot I marked with an anchor tag
"."	Stay in this directory and go to the home page or default index page

Table 5.2

Relative Link and Anchor Cheat Sheet

Hyperlinking

Hyperlinking is what makes the Web so cool. However, it's a great responsibility to author in such a way that the links you create enhance your documents rather than disrupt your reader's train of thought. For instance, you may be posting on your Internal Web for the Human Resources Department a document that contains information about retirement benefits. This document mentions how the IRS taxes deferred accounts. You could link the word *IRS* to the IRS home page at `http://www.irs.ustreas.gov/prod/`. But what's the point? Sending users to that location just because it exists may be a proverbial rabbit trail. On the other hand, if a recent change in a tax law affects the way your company does business, a specific IRS page may be totally appropriate and helpful.

Definition Hypertext *is text that is coded to jump to another location when you click on it. It's usually indicated with underlining and a different colored font.*

There are several good reasons to use hyperlinks:

- to conserve bandwidth
- to take advantage of existing Web information
- to update chunks, thus keeping content current
- to help users find the right information

Bandwidth should always be a consideration to Web authors. You have the power in a popular document to slow all servers within your Internal Web to a frustrating near-halt. If a document can be downloaded in chunks, it's faster for the user and more prudent for the network. Chunking is breaking a document into connected smaller pages with hyperlinks to other sections of the document. For example, I often create a hypertext table of contents on a separate Web page that links each heading listed in the table of contents to the actual heading of a multi-page document.

Another way to save bandwidth is to embed hyperlinks to images, making them available at the user's request, rather than downloading them with the document. This greatly reduces the main document load time. If visitors do not need the images to fully understand the prose, they may not need to access the image at all.

Take advantage of existing information. Why reinvent or rewrite what already exists when you can jump to it? For example, Pacific Bell's Internal Web publishes Help documents with instructions on how to configure the Pacific Bell standard browser to launch a document's native application (such as launching Word when you click on a Word file). Each time someone puts in a link to a document that is intended to launch the user's copy of the native application, there is always the chance that the user who wants to do so has not yet configured his browser to do so. With the Help information pages, already in place, the Pacific Bell author need not write instructions for the user. Instead, the author creates a link to "How to Configure Your Browser for Helper Applications."

Chunked updates. Another efficient use of hyperlinking is to single out pages that need to be updated regularly and separate them from parts of the same document that remain more or less static. For example, on the home pages for technical teams you may be tempted to list the team members, their phone numbers, and e-mail addresses. Instead, consider hyperlinking the word *team* to a spot on another Web page that contains a list of several technical teams. That way when you update the team list, the information on each technical team home page is up-to-date sans maintenance. The same is true for resource information "out there" that other people keep up-to-date. For example, on Silicon Graphics's Internal Web site the stock price is automatically updated by fetching the information from Yahoo every 15 minutes—the responsibility of updating the resource lies with Yahoo.

Recommendations for Hyperlink Authoring

Click Here. I once read criticism of Web authors who use "Click Here" instead of incorporating the link into the prose. I took the criticism to heart, criticized another person's work (at her request) passing along what I had read. Then I found that sometimes "Click Here" was clear, concise, to the point, and preferable. As mentioned earlier, one reason you might want to add a hyperlink is to have an image be optional or on "click-demand." Putting diagrams, screen captures, and other images in a separate file makes you a good Netizen. "Click *here* for a picture of the database input dialog box" might be preferable to just linking the words *database input dialog box* in the middle of a sentence.

Copying Source HTML

When you see a page that has the formatting you've been dying to "create," it's really easy to borrow it. For example, from a Windows machine go to the URL where the document is and then do the following:

1. Open your HTML editor to a new page (or Notepad or word processor if you wish).

2. Choose View, Source from the browser menu.

3. Select the area you want to copy with the mouse.

4. Press Ctrl+C to copy.

5. Hold down the Alt key and press the Tab key until you're back in your editing application.

6. Press Ctrl+V to paste the selection into your file.

7. Replace their data with yours.

Another option is to copy the whole page. To do that you simply choose File, Save As Source, and download it to one of your computer drives. With these instructions, let me warn that just because something is on the Web it is not necessarily free. Copyrights are enforced, and permission to copy is easy to obtain.

Testing Your HTML Code

After you have created a Web page, you will want to test it by looking at it in your browser.

Some HTML editors, like the one I use, have a test button that automatically opens a copy of your default browser and displays your document. I only use the test button once with each document. I see the page displayed, go back to my file and make the changes, save them. I then switch to the editor and click on the Reload or Refresh button. Also, working in this environment I find that the editor puts a less logical string in the Location or Address textbox than my browser can recognize for relative links. For example, it may put `file/local host` rather than just `file:c:\filename.htm`. When I click on relative links, my computer doesn't recognize that "local host" stuff. Therefore, if I really want to test my files, including all my links, I open the browser and choose File, Open or File, Open File (depending on my browser du jour) and keep all my test files with relative URLs in the same subdirectories that I will duplicate on the server. If your editor does not have the test feature, or if you are using Notepad or word processing software, you will need to display the file in your browser this way in the first place.

For some people, an HTML editor, conversion utilities, and WYSIWYG editors are way overkill. If you are one of those people who needs to create only a simple HTML page on rare occasions, you may choose to read a little about HTML, consider the freeware conversion utilities later in this chapter that convert documents and Excel spreadsheets, and then create/edit your pages in Notepad or your word processor. You will still need to test your code. If you are on a 16-bit system, you may run into a little trouble using your word processing software, but not if you follow these instructions:

- Save your file.
- Close the file out of your word processor.
- Choose File, Open or File, Open File from your browser menu.
- If you need to make changes to the file, you will need to open it again in your word processor, but you can leave it open in your browser. Make the changes, close the file in the word processor each time you want to test it, and then switch to your browser and press the Reload or Refresh button.

For these test scenarios, you may want to tile two windows, one with your editor open, the other with the browser open, and switch between them.

If you are using Notepad or have a 32-bit system or a Mac, you should not need to close the file to open it in your browser. When you want to see the changes you are making, switch to the editor you are using, make the changes, switch back to the browser, and then choose Reload or Refresh from the browser menu.

Tips for Using Images

Copying Images

Downloading images from the Web is easy. Background images can be a little tricky or not accessible, but here's how to copy most images sitting in full view:

1. Click on the image with the right mouse button (MacPeople hold down the only button).
2. Choose Save This Image As . . . or Save Picture As . . .

Background images are a little harder to capture, and sometimes the directory in which they are stored is not accessible. For example, you might want the beautiful gradient background of Addison Wesley Longman's parent company, Pearson, located at `http://www.pearson-plc.com` shown in Figure 5.1.

You need to get the image "alone" as the only file open in your browser screen, then choose File, Save As from your browser menu. To do this, you need to read the HTML code on the page where you found it:

1. Open the page in your browser that contains the image you want.
2. Choose View, Source from the menu.
3. Look near the top of the page for the `<BODY BACKGROUND=...>` tag, for example,

   ```
   <BODY BACKGROUND="/pics/bground.gif">
   ```

   Often these images are stored in relative addresses as in this example. Therefore, it may take some figuring out. (See Relative URLs earlier in this chapter.)
4. Use this information to change the address of the URL to open the image. In other words, get the Location or Address to read the full path to the image, and then the image name, for example,

   ```
   http://www.pearson-plc.com/pics/bground.gif
   ```

Figure 5.1

Pearson's home
page, which is much
prettier in color

In this case you would add `pic/bground.gif` to the end of
the present URL in the Location or Address text box of your
browser.

5. Then press Enter. The image should appear on your screen. The
   Pearson home page background is shown in Figure 5.2.

6. Choose File, Save As from the browser menu to save the image
   on one of your own hard disks with whatever name you wish.

I am not advocating the use of background images and rarely use
them for Intranet documents. This is at the request of a broadband
narc I know who counted how many hours it would use each day for
X number of employees to "hit" the home page and wait for "gratuitous graphics" to download. I make a concerted effort to make sure
the graphic images that are added to the pages I author have meaning
and/or value. See Chapter 7 for tips on shrinking the size of
documents.

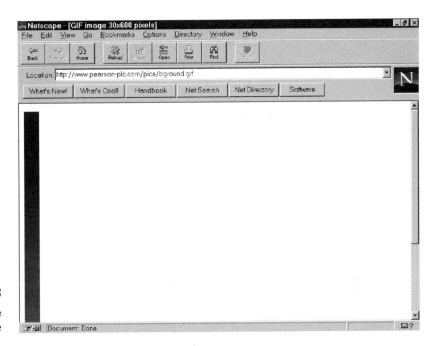

Figure 5.2

Pearson's home page
background image

Finding a Whole Library of Images

If the subdirectory where images are stored is at a different level than
the one you are in, you may discover a whole library of images while
you are going through the downloading process. For example, in the
Pearson home page, notice that the background image was stored in a
subdirectory called `pics`. Apparently the Pearson Webmaster stores all
the graphics for the Web site here. Many Webmasters wisely organize
their sites this way. You may see a subdirectory such as `images`,
`icons`, or `gifs` that will give you a clue about the contents. In this example, if you remove `bground.gif` from the URL you will see the
index of Pearson's `pics` as shown in Figure 5.3.

Linking Images

If you have done any Web surfing at all, you have probably clicked on
an image instead of text to jump to another place on the Web. I call
these *hyperimages*. When part of an image jumps one place and another part of the same image jumps somewhere else, the image is called
an *image map*. For more about creating image maps, see Chapter 6.

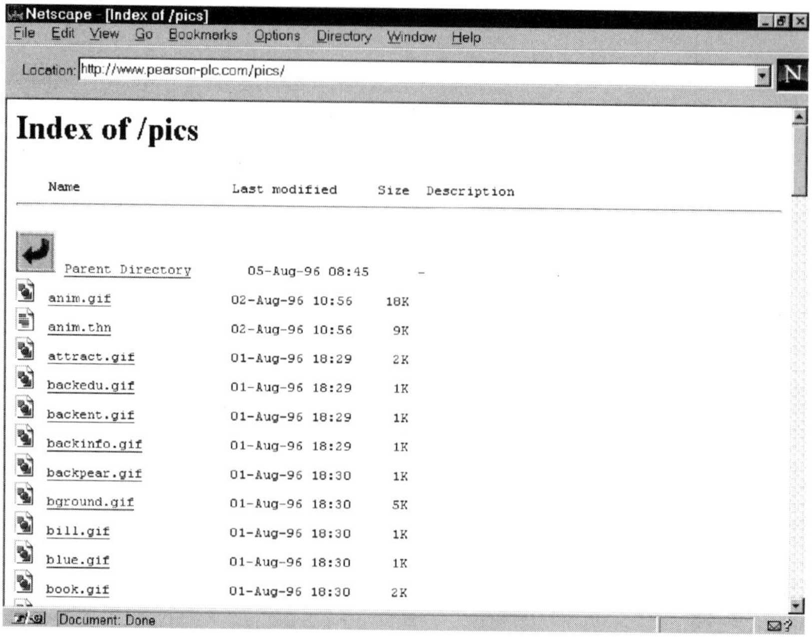

Figure 5.3

A whole library of images

Definition   A hyperimage *or* hypergraphic *is a graphic that jumps to another location when you click on it. An image map is a graphic with sections (defined by coordinates) that hyperlink to other locations.*

When you author documents containing hyperimages you can code the link with BORDER=0, which causes the outline to disappear. For instance, in Figure 5.4, the image at the top is coded with BORDER=0 so it will display without a halo box and look as it was originally designed to look.

A conscientious HTML author will also faithfully use ALT text with every graphic. Users who are on a slow link often prefer to turn graphics off completely or press Stop after the browser receives the main document.

This means if you get tired of waiting for all the graphics of an HTML page to download and you press Stop after the main document is downloaded, you will have an idea of what the pictures are even though you couldn't wait any longer to see them. More importantly, if the graphics are hyperlinked, you will still have all the navigational savvy to know where the graphic might link to. For instance, the ALT text of a little button with "TOC" on it should probably be "Table of Contents." This is a human factor consideration as well. Blind users turn all images off in their browser. The reading tools they use that send messages to be read by touch cannot view graphics.

Definition   *A good HTML author will always put in* ALT *text that describes the image.*

Slow-link users may also be Intranet users in outlying offices or telecommuters who are dialing in. Figure 5.5 shows how the ALT text of the images in Figure 5.4 would look if the user interrupted the transfer of the document. The file cabinet is replaced by a broken image, but the ALT text tells the user what the image represented. Notice that the top two images include the word *hyperimage* in the ALT text to clue users in.

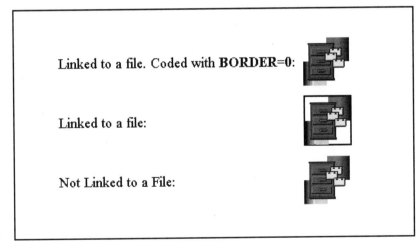

Figure 5.4

Two linked images—
one with a border—
and one unlinked
image

Text Files

Browsers can read text files. So, if you just want to get information posted to the Web, you don't really have to convert it to HTML. This is nice to know if you have a page of information that does not require

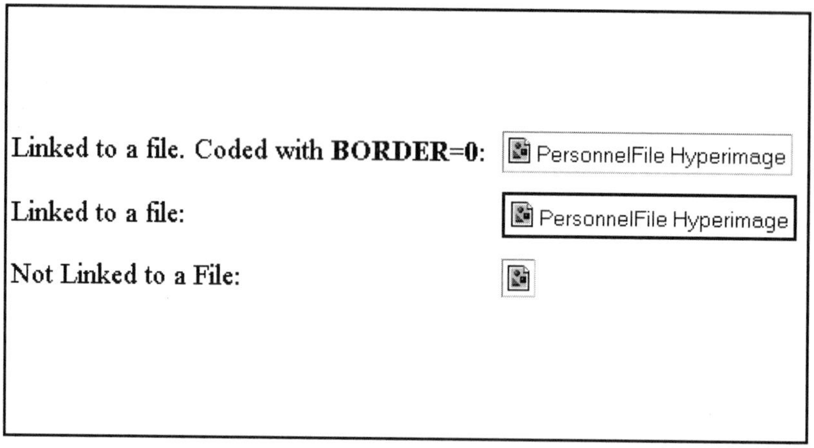

Linked to a file. Coded with **BORDER=0:** PersonnelFile Hyperimage

Linked to a file: PersonnelFile Hyperimage

Not Linked to a File:

Figure 5.5

The ALT text of the images in Figure 5.4

fancy formatting, hypertext links to other documents, graphics, or anything special. For instance, if you have simple news flashes or other items that you would like to post to a Web site and your main concern is merely content, all you have to do is save it as a text file in your word processing program or from an e-mail message and then upload it to your Web server.

Three Examples of Text Files Loaded on the Web

To get the best readability in a Web browser, your text files need a little bit of preparation. For example, the previous paragraph was saved with no preparation using File, Save As Text Only from a Microsoft Word 6.0 document. Figure 5.6 shows how hard it would be to read this file in a browser because it doesn't wrap the sentences to the next line.

With just a slight change using File, Save As Text Only with Line Breaks, the paragraph returns at the end of each line and readability improves considerably as shown in Figure 5.7.

As a content provider you will always want to consider the "lowest common denominator" of viewers. In most cases this will be users with laptops. There is one other slight improvement you can make before you save a text file destined for Web browsing. Reduce the width of the lines on the word processing page by increasing the right and/or left margins before saving as Text Only with Line Breaks. This will cause the line breaks to "wrap" so users can read the text without scrolling, as shown in Figure 5.8.

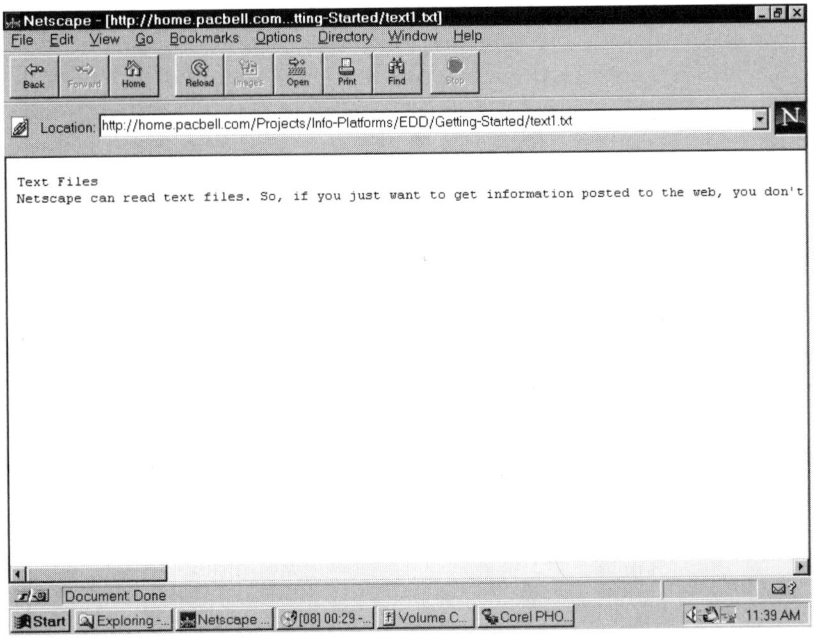

Figure 5.6

Saved as Text Only
with no preparation

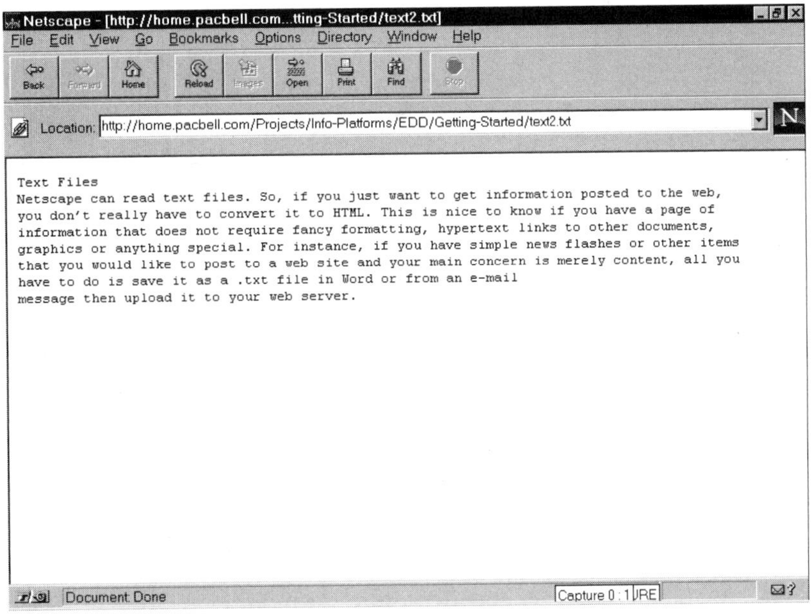

Figure 5.7

Saved as Text Only
with Line Breaks

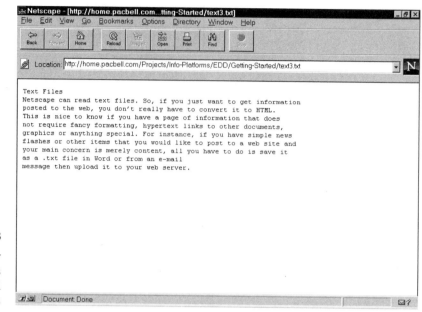

Figure 5.8

Saved as Text Only
with Line Breaks
and reduced
margins

Alternative Viewing Possibilities

It's hard to compete with HTML for low bandwidth and hypertext capability. And each new generation of HTML comes up with new formatting capabilities. As several companies scrambled to create programs that would present desktop publishing–like formats on the Web, HTML evolved with features such as tables, frames, and text wraparound images. However, converting everything to HTML is time consuming and therefore expensive. It is also unnecessary, but text documents can be really boring.

Portable Documents

The first alternative viewing possibility is *portable documents,* which basically aimed for a "fax on glass" approach using Web browsers as a printer. You may recognize this type of product as Adobe's PDF, Tumbleweed's Envoy, or Common Ground's Web Publishing System. These portable documents are like HTML in that they are platform independent but they require proprietary viewer programs for accessing files. Their big plus is that they allow authors to control type, design, and layout. They are easy for authors but not so easy for users. Just as I'm sure you've experienced difficulty reading small print or graphics on a fax, viewing is sometimes limited. This requires special software, skills, and extra effort for HTML functions such as hypertext links or "hotspots." Also, it is impossible to implement forms using this format. But they definitely have their place. For instance, you may have documents such as timelines produced by applications such as Microsoft Project that you want to link to other documents. Using portable document formats is the only way to accomplish this.

Universal Viewers

Another wonderful technology that is rising to the occasion of Internal Web Document Management is universal viewers (mentioned in Chapter 9 as a document management solution). Some products that you may recognize in this area are Quick View Plus from INSO, KEYview from FTP, and Adobe File Utilities. These are plug-ins or add-ons to browser client software. There are presently a lot for Windows, a few for the Mac, and very few for UNIX. Plug-ins allow you to view documents in their native format without launching the native application. All you can do is view, but for many legacy documents viewing is all that would be necessary anyway. It's a real plus to be able to view documents without having the threat of Trojan horse viruses lurking in open and close macros and sans the waiting time of launching an application. Table 5.3 compares the various document formats for viewing Web documents.

Authoring Tools
HTML Editors

I work on the Windows platform and after evaluating several editors, I chose HTML Assistant Pro (`http://www.brooknorth.com/htmlpro2.html`). After I was pretty locked into its familiarity, Hot Dog (`http://www.sausage.com/`) entered the market. I tried it out and considered it better than many editors I had previously rejected, but I stayed with HTML Assistant Pro because I was used to it and had already purchased it.

There are several Web pages that have lists and comparisons of editors. Two URLs where you can find such lists are shown in Table 5.4.

	Document Format	Hypertext	Launches Another Application	Drawbacks
	HTML	Yes	No	Requires author expertise
	Text	No	No	Boring
	Portable documents	Yes, but not easy	Yes	Need conversion software (expensive) and viewing software (free)
	Native file format	No	Yes, the native application	Consumes time and machine resources; possible vehicle for Trojan horses and viruses
Table 5.3 Viewing Web Documents	Universal viewer	No	Sort of, it's a plug-in or add-on	Possible interference with other installed applications on the client PC

	URL	What You Will Find There
	http://204.91.49.11/hteds.html	Public HTML editors
Table 5.4 HTML Editors	(http://www.columbia. edu/~rk35/www/editors.html)	Suggested editors

WYSIWYG Editors

Every day more products are entering the market, so I don't dare tout one too highly because I might have a new favorite before the copyeditor gets through with this chapter. But, because as I said in the introduction, I want to give you the wherewithal to make the right choices, so here are my opinions about the WYSIWYG editors I have used.

Some of the big names are Netscape Gold, Microsoft Front Page, and Microsoft Internet Assistant. They are wonderful, especially if you are creating tables. They are terrible if you want to see what's going on with the HTML. Actually you can see what's going on with the HTML by viewing the source in your browser, but you cannot edit the HTML, which to me is a huge drawback.

WYSIWYG editors decide what META data to include, and they always say they are "created by this wonderful editor" even if you open the document you created another way to make a few additions to a table. This means if you want to put "Subject Matter Expert" in the META field, or duo authoring credits, or your e-mail user ID as comments in the source, you need to add these changes in Notepad or another editor. If you are using one of the many plug-in/add-ons WYSIWYG editors to Word and you want to edit the HTML in Word, you will have to rename the file as a `.txt` file, then open it in Word in order to see the HTML. Otherwise if you open the file as an `.htm` it will automatically launch your plug-in/add-on.

Now I don't want to be rude, but I also found a few bugs. I will not name products because both bugs I am about to mention are in two major players, who battle each other in the press, and sometimes in court, daily. These two major players are so competitive that they will probably fix these bugs before this book goes to press. Nevertheless, I recommend that you download free software and test it before you buy it or if it is free, that you make sure you can uninstall it if you don't like it.

Bug Alert #1. Test to see how it converts legacy documents. My testing of duo purpose editors showed that they were good at one thing but not good at another. I basically got a mess and had to invest way more work clean-up time than it would have taken to create a new document.

Bug Alert #2. Test to see how links are formatted. One WYSIWYG editor that uses drag-and-drop technology automatically chose to insert relative links in all caps. These relative links retained the original file source. This means that they contained information that became obsolete as soon as they were on the server, some such nonsense like `c:\|file///` which of course caused lots of "404 Not Found" consternation. And, since different operating systems pass along filenames in various ways when you move your documents to the server, they often end up as lowercase filenames, and therefore unreadable by these documents. Way, way, way too much postprocessing for my taste.

What to Look for in an Editor. There were three main drawbacks that I encountered while evaluating HTML editors:

1. Most of the editors choked on documents over 32K. (HTML Assistant Pro's free version has this limitation, but the licensed version does not.)

2. The editor was a "plug-in" or "add-on" to Word. This is really cumbersome because Word for Windows "holds onto" the document if you are on a 16-bit operating system. This means that if you want to look at your document in a browser you will get a message that says it's already open or not available. You have to close the document, open it in a browser, then if you have any corrections open the document again, and so forth. The 32-bit version doesn't hold onto the document and neither does the Mac version, according to my MacFriends. I also personally do not like Word plug-ins and add-ons because they are often difficult to uninstall.

3. I didn't like the editors that "validated" the code for me. It took too long to figure out what messages the editor was reporting. In the meantime, the editor would not let me proceed. I prefer to debug the HTML myself after proudly displaying my mistakes in my browser :-).

Conversion Utilities

You can actually create your online documents in the familiar environment of word processing or create tables in Excel and then convert them to HTML.

Advantages to Using Conversion Utilities

Here are some advantages to using conversion utilities:

- You can maintain a printed version and an HTML version of your document in a "one-button publishing" format. Sort of. (See the Drawbacks to the Advantages section.)
- Conversion utilities often have other perks, like automatically building a hypertext table of contents or an index. They can break the document into smaller bytes, create HTML tables, and do a great job of converting graphics.
- You can work in the familiar word processing, WYSIWYG environment.

Drawbacks to the Advantages

You'll want to weigh the advantages of using conversion utilities against a couple of drawbacks:

- The names that conversion utilities give to anchors and converted graphics are not as intuitive as the ones you choose. For instance, within a team phone list you may want to have a table of contents that hyperlinks to each subteam. If you were naming the anchor for the LAN team, the Messaging team, and the Remote Access team, you would probably choose names like `lan`, `messaging`, and `remote`. Conversion utilities generate names like `l1`, `l2`, and `l3`. They also use a preponderance of lowercase *L*s, which look a lot like the numeral one. This makes reading the HTML code nearly impossible. So I use Edit, Find a lot once I've converted a document and want to tweak it in my HTML editor. Likewise, a graphic that you name `bell-curve` might be named `l13.gif` by a conversion utility.

- Don't be fooled into thinking you don't need to know at least a little about HTML—it rarely converts seamlessly.

Three Utilities

There are a lot of conversion utilities out on the Web and more appearing every day. As mentioned earlier, some HTML editors (including my fave, HTML Assistant Pro) now contain conversion utilities. But I would be amiss if I didn't tout the one that I think will lead the pack for a long time: HTML Transit.

HTML Transit. HTML Transit maps word processing styles to HTML tags. The better you "style" the document up front (see the next section), the better results you will get after conversion. It also converts tables and graphics in the process. I think the feature I like best is that I can mark index items in a word processing application and when I run the document through HTML Transit, it creates a hypertext index. Way cool. The latest version even allows you to put HTML code in a word processing document, hide it so the printed version doesn't print it, but the converted HTML version has a link. You can download an evaluation copy at `http://www.infoaccess.com`.

RTFTOHTML. This is a free utility that works on Windows, UNIX, and Macintosh platforms. After you create a document in Word, you save it in RTF (Rich Text Format) and then run the conversion. It does not do a great job of converting tables, and it doesn't do graphics at all. It does, however, create an automatic link to all the graphics it finds in a document. This means that once you convert the graphics to a GIF or JPG format, you can "plug them in" the spot RTFTOHTML creates, using a "click here for picture" remark. This free utility combined with XL2HTML and a good graphics application would be sufficient for someone who doesn't have a lot of Web-head responsibilities. (See Chapter 7 for some tips on converting graphic images.)

XL2HTML. Not only is this utility useful for converting Excel tables to HTML tables, but you can also drop a Word table into a spreadsheet to get some extra mileage out of it. It's free and easy to use. Directions for using it are on the same page where you can download it:

```
http://rs712b.gsfc.nasa.gov/704/dgd/xl2html.html
```

Using Word Processing Styles for Mapping

Word processing styles are a saved set of formatting for a paragraph or characters that have a name. They not only help with conversion; they make it easier to author documents because you simply choose a pre-defined format. For example, making a title big, bold, and blue takes only one step when applying a style rather than selecting three different formatting properties.

From a word processing point of view, styles save time. Here are the main advantages to using styles while word processing:

- It's easy to format more than one paragraph or set of characters to look the same.
- You can change all instances of a style in one fell swoop.

Tables 5.5 and 5.6 show examples of paragraph and character style names and their associated formatting styles.

Style Name	Formatting Associated with the Style
Heading 1	Arial, 20 point and bold
Heading 2	Arial, 14 point, bold italic
Normal	12 point, Times New Roman
Quotes	12 point, Times New Roman, indented ½ inch on each margin

Table 5.5
Paragraph Style Examples

Style Name	Formatting Associated with the Style
WARNING	Bold, Small Caps
Author	Bold, Italic

Table 5.6
Character Style
Examples

One-Button Publishing

For the Web publisher a big advantage to using word processing
styles is that they can be mapped to electronic publishing. Here are a
few of the existing tools that convert word processing styles into
HTML tags:

- HTML Transit
- HTML Assistant Pro
- Internet Assistant
- OmniMark
- RTFTOHTML

This is not a complete list; in fact most of the HTML editors have a
conversion feature. That is, you can have a printed version and an electronic version of the same document. When you need to update the
document, theoretically you need to update only one version, and then
run the mapping program. Unfortunately this process is not seamless
and usually requires posttranslation processing on the electronic copy
that will need to be repeated after each update.

Summary

There are lots of ways to view documents on the Web besides author-
ing them or converting them to HTML. You will want at least a few
HTML documents, however, to make your site a cool hypertexted
Web. You don't have to master HTML to author these documents.
WYSIWYG editors and conversion tools simplify the process of
authoring, but someone in your organization will need to know how to

read the HTML source. Using relative URLs within documents allows you to move a set of Web documents from local drives to the server or to a different spot on the server without recoding the links within each document. Conversion tools make it possible to have one-button publishing as well as a printable document and an HTML version. Finally, the quality of these documents, especially the hypertext capability, is greatly improved if you use styles in the word processing version.

Effective
Web Design

What You Can Do

You're surfing on your corporate Internal Web looking for information on a soon-to-be-released product. You find the internal search engine, type in "play-dough" (a code name for your next-generation Internet toaster appliance) and voilà—600 pages return. Hmmm, not so useful. However, you click on one of the links the search engine returned, and you find something very close to what you're looking for. But the page is "orphaned." It leaves you clueless about its hierarchy or any other related information. You look up at the Location or Address textbox of your browser, and even the URL is strange looking:

```
http://www.sillyvalleycompany.corp.com/~pinktofu/
schpiddle/schpaddle/reallylongfilename.CGI?what#
the*heck?is+allthis?stuff$anyway?
```

Does this sound silly and far-fetched? At many of the companies with more mature Internal Webs, over 400,000 URLs exist. *Web glut* and poor design are already very serious issues. It's not uncommon for some organizations to have upwards of a million static pages, not to mention those created on the fly via CGI scripts or Java, or JavaScripts.

Definition   Web glut *refers to sites full of hype, nonsense, trivia, and/or gaudy, poorly executed Web applications.*

101

The Internet is full of sites that are full of hype and void of actual value. Similarly, a poorly designed Internal Web can quickly become glutted with gaudy, confusing documents and poorly executed Web applications. This chapter focuses on good Intranet Web site architecture to help you, the site designer, create useful, appealing sites that will benefit end users in their web experience.

What You Will Need

You don't have to spend weeks analyzing click patterns from someone else's Web site before you're ready to design your own. Although analyzing statistics can help you evolve your Web site once it's designed (see Chapter 7 for more on gathering and analyzing statistics), designing a great site comes down to a few basics:

- Know your audience.
- Be consistent.
- Use basic graphic arts paradigms.
- Keep it simple and predictable.
- Design navigation.

How to Design Effective Web Documents

Know Your Audience

People learn in different manners. We're all different. Yet many studies have shown that despite our uniqueness, we learn in three major ways: visual, auditory, and kinesthetic.

Visual people are like Data on "Star Trek, the Next Generation." They take in data quickly and visually. They love to TV-channel surf.

They love the Web. They often are here-and-now focused and talk quickly, using their hands to actively "draw" pictures as they speak. See what I'm saying?

Auditory people like to hear themselves (and others) talk. You have to match pace with their speech to relate to them. How you say things is as important (more so?) as what you are saying. Hear what I mean?

Kinesthetic people can drive visual people crazy, as they often get into the visual person's space. These are hands-on, often naturally affectionate, feeling-oriented people. I feel like I understand.

Each of us has some of each type in us, but we tend to favor one of the three in learning situations. What this means to Web design is that you need to target all three audiences. Appropriate visuals and clean text layout will appeal to those who see your pages. (See the section Use Basic Graphic Arts Paradigms for hints on aesthetically appealing design.) Because the Web is interactive, it lends itself to satisfying your kinesthetic audience, but too many links can disrupt your users' continuity of thought. The best way to appeal to those who "hear" what's going on is to focus on good writing punctuated with appropriate hyperlinks. Use strong active verbs rather than a passive voice. In fact, clear, concise writing appeals to all three. So often organizations expect the Webmaster gurus to double as Web content providers. While coding text and creating slick scripts may come easier to them, remember that good programmers are not necessarily good writers or editors. Very technical writing that is to be shared with a wider audience can, and should, be replaced with clear, understandable prose. For example, take a look at a job description written by an unnamed programmer:

Site Curator: This is an architectural position responsible for the overall integration and continuity of an entire Web site that addresses the information needs of a business area. This individual is responsible for the integration and integrity of the Page Curators' individual deliverables. They have managerial responsibility to the business to assure that the components of the Web site come together to meet the overall business need, and that the information and functionality of the individual pages combine with logical integrity as an integrated and usable whole. Depending upon the extent of interactivity and the complexity of the technology, as well as the extent of business functionality supported, make this a D or E level job.

Huh? I think the only techno word this person left out is *utilize* which far too often replaces its kissing cousin synonym, *use*. Sometimes writers use *utilize* instead of *use* because they appropriately say that a program is utilizing code or a system function, but some people just utilize the word because they think it is more impressive, often losing their audience.

So if you are putting technical information on your Internal Web, remember your full audience. Some of it can go up, "as is" for the techies to access easily, but if your audience is broader, you may need to capsulize portions in simple layout with clear writing. It might be a good idea to have a focus group of less technical people review it before it goes live.

Be Consistent

Being ever mindful of your audience, make your Web as intuitive as possible, starting with your directory structure.

Structure and Naming Conventions of Directories and Subdirectories

Although Windows and Macintosh Web servers do exist, the Internet is primarily a UNIX environment, and therefore UNIX has set precedence in directory-naming conventions. UNIX also still dominates other Internet communication that existed before the plethora of fonts and formats entered the e-mail, newsgroup, and Web page arenas. For example, using all uppercase letters implies YELLING on the Internet. UNIX is case sensitive, so INDEX.HTML, Index.html, and index.html are all different files.

The naming convention that I follow is to start the names of directories with initial caps. For instance the directory for the personnel department is `Personnel`. The directory for remote access is `Remote-Access`. My convention for files is lowercase, such as `filename.htm` or `filename.html`. If an organization is well known by an acronym, such as, say, Core Process Reengineering, I name the subdirectory `CPR`. Though it is easier for users if everything is lowercase, which could certainly be the choice you make for your Internal Web, please consider the following: Uppercase names are sorted first when your operating system lists files in a directory. Therefore, when you capitalize the first letter of the directories on your Web server, it is easier to identify directories in the sort results. For example, typing `ls` (the UNIX command to list files) results in the following:

```
Art
BobsStuff
Images
Sample-Directory
index.html
feedback.html
team.html
```

Note that `Sample-Directory` comes before `index.html`. While it may seem a moot point when you are first setting up your files, you'll begin to appreciate the order as your Web portfolio expands.

Typically, the Web server is set up by default to look for `index.html` and/or `home.html` in every directory. This gives you the opportunity to use shorter and clearer URLs. For example, say you have a URL of `http://Random.com/Number/random.html` as your home page. Copy and/or move `random.html` to `index.html`, and your URL is now `http://Random.com/Number/`. The `index.html` file is no longer needed. Though you may prefer to expose the index of the entire directory to Web surfers to avail them of the server's automatic index capability, it usually makes more sense to have an HTML page to explain (or tout) what is in the directory and offer logical hyperlinked direction to the rest of the subdirectory. To set up a home page for a directory you can either name that page, `index.html`, `home.html` (whichever your server recognizes), or set up a symbolic link from `index.html` to the name of your home page. (For more about symbolic links, see Chapter 7.)

Templates and Scripts

Depending on the size of your company and its Internal Web, you may have a great deal of control over consistency, using templates and scripts to add predictability. Once you have decided on a look and feel of headers, footers, relative font sizes, image placement, and so forth, you can create templates and/or scripts to ensure that this stays consistent. For example, you may encourage employees and consultants to post personal home pages and give them a template to get them started. All they need to do is fill in the blanks. These suggested "blanks" might prompt for key searchable information such as "areas of expertise," "areas of interest," or "project names." Templates have the benefit of being fairly easy to distribute, and people generally like the ease of just filling in the blanks (except when it comes to taxes).

Scripts have the power to change the look and feel of documents as they are posted. This passes the responsibility from the authors to centralized Web site administration. You may prefer this to distributing templates company-wide and supporting a large number of fledgling Web authors. Scripts can also sense the hierarchy of pages. For example, you could create a script to provide header, footer, and perhaps a background, while calling specific content for the heart of the page. Such a script's pseudocode might look something like this:

```
begin
    pass argument of content text file
    read and print header file
    read and print content file
    read and print footer file
end
```

One excellent case history example is from the genius designers of SGI's Internal Web. They use a script to present three views of an index page shown in Figure 6.1. The same content is sorted no matter which view a user clicks on, but the results are alphabetical, chronological, or topical.

To use scripts effectively, you might need to broaden your view if you are in the habit of doing everything manually. You may only be able to visualize producing the SGI site by maintaining three HTML pages: an alphabetical listing, a chronological listing, and a topical listing. It takes a little longer up front to automate the process, but com-

Figure 6.1

SGI's Internal Web, viewable alphabetically, by date, or by topic

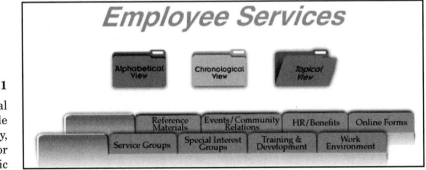

puters are better suited for such menial tasks. The time you save on maintenance will pay you back in triplicate.

You'll need the following data for every page: the URL, the topic/category it fits under, the date created/added, and the text you want printed out as the hypertext link for that respective URL. For example, a data set for Netscape Communications to be listed topically under browsers might look something like this:

```
http://www.netscape.com,Browsers,12/1/95,Netscape
Communications
```

You can use a spreadsheet and save it as comma-delimited text, or use a simple text file with the information. Once you create the data set, all you need is a script to create pages on the fly based on what type of data is requested by the user. Once you create the scripts, you can maintain three directories, by updating the data set and running the script. There are of course many ways to do this. The following is some simplistic pseudocode that you and your local Web gurus can interpret. This assumes that your server is set up to understand CGI scripts as a file type (your system administrator or Webmaster will know), and that someone helping you write the script can use a scripting language such as PERL. This can be done using one script. Here's the pseudocode to turn out three different views of the data based on the user's request:

```
open data
determine if alpha, topic or datefile is wanted
sort appropriately
print html to browser (navigation at
top/bottom/side as appropriate)
close data file
```

Of course, you are now hoping that your server can handle the load of CGI scripts you would like to run and that you can muster the resources of people who know some simple scripting techniques. Typically, CGI scripts cause the Web server to spawn another process (taking up processor and I/O time) to launch the script. Many Web servers that seemingly do fine running only HTML and image files choke under the load of too many CGI scripts. You may therefore need to limit the number you use. For more about CGI scripts and what languages they can be written in, see Chapter 8.

Style Sheets

Microsoft's Internet Explorer has proprietary style sheets to help with common design and layout templates. By the time this book goes to print Netscape will incorporate style sheets in Netscape Navigator as well. Style sheets are especially useful in massive Web authoring environments where you want to have a common look and feel in your documents. The original concept of style sheets is found at the World Wide Web Consortium at `http://www.w3.orgas`, as well as the suggested open standard for deploying style sheets. The WWW Consortium home page is shown in Figure 6.2.

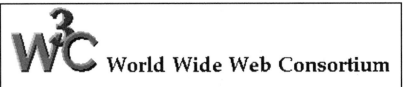

Figure 6.2

The WWW Consortium advances Web technology, including style sheets

Style sheets let you create several flavors of formats you want to see on each Web page of a site, such as a series of headings or paragraph formats. However, in addition to font size and spacing, you can add things such as color, alignment, and text. For example, you could create a style sheet that publishes your main headings in fuchsia, aligned left, with a font size of 16. Your subheads would be say, gray, italic, aligned left, with a font size of 14. Style sheets free you from using complex coding within the tags of your Web pages. You define styles once at the top of your document or in a separate file and then use the style sheet tag (`<myheading> </myheading>`) throughout your document. Similar to a word processing style sheet, if you want to change all instances of the style, you need to change it only in the style sheet rather than reformatting each tag. Pretty powerful stuff.

Use Basic Graphic Arts Paradigms

Graphic design is an important part of Web design, but you don't necessarily need to be (or hire) a graphic artist or page layout specialist. With a few simple guidelines, such as the "rule of thirds" and the "rule of odds," you're well on your way to decent page layout.

Rule of Thirds and Rule of Odds

In almost all basic photography courses and books, you hear about the *Rule of Thirds.* Instead of putting your subject dead-center, you put it where the thirds intersect. The same holds true for Web page layout. A completely centered page breaks this rule and can easily become monotonous. A little off-center, as long as it's consistent and predictable, can really bring your readers in. Figure 6.3 shows the "tic-tac-toe" splitting of the page into thirds, placing objects at the intersection of the lines to present results pleasing to the eyes.

The *Rule of Odds* is simply to use an odd number of pieces in the whole of your Web picture. So an image and two blocks of text would

Figure 6.3

Using the Rule of Thirds

equal three elements. These unequal weights to your page are more appealing to the human eye and even help that right brain of yours (oh no, not that) to kick in. Again, you'll engage your users much more with this simple technique.

Two Web zines that use these rules quite well are `http://www.suck.com` and `http://www.word.com` (see Figures 6.4 and 6.5).

Figure 6.4

Table layout using Rule of Odds

Figure 6.5

Tables, text, and images using the Rule of Thirds

You can experiment with layout using image alignment, transparent images, and tables. For example, if you want to align a column of text to the right-most third line (as in Rule of Thirds), you could write code as follows, and produce the table shown in Figure 6.6:

```
<table border=5 cellpadding=20>
  <tr>
  <td width="350">
  <!Use a width tag to hold a nice wide left column
open for 350 pixels></td>
  <td width="100">
  <p><font size="4">
```

```
    Add your wonderful, lengthy, intellectual, bril-
liant text quote here - to get a newspaper column
effect.
    </font></p>
    </td>
    </tr>
</table>
```

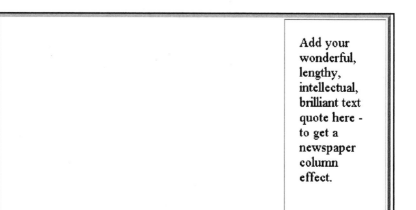

Figure 6.6

Using a table to
produce the Rule
of Thirds effect

Keep It Simple and Predictable

Use your imagination and think of an application that seems graceful, elegant, fun, and simple. In this day of "value-added" bloated applications, this is a fairly rough exercise. Truly graceful and useful applications are a seamless extension of the user. For example, if an application has 45 icons, drop-down menus that change frequently (where was that Save button?), and no sense of what the user needs, it quickly becomes useless. Some Web page designers attempt to put every possible HTML feature in their site. However, a graceful, simple, clean, logical, predictable, friendly, surprise-free design will go a very long way. Here are a few suggestions to ensure success.

Colored Backgrounds, Fonts, and Links

Backgrounds colors need to be used with care. They can add a lot of appeal to your site. But you need to be mindful that once you've changed your background scheme, it's likely that you'll need to change your font and link colors to make the page readable. This is especially true if you decide on a darker background. Font and link colors that remain consistent and predictable are more user friendly. If you are coming from a desktop publishing or word processing mind-set, you may need to consider a completely different paradigm for highlighting text in the Web environment. For example, because a linked word is an underlined word on the Web, you would not want to underline for emphasis—better to choose italic, bold, all caps, or use a different font color. Then, when you do use a different font color, keep in mind what color is being used for a link or a visited link so your font color doesn't cause confusion. For example, users who have become accustomed to the familiar magenta/purple default color for a visited link may come to a page that has this same color used for emphasis and experience "user interface crisis" when they click on it and nothing happens. This is not to say that well-thought-out use of color can't be useful, enjoyable, and convey meaning. But I recommend that you not only test your choices by taking a fresh look at it a few hours after completion, but also enlist the help of a second set of discriminating eyes before your pages go live. I've found that as a rule of thumb, if I have a light background that doesn't conflict with the default blue and purple/magenta link and visited link that the most intuitive choice is to stick with the default. An example of conflict would be a pink background that would cause the magenta visited link text to be nearly invisible. When you decide to go with the drama of a dark background, such as say, black, deep blue, or dark purple, you can pretty much disregard default text colors. Most likely white will show up the best. Yellow is a close second. At this point you will need to test each color to see what seems to show up. Keep in mind that if you do not follow the default convention, your users may need to guess which links are visited links and which are not. When you would like to do something different, carry consistency throughout related pages. Consider that users arriving at your site are surfing multiple sites, each with a different background, hot link, and navigation scheme. When they arrive at your site, they must figure out how your navigation scheme works. Make it easy for them; stay with the same theme. Don't make them figure it out again on your next page.

Substitute Color for Graphics

You need to remember than some of your users are on a 14.4 or 28.8 modem connection, and it takes valuable seconds (the World Wide

Wait?) to download some graphics, so please take the following into consideration:

- Conserve the bandwidth—think of your audience and how long it takes to load your pages.
- Remember that your monitor (at say, thousands of colors) will display color differently than 8-bit (256 color) and 24-bit (millions) monitors, especially across platforms. Test your pages on different platforms and in different environments. Consider using a product like Silicon Graphics's Cosmo Color, which ensures that what you see is what your audience sees using a special blend of color palettes that works cross-platform on the Web. The Cosmo Color Web page is shown in Figure 6.7 and is located at:

```
http://www.sgi.com/
```

Use a background color rather than a background image. Color loads instantly, and the absence of a pattern makes your page easier to read.

Figure 6.7

Silicon Graphics's
Cosmo Color

Get Complex If You Dare

At this point, I'm going to assume that you are conscientious Web professionals who are keeping in mind your users' needs and server overload but that you also want a touch of panache on your site.

Frames and Flames

By now you have seen HTML frames on Web pages. Frames are basically little Web pages within the browser window. Sometimes each frame is coded to operate as an independent window. When you click a link within the frame it changes the content of the frame you are in, just as if it were in its own window. More often, frames are coded so that when you click the contents of one frame, the contents of another frame on the same screen changes. The latter is true when you take advantage of HTML Transit's nifty new feature that places the hypertext index it creates into a frame as it converts documents from word processing to HTML. For more about HTML Transit and other conversion utilities, see Chapter 5. Frames are getting more prevalent as browsers are getting better at presenting and debugging them, but some people still hate frames and say so. See Table 6.1 for excellent Web resources where you can learn how to create frames and read flames from users who hate them.

URL	What You Can Get There
http://home.netscape.com/assist/net_sites/frame_syntax.html	Netscape's help pages frames tutorial
http://www.newbie.net/frames/index.html	The Netscape Frames Tutorial by Charlton Douglas Rose
http://www.physics.iastate.edu/numaps/96/days/04/frames2.html	Sample code from FRAMES AND ANCHORS - NUMAPS96
http://ucunix.san.uc.edu/~solkode/w3guide/frames.html	All about Frames by Dave Solko
http://www.websight.com/current/usecool/usecool.html reason why	Two opinions about frames: one says, "No" and the other says, "Cool."
http://wwwvoice.com/hatefrm.html	I Hate Frames Club
http://www.ummed.edu:8000/pub/i/ijosh/frames/	Why frames suck

Table 6.1
Frames and Flames
Resources

Three Low-Bandwidth Image Types: JPEG, GIF, and PNG

A *JPEG* handles 24-bit color (16.7 million colors) and is one of the smallest image file sizes on disk. It derives its name from the Joint Photographic Experts Group, which created the standard. However, JPEGs take a bit longer to decompress than a GIF. PJPG, Progressive JPEGs, a format supported by the Netscape browser, are a happy medium between the speed of GIF and the quality of JPEG. JPEGs are great for scanned-in photos, digital camera images, or photos with important subtleties. Keep in mind that many machines still do not support 24-bit color, so you might not see the spectrum of quality JPEG offers. However, you'll notice that many digital cameras now save directly to JPEG instead of a proprietary format.

Definition   JPEG *derives its name from the Joint Photographic Experts Group who created the standard. JPEG, JPG, or* JFIF *handles 24-bit color (or 16.7 million colors) and is one of the smallest image file sizes on disk.*

GIF files, originally created by CompuServe, handle 8-bit color (256 colors), are great for navigation icons, button bars, and probably represent 80 percent of the images you use for your site. GIF images can be interlaced, made transparent, and manipulated with other techniques to load quickly. For the full history, and a bit of humor, check out the "Great GIF licensing controversy" at `http://www.xmission.com/ ~mgm/gif/`.

Definition   GIF, Graphic Interchange Format, *was originally created by the CompuServe Online Service.*

PNG (Portable Network Graphic) is a new format, currently supported by plug-ins in the Netscape and Internet Explorer browsers. PNG combines the quality and size of JPEGs with the speed of viewing of GIFs producing quality results. The PNG effort is an open standard created by research efforts and critiqued openly in the Internet Engineering Task Force (IETF). For more details, check out `http:// boutell.com/boutell/png/` and expect to see more on PNG in the future.

There is a great list of general information about all file formats found on the Internet at `http://www.matisse.net/files/formats.html`. It also lists their respective viewers and creation tools.

Definition PNG (Portable Network Graphic) *is a new format, currently supported by plug-ins in the Netscape and Microsoft Internet Explorer browsers. PNG combines the quality and size of JPEGs with the viewing speed of GIFs to produce quality results.*

Finding Ready-Made Graphics

Many sites offer ready-made graphic images and instruction on how to razzle dazzle your users. Some of these great sites are shown in Table 6.2, but you can find many more by doing an Internet search.

URL	What You Can Get There
http://www.stars.com/Vlib/Providers/Images_and_Icons.html	Resources for Web development including a library of graphic images
http://www.pixelsite.com/.	Images and clip art, and how to modify your images on the fly
http://innovate.sgi.com/listings/summarysearch.CGI/gif	Innovate Online!—another great Silicon Graphics site, creates a virtual Web development environment and has a place to exchange tools, content, and documentation with other members

Table 6.2
Some Graphic Image Libraries

Special Effect Graphics

Image maps are images with hot spots that link to other locations or addresses on the Web. Image map creation is included in a lot of HTML editors including Microsoft Front Page and Netscape Gold. Basically, you need to create a map file with coordinates. Usually, this map file is kept on the server machine; however HTML 3.0 allows it to reside on the client side (client-side image maps). Regardless of where the map info resides, your HTML page is then coded to call the map file coordinates and associated image file on which you "drew" the coordinates. A map file with three rectangle coordinates linked to three URLs could look something like this:

```
rect 1,70 80, 141 http://www.yourcompany.com/yapp
rect 141,1 222, 34 /ANC/html/anc-news.html
rect 81,35 222, 141 /ANC/html
```

Here's the code within your HTML page that calls this map and image:

```
<a href="anc-logo.map"><IMG SRC="news.jpg"
alt="[News Icon/Map]" ismap></a></TD>
```

There is a lot of instruction about image maps out on the Web; so much so that it's a tedious search to find those applicable to your needs. Table 6.3 gives the URLs of a few places to begin your search.

URL	What You Can Get There
http://www.sesd.stsci.edu/latex2html/ manual/node29.html	Good definition and step-by-step how-to
http://www.w3.org/pub/WWW/ Daemon/User/CGI/HTImageDoc. html	W3C httpd clickable image support
http://hoohoo.ncsa.uiuc.edu/docs/ tutorials/imagemapping.html	NCSA image map tutorial
http://www.ecaetc.ohio state.edu/tc/ mt/	MAP THIS home page
http://www.ncsa.uiuc.edu/Edu/ MMM/MacMapMaker.html#CanDo	Instructions for MacUsers
http://netware.novell.co.jp/img4.htm	Image map scripts test page

Table 6.3

Image Map Resources

Definition   Image map*s are a single image with different hot spots that link to corresponding URLs.*

Transparent GIFs are GIFs with a single RGB (Red Green Blue) value invisible. They allow images to appear in shapes other than a square on your Web page. In order for them to work properly you will need to code them as BORDER=0 in your SRC IMG tag. Check out the sites in Table 6.4 for more transparent GIF info.

URL	What You Can Get There
http://www.magi.com/~kk//tbi.html	Creating transparent background images, freeware
http://members.aol.com/htmlguru/transparent_images.html	FREE WEB TOOLS transparent background images
http://www.best.com/~adamb/GIFpage.html	The transparent/interlaced GIF resource page
http://www.mit.edu:8001/people/nocturne/transparent.html	Transparency, what is it? about making the background of your .gif transparent with the GIF89 file extension.
http://www.globalx.net/kerry/tbi.html	Offers a step-by-step how-to for transparent images
http://www.mccannas.com/	A beautiful, free art Web site, with excellent Photoshop tips to boot!

Table 6.4
Transparent GIF
Resources

Definition   Transparent GIFs *are GIFs with a single color (Red Green Blue value) invisible. They allow images to appear in shapes other than a square on your Web page.*

Animated GIFs are essentially a sequence of standard GIFS, grouped together in a single GIF file with some instructions on time delay, looping, and so forth. Think of an animated GIF as a single-cell animation for the Web. The end result is that your users view a short animation. You can find more information and tools here (among other places):

```
http://www.webdiner.com/annexc/gif89/snowstpl.htm
```

Definition   Animated GIFs *are a sequence of standard GIFs, grouped together in a single GIF file with instructions on time delay, looping, and so forth.*

Workaround for Slow-Loading Graphics

If you really gotta have a "wow" picture but you know nobody in the world has the patience to wait for it to load, you can load two versions of it. The image that will finally get there is coded normally with `src=`. The image that loads first is included in the same tag, directly after the `src` coded `lowsrc`:

```
<img src="bigcheesey.jpg" lowsrc="quickdirty.jpg">
```

For example, take a look at the cover of this book on the Addison-Wesley Web site for a demonstration of this technology:

```
http://www.bannan.com/Intranet-Doc-Mgt
```

These pages allow a quick loading of an image, so you "get the picture" (sorry, bad pun—couldn't resist) almost immediately and then eventually load the high-resolution version. The low-resolution image is 20K and loads in less than half a second. The high-resolution version is 52K and takes much longer. Of course, this technology requires you to use your favorite image manipulation package to save a second version of your high-resolution image. Usually, you'll want to save it as gray scale and maybe drop the resolution quality. This will result in a much smaller image and a very happy international audience.

You can increase browser performance and make images load more quickly if you include height and width coordinates within each image tag. Without this information, the browser must perform three different steps when it encounters an image. It must first download the image, then determine its size, and finally display the image. The second step is time-consuming and memory intensive.

Use Java and JavaScript

JavaScript is usually non-compiled (readable code) included right in the source HTML file. Therefore, you can choose View Source from your browser menu to see JavaScript code and then copy and paste it to your own document. Remember though, just because this is possible doesn't mean that it's not stealing. It's only fair that you use it to learn and practice so you develop your own code and then others can borrow from you. For more robust use of JavaScript, you can use Netscape's LiveWire Pro to compile it. To find Java source you need to find a link to it on a Web page. Java is a language that runs on the client, as opposed to CGI scripts, which run on the server. It is flexible, scaleable, and object oriented. In other words, it can be confusing and requires a considerable learning curve. You'll need to set aside time to learn Java, either from a book, a class, or look over the shoulder of a Java programmer combo. For more about Java and JavaScript, see Chapter 8. A great place to learn from others is the HUGE repository at gamelan:

```
http://www.gamelan.com
```

The "Mission Impossible" GIF

Speaking of Java, Raj Sarasa has written a simple Java applet that essentially does a time-dependent expiration of a "New" sign. You can supply parameters to customize this applet. Check it out at

```
http://www.cybes.com/expsign.html
```

Be aware though that Java and JavaScript can put a heavy load on your server and even give client workstations a workout. It can drastically slow the WWW experience, so be sure to use them sparingly and appropriately.

A Site Sampler

Remember that I don't recommend lots of gimmicks for the average Internal Web, but never let it be said that I didn't tell you about where to find them. There's a site out on the Net that uses most of the gimmicks mentioned in this chapter and gives instructions on how to create them:

```
http://members.aol.com/sportfan69/Helpme.html
```

Design Navigation

In the beginning of this chapter, I mentioned "orphaned" pages. While search and catalog engines can help by finding pages that may be orphaned, it's important to give careful consideration to each navigational link you include in a document. (For more about search engines, see Chapter 11.) You may notice that I also discussed some of the navigational design issues in Chapter 5, but just in case you are selectively reading as an author or as a designer these are worth mentioning in both places.

Be Sure to Include

Your Name and E-Mail Address. The easiest way to include this information is to use a `MAILTO`: tag for the owner of each Web page, so folks can click to send you an e-mail rather than merely read your e-mail address as text within the document. For example, my friend Chris Reavis at SGI wouldn't think of posting a page that he is responsible for without giving users this feedback opportunity:

```
<a href="mailto:chrisr@sgi.com">Chris Reavis</a>
```

Another option is to set up a feedback form that is delivered to you or a group of recipients. The advantage of this system is when personnel changes, the alteration is made only in the script that reads the form rather than on each Web page that links to it.

Your Organization, and a Link to Its Home Pages. Be sure to include the current hierarchy and related context of all pages. For example, if you are talking about minestrone soup on your canning company's internal pages, they may refer to canning, soup making, marketing, and the like. If you don't make the associations for your Web users, don't assume they'll be able to figure it out for themselves. Something that is clear within a single organization may be confusing if you're working on a team that crosses organizations.

For example, last year Silicon Graphics, Inc. acquired Cray Research. Many people from each organization worked two positions during the merger—their original one and their merger-related one. Many short-term, highly focused teams were created, and their Web pages didn't fit in any group's hierarchy. Instead, a suite of pages specifically related to the merger were created, so Finance, HR, IS, Engineering, and Marketing merger teams linked into these pages, rather than formal work-groups. These pages kept their users aware of changes in product lines (manufacturing and marketing), work groups (engineering), service models (customer service), benefits (HR), and network infrastructure and databases (IS).

Date and Time Last Modified. This ensures the freshness of the data on the page or at least let your users know that it's not fresh (if the owner won the lottery and left the company before a replacement was found), provide the date and time the page was last modified.

Be Sure to Avoid

Unnecessary Links. As a designer you need to be aware that you can overwhelm your audience with too many links, which break up the continuity of your content.

Hard to Read, Complex, Nonintuitive Graphical Interfaces. Graphics are great for navigation, especially simple, clean icons and image maps. Make sure you also have a text-based navigation scheme for your images and image-maps. This will ensure that bandwidth-challenged (and perhaps browser-challenged) users have access to the same data.

Unnecessary Graphics. One way to minimize graphics is to use what I call "pseudo buttons." It's common to use an image that looks like a button for navigation, but you can create "tables within tables" to look a lot like buttons. They have the added advantage of displaying visited link status. The following code will produce the pseudo buttons shown in Figure 6.8:

```
<table>
<tr>
<td><TABLE BORDER=5 padding=10>
<th>
<A
HREF="http://www.yourcompany.com/directry.htm">
Index</A>
</th></table></td>
<td><TABLE BORDER=5 padding=10>
<th><A HREF="http://www.yourcompany.com/">Your
Company Home</A></th></table></td>
<td><TABLE BORDER=5 padding=10><th>
<A HREF="http://www.yourcompany.com/cool.htm">Cool
Tools</A></td></th></table>
</tr>
</table>
```

Figure 6.8

Pseudo Buttons Created by Embedding Tables within Tables

Check for Visually Impaired Web Site Accessibility

As you design your site, be aware that some people with physical handicaps may be viewing it. Blind users configure their browsers to reverse the screen colors from the basic dark print on light background to a white on black. From this format the text is converted to a Braille reader. If you do not put ALT tags on your linked images or image maps, the visually impaired cannot read them. If you are conscientious about designing your Internal Web for all, you might want to check out the links for the visually impaired at

```
http://www.brailler.com/
```

Summary

You have learned that effective Web design requires being mindful of your audience. Be artistic, consistent, and innovative. Use basic graphic arts paradigms to appeal to the right brain but keep it simple and predictable, creating clear navigational paths. Be aware also that Web technology is evolving at an incredible pace, and there is still a lot of pioneering to do. Conserve bandwidth—don't subject users to the "World Wide Wait." Copy, paste, and create new stuff. Many of the ideas and instructions in this chapter are gifts that were placed out on the Web by others. Learn from them and use their tools to make new ones so that others can copy, paste, and create new stuff with your tools!

Web Site
Management

What You Can Do

The evolution of your Web site is inevitable. Once you've authored documents and designed your site, there's still a lot more you need to know. In the rest of the chapters in this book we discuss ways to orchestrate the symphony of formatted and huge documents on your Intranet. As always, the size of your company and its Intranet will help determine the choices you will need to make. In small companies it only takes a person or two to run a Web site. If you are in a high-tech environment, however, with lots of workstations and lots of employees, the payoff is greater but so is the effort and cost to keep things managed and running smoothly.

As you may remember from Chapter 1, for simplicity of reference, this book categorizes documents in three ways: *unformatted* (for example, e-mail kinda docs), *formatted* (primarily the kind we are used to seeing produced by a word processor), and *huge* or *self-describing* documents (SGML). This chapter deals primarily with managing the formatted variety on an Internal Web.

What You Will Need

You need to do a lot of planning to make all this work. For one thing, you need to know how to load documents on the Web, which documents should go on the Web, and who controls the decisions. This chapter will overview the distributed hypermedia system and discuss how to plan for the following:

- uploading files to your Web servers
- home pages, "What's New" pages, and symbolic links
- managing common Web site tasks
- managing changes in Web site design and strategy
- managing user help
- pushing information to users

How to Manage a Web Site

We'll begin our discussion with the most basic task: getting your files on the server.

Uploading Files to Your Web Server

Before you can copy your files to the server, you must have write privileges to the directory and an application for uploading files.

Depending on the size of your company and your Web site needs, you will need to determine who can write to the site and set privileges or create accounts accordingly. Chapter 11 discusses plans for setting up write privileges.

As always, we cannot list all file-loading applications, but we'll discuss some of your options.

FTP

The most frequently asked question I get from neophyte Web site managers is "How do I load the files from my local drive to the Web server?" Most networking software, like Windows for Workgroups, includes an FTP (File Transfer Protocol) client. With luck this section will explore enough possibilities that no matter what platform you operate from, the mystery of loading files will be solved. First of all, if you are a UNIX guru you probably have skipped this section. You already know how to sit at a UNIX prompt and use FTP, typing one line at a time to transfer files all over the world. Once in a while, some wannabe geek, like me, stops by to ask you a question so you give her an answer as you continue to type commands and laudably interpret each command. After a year of stopping by the desk of my favorite UNIX prince and asking questions about FTP, it finally dawned on me to ask this question: "Is there a list somewhere of FTP commands?" The answer I received was something like this: "FTP is FTP is FTP is FTP. There may be some annoying Microsnotisms on NT, but it's a simple protocol (in terms of the relatively limited command set) and is supposed to stay that way, so I doubt there are many, if any." I said "Huh?" So I searched the Net. I don't know why it took me a year to figure that one out. Just in case you haven't thought of it yourself, I have something important to tell you: FTP commands *are* UNIX commands. That's why FTP is easy for UNIX princes and princesses and confusing to the rest of us. Table 7.1 lists some URLs where you can find info about FTP commands and how to use them.

	URL	What You Will Find There
	http://www.cbu.edu/~ewelch/ Unixhelp/tasks_ftp2.html#ftp2	Transferring files using the FTP program
	http://www.cbu.edu/~ewelch/ Unixhelp/tasks_ftp2.1.1.html	List of FTP commands
	http://iew3.technion.ac.il:8080/ Home/CC/Comp_news/UXhelp/tasks _ftp2.1.1.html	List of FTP commands and how to get help
	http://www.dee.uc.pt/UnixHelp/tasks _ftp2.1.3.html	List of useful FTP commands
Table 7.1 Take the Mystery Out of FTP Commands	http://freenet.vcu.edu/ help/file_maint/ftp.html	FTP commands and tutorial

Using FTP. If you have a DOS background you will find using a non-Windows FTP client a lot like executing commands from a DOS prompt. As I said earlier, if you are a UNIX user you have probably skipped this section. If you are a MacUser see the MacLoading section later in this chapter.

The first thing you need to do is open your FTP application. You then type "open" and the name of the computer you would like to FTP to:

```
ftp home.yourcompany.com
```

You will then be connected to two computers:

- *Local host:* the one you have the FTP application loaded on. This is probably the computer on your desk where you execute the commands of most of the software applications you run. This computer may also be connected to shared drives on a network, which are of course on other computers. This means that even though you are a "local host" you can transfer files from any drive you can open on your computer. For instance, you may have a group shared drive called g:\. As Web site manager you can instruct others who have access to this drive to put their files on the shared drive for you to load to the server.

- *Remote host:* the Web server. You get the name of the remote host from the Webmaster who gives you write privileges.

Usually after a brief network delay, you will get a message that says you are connected to your remote host, probably some warning message, some server operating system information, good news that it's "ready," and a prompt for you to type in your password:

```
connected to home.yourcompany.com
Use of this FTP server is limited to Your Company
business activities.
ComputerName FTP server (Version wu-2.4(3) Sun Mar
26 12:34:57 PST 1995) ready.
User (ComputerName.yourcompany.com:(none)):
```

At the prompt, type in your user ID (depending on the security setup at your company, you may be able to log on to this computer as anonymous and enter your user ID as your password):

```
User (ComputerName.yourcompany.com:(none)):
joanbann
Password required for joanbann.
Password:
```

Once you type in your password the computer should answer with something like this:

```
User joanbann logged in.
```

Now it's time to use all those great commands that you can find using Table 7.1. The most common ones are listed in Table 7.2.

FTP Command	What It Does
cd (change directory)	Moves to whatever directory you would like to send files to on the remote host.
lcd (local change directory)	Goes to the directory on your local host where all the cool HTML and GIF files you have created and tested are anxiously waiting for their public appearance.
binary	Sends the next files in binary exchange. For example, I want to upload graphics, which are binary files.
ascii	Sends the next files in ASCII format. The best way to send HTML files is in ASCII format. The FTP client I use defaults to ASCII when it opens.
put	Followed by the filename. This loads your file or files if you use mput.
get	Reverse of put

Table 7.2

Common FTP Commands and Their Purpose

Definition ASCII (American Standard Code for Information Interchange).

Definition Binary *is the basic numbering system for calculations, codes, and data in all computers, consisting only of the digits 0 and 1, in contrast to the 10-digit decimal system.*

WS_FTP. WS_FTP is an intuitive program available for 16- and 32-bit Windows machines. You still have to set up the "open" process in the same way you do in the command-line version of FTP, but you only have to do it once. You can save access to each FTP server, including your password, if that is prudent. It is not prudent if your local host computer is not in a secure location.

Once you are logged on to the remote host, you can select your local drives and server drives with the mouse and view everything that is in them. You can load a whole bunch of documents and graphics at the same time by selecting them the way you do in File Manager or NT or the Win95 Explorer: Use the Shift key to select consecutive entries, and the Ctrl key to select one at a time. Then click the arrow and the files go to the server one at a time (my computer announces each arrival with a pleasant little "gong"). If you click on the Auto checkbox it detects whether the files you are loading are ASCII or binary friendly and ports them accordingly. Figure 7.1 shows the WS_FTP connected to a public drive at ftp.pacbell.com. You can order a licensed copy of WS_FTP or download an evaluation copy, which will expire after 30 days, at

```
http://www.csra.net/junodj/ws_ftp32.htm
```

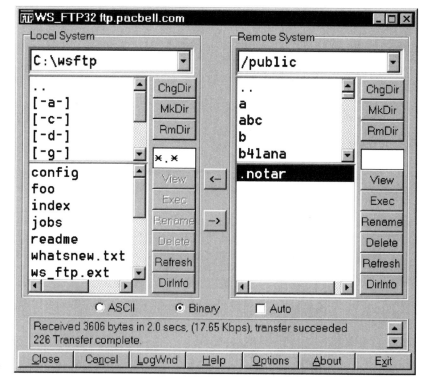

Figure 7.1

The WS_FTP window

Other FTP Applications. There are other FTP applications out on the Web. For example, I hear that Win_FTP is almost like WS_FTP. Please do not limit your search to the products I mention in this book. As stated earlier, I just want to get you started.

MacLoading

"Fetch" is the overwhelming favorite uploading tool among my MacFriends. Since I rarely have the opportunity to sit down at a Mac, I asked my friend John Pendleton to write the following steps on how to MacUse it. This is the formula for first-time use. Thereafter, steps 1–10 can be eliminated:

1. Double-click on the Fetch icon.
2. A dialog box appears with the Dartmouth Archives or the Info-Mac Archives as a default address.
3. Hit Cancel.
4. Select Add Shortcut from the Customize pull-down menu.
5. Enter the name of your host server under both Shortcut and Host.
6. Enter your user ID and password in the appropriate windows.
7. Enter the exact directory path to your folder in the appropriate windows.
8. Click OK.
9. Go to Edit Shortcuts in the Customize pull-down menu.
10. Highlight the shortcut name you have entered and click on the Make Default button. From this time on, you will always start at the chosen address.
11. The name of your folder will appear in a window on the left of the dialog box, with your options displayed on the right.
12. To send files to the server, go to the pull-down menu marked Remote at the top of your screen.
13. Select Put Folders and Files and a new dialog box will appear.
14. Select the appropriate files from their folders on your hard disk by highlighting them in the window on the upper-left side of the dialog box and click on the Add button in the lower-right corner. When you have assembled a complete list, click on Done.

15. Yet another dialog box will appear, asking in which mode you wish to send your text and files. Set both to `raw data`.

16. When the doggie stops running, you're done. Click `Close Connection` and then quit the program.

When sending a mapped image and the associated map to some servers, send the image as raw data and the map document as text. The map document will have the same name as the associated image, except that the suffix will be `.map` instead of `.gif`. Once the map document gets to the server, it will have acquired a new, additional suffix. If it started out as `acme.map`, it will now be `acme.map.txt`. You need to go into the server and rename the file as `acme.map` before it will work. Why this happens is beyond me, but it is important to remember to fix it.

Home Pages, Symbolic Links, and "What's New" Pages

Home Pages

One of the Web site management tasks you will do often is set up what's commonly called a "home page." This can be the front page of an organizational Web site, the first page of a chunked multipage document, or an employee's "personal home page." When you post a home page you will want it to be the default first page users see when they get to a subdirectory. For example, here's the URL for the Addison-Wesley Developers Press Web site. Notice in Figure 7.2 that the URL in the Location text bar at the top of the Netscape window is

```
http://www.awl.com/devpress/
```

More powerful Web servers, such as Netscape's Enterprise, use a "~" mechanism for denoting personal directories and home page areas. It's commonly used for client-site directories and can be pressed into service for departmental, group-level, or personal home pages.

Figure 7.2

A home page that defaults to the subdirectory

Definition   A home page *is often used to refer to the main document or top page in a collection of organized information. For example, the Addison-Wesley Developers Press home page in Figure 7.2 is a front page to all that Addison-Wesley Developers Press on their Web site including info about them, what's new, what's coming up, how to contact them, and how to order books, like this one, directly.*

In the truest sense, many "personal home pages" are not "home pages" at all but any page that contains biographical and sometimes personal information about a person. A page about a person has become known as a personal "home page" even if it has no introductory links to anything else. Far be it for me to defy what people readily understand even if it doesn't fit a mold.

The Addison-Wesley Developers Press home page has no `.htm` or `.html` file listed after the last forward slash, yet the Web server default for a URL like that is to display an index of all files in the subdirectory such as the list shown in Figure 7.3. So how did they do that? There are two ways. The index has a name that the Web server creates automatically. On UNIX servers it's called `index.html`. You can rename your home page `index.html` and it will come up instead of the default list of files. However, if you have a large site and edit pages locally and then move them to the server (as opposed to super-UNIX users who make edits directly on the server copy), it's possible that you might forget which subdirectory you're in. It would therefore be very easy on some late night (geeks do that) to accidentally overwrite the one department's home page with another department's home page. The way to avoid this confusion is to create a symbolic link.

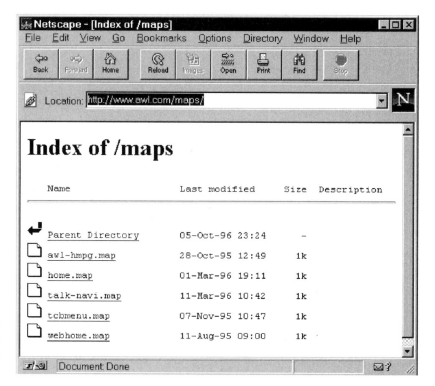

Figure 7.3

An index of a subdirectory is the usual default.

Symbolic Links

There are two kinds of symbolic links that I find most handy. The first is a symbolic link from a subdirectory index to a home page. The syntax for this command in UNIX is

```
ln -s homepage.htm index.html
```

As soon as you create a symbolic link (I use Telnet to execute that command) you can go into your browser to the subdirectory where you created the symbolic link and click on Reload. If all has gone well, sans typos and all that, the index (similar to the one in Figure 7.3) will be replaced by the home page you linked it to. Now when you want to update the home page, all you have to do is update it on your local host and then upload it to the server using its more descriptive name. Click on Reload again and you will see the updated home page.

The second symbolic link I use is one that saves new Web site managers a lot of time and confusion. It links their entry into the Web server to the site on the server where they have write privileges. For instance, you may "own" a server subdirectory called Security. When you FTP or Telnet into a session with the Web server, you may need to change directories by typing a lengthy string (or clicking several times in a Windows FTP client) to get to the Security directory, for example,

```
cd home.company.com/Maindir/Organizations/Security
```

Added to this confusion, it's very likely that when you gain entry to the remote host, you enter buried in a subdirectory whose user IDs are stored and have to figure out how to get to the root. So the answer is to set up a symbolic link to the directory the user owns. For example, say you're in pop/joanbann; to set up a symbolic link in this directory to "security" use the following syntax:

```
ln -s home.company.com/Maindir/Organizations/
Security
```

Then the next time you log in you can just change directories by typing

```
cd Security
```

After changing to the directory, if you type pwd you will see that you have jumped into the full path of the directory you own. If you use a Windows FTP client you will see Security as one of the directories on the remote host side of the window. When you click on it, the path at the top of the Windows FTP client will be the full path—so much easier.

Loading Multipage Documents

Chunking documents is a good habit. It saves bandwidth and user consternation. With conversion utilities like HTML Transit (listed in Chapter 5) chunked documents can be easily hyperlinked together and formatted with a hyperlinked table of contents and/or index. The easiest way to orchestrate loading multipage documents to the Web is to create a separate subdirectory for the set of documents, which make up the whole, use relative URLs, and then create a home page symbolic link from the server index page to the most logical home page of the set, which may be the table of contents. For example, if I were to put this chapter in its own subdirectory, I would break it into small hyperlinked documents. If I did not index the title page as the home page, a default `index.html` page would appear similar to the one shown in Figure 7.4. However, if I create a symbolic link to the table of contents page, when a user gets to the URL they will see the page shown in Figure 7.5.

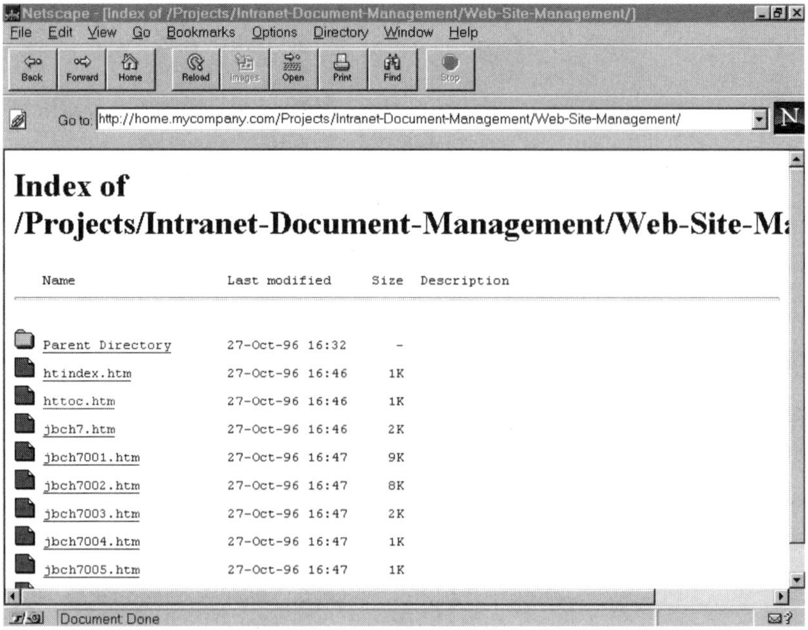

Figure 7.4

Default index of a chunked document

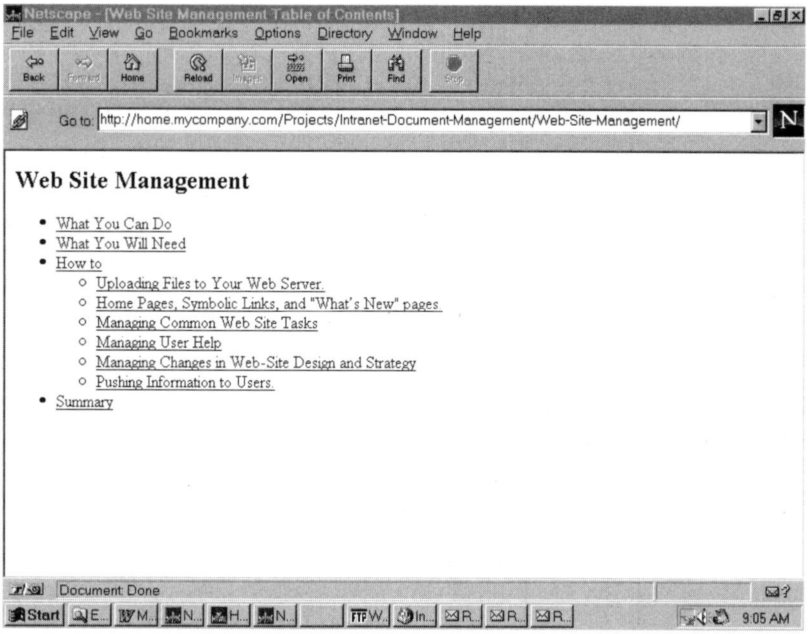

Figure 7.5

A symbolic link
brings up the
home page of the
chunked document
in Figure 7.4

Multiple Versions of the Same Document

So what if a user would like to have a printed copy of your multipage
documents? If you have chunked it, and they want the whole thing,
they have a small hassle ahead, printing it page by page and then trying
to figure out which page 1 is really page 1 and which page 1 is page 10.
The nonintuitive, browser-generated headers on them such as
`http://home.mycompany.Projects/Intranet-Document-`
`Management/jbch07.htm` will probably offer little help. If it's likely
that a lot of your users will need a hard copy of your document, the
easiest way to offer it to them is to save it in word processing format,
with an FTP link to it. If you `zip`, `tar`, or `stuff` the document, when
they click on the link they will be prompted to save it to disk. Depending on the way you have users set up on your Intranet, you can also ad-
vise them to configure their browser to launch helper applications. For
example, if they are configured to, say, launch Word when they click on
`.doc` files, their local copy of Word will open when they click on a
`.doc` file. They can then use their word processor to print a complete
copy of the document, which includes a logical paper-friendly table of

contents, headers, footers, and page numbers. Warning: When you teach your users to configure their browsers to launch native format documents from within their Web browser, you may be opening up your Intranet to Trojan horse viruses. As always, depending on the size of your Intranet, the number of users you need to educate, and the likelihood that they will grab documents from the Internet, you might prefer to keep this to a minimum and use anti-virus software. Even if documents are downloaded in zipped versions and opened later, they can carry viruses.

Managing Common Web Site Tasks

This discussion is not exhaustive, but with luck it will get you jump-started if managing a Web site is new to you.

Managing "What's New" Items

Your Intranet can be a very "newsy" place, especially if you are doing a great job managing users' expectations that it's the place to find the latest version of documents and the latest company news. You may find that some "What's New" items should be "Important Announcements," and if you have a lot of both you might consider maintaining two separate pages. Either way, you want What's New to be new and to be posted fast. My recommendation is that you establish a feedback form, and depending on how much you trust your audience, perhaps even an automatic upload procedure programmed to post the form to What's New. Your feedback form could even be precoded with HTML, so your users merely fill in the actual words in the blanks of the form with information such as the date, the announcement, the URL of the announcement, the person's name, and their e-mail address. The form could then code the data in HTML. The other option, which I actually prefer, is to have the form come to me and let me take a look at it before I code it. Regardless of how busy I am, I usually can post within an hour after I receive them.

So what about the old What's New? Good question. You can have things just "fall off" the list after a certain amount of time. But it's amazing how many users find What's New items and bookmark so they can use that route to get to the site long after the item is no longer new. You can imagine how confused that visitor is when he comes to your What's New page looking for that "new" Job Aids page (now two months old). Not only can he no longer find it; he can't remember the name of the organization who hosted it. One way to accommodate this kind of dilemma is to phase pages out but make an archive of "old What's New items" and of course link the history to the end of the new.

A Place for Everything and Everything in Its Place

Was my grandmother the only one who repeatedly drilled that phrase into an offspring's head? I hope not; it's a good plan. One of the advantages you have of placing documents on a Web server is that they can be accessed from everywhere else on the Web. This goes for graphics, too, of course. This means that you can have a central repository for images and icons that can be reused throughout your Internal Web, and you only need to post one copy. Just put them into an "images" subdirectory. This also goes for personal home pages, stats, and any other items with commonality. Centralizing and depositing stores of files makes it easier not only to find them but also to purge them when they're no longer useful.

Setting Up Downloadable Licensed Software

If your company licenses software, your Internal Web is the perfect place to set up a company "Tool Store." Not only can you set the expectation that this is the place to find the latest versions; you also have the convenience of configuring the software with your company-specific preferences previous to distribution. For example, you could program your browser software to automatically recognize proxy setups or to open your company's Internal Web home page.

Company Discounts and Your Approved Product List du Jour

One of the things you will want to get set up as soon as possible is access to any vendors or suppliers who give you discounts. Having this information up-to-date and readily available can save your company big bucks. This can be everything from a corporate travel plan discounted by particular travel agents, to your approved product lists and suppliers. It may not be your responsibility as Web site manager to actually keep these pages up-to-date, but having links to them should be a high priority. Your part of this important Intranet tool will be to make these kinds of things as easy to find as possible. It may not be intuitive for users to find these documents buried in the procurement organization's Web site. They should probably be hosted there, but your high-level company home page directories should have them listed with easy-to-find titles. For instance, think about what you would like to display in an alpha sort directory, like "Travel" instead of "Corporate Travel Plan" or "Training" rather than "Software Instruction Totally Cool School and Vendor." You also should counsel authors to put in meta keywords to help the search engines find them. Your Corporate Travel page might have keywords and description information such as the following:

```
<META NAME="keywords" CONTENT="car rental airlines
travel discounts hotel reservations travel tips
travel policies">
```

```
<META NAME="description" CONTENT="The General
Contracting Organization has created this Travel
Page as a means of communicating to everyone in-
formation regarding the Corporate Travel Program.">
```

Managing Changes in Web Site Design and Strategy

Just when you think everything is beautifully organized on your site something is bound to change. There are several factors to consider that can help you anticipate change and even be one of the change agents to meet the evolving needs of your company.

Using Stats

There are a ton of statistics applications that can help you identify who is accessing what page and how often. The results can be dispersed to individual site owners on a regular basis to keep them apprised of which documents are the most visited. Once you have this information you may decide to give a more popular document a shorter path so people can have the convenience of accessing it in one click instead of two or three. If you cannot find a logical way to categorize these documents at the top level of your site, you might consider giving them their own category just because they are popular, like "Top Ten Sites." This categorization not only helps the users who are already accessing the sites regularly; it might also point out to others that these really handy sites exist. For example, pages that contain phone lists or cafeteria menus have a tendency to be very popular, but they also have a tendency to be buried within the site of the department that produces them. Table 7.3 lists a number of places where you can find stats applications, and, BTW, there are lots more than these.

URL	What You Will Find There
http://www.bazaarsuite.com/	Bazaar Analyzer: Java-based, platform independent
http://www.webtrends.com/	Web Trends: compatible with any WebServer that supports the Common or Combined Log Format
http://www.marketwave.com/	Hit List: for UNIX and NT servers
http://www.CQMInc.com/webtrack/webtrack.htm	Web Tracker: looks like it only does NT; not sure if it does UNIX

Table 7.3
Stats Applications

Definition   BTW (by the way) *is a very common Internet acronym.*

Requesting and Responding to Feedback

Many times in this book I recommend feedback forms or an opportunity for users to `mailto:` Web page authors. So what do you do with the mail you get from these? You evolve the site. Some feedback requires an obvious response—you have proudly displayed your mistakes, or a link you originally tested no longer works, and a frustrated user sends e-mail to let you know. Some feedback, however, requires a not so obvious response—users can request the darndest things. Sometimes they write three full pages on how they think the site should be completely reorganized. Sometimes they want to see more of something and less of something else. The "more of something" is often information out of your control and needs to be referred to departments that handle it. For instance, I have often received requests for specific human resources information to be added to the Web site, so I refer the request to the HR Webmaster. The "less of something" is usually graphics. As beautiful and entertaining as they can be, they slow people down, and that's not why people go online. The next section in this chapter, Reducing the Size of Graphics, might be a big help if you gotta have 'em.

One effective way to respond to feedback forms is to have them delivered to everyone on a task force. The task force can then respond in several ways. One way is to have individuals who have a particular area of expertise grab the appropriate request. This first way would be ad hoc: "I'll take this one" with a cc to everyone else on the team. Another way is to have someone on call this week to answer. Either way, some requests will need to be set aside for consideration at the next task force meeting because it is not appropriate for one person to respond. This would certainly include requests for changes in the next Web site enhancement. Strategizing a path forward is not an easy process. It's my experience that if there are five people in a room deciding the direction of a Web site, I can count on at least six opinions to be shared about each issue. Be prepared for long discussions and disagreements about how the site should look and feel. Also be prepared to make some changes now and let others lie for a while till the next enhancement. You might consider test users to see if your projected plans seem right. For example, you might give them a subject to look up and see where they intuitively start looking to find it on your site. It may surprise you how illogical your logical path is to someone else. Another good test is to see what your users see; that is, how does the site perform on various sizes and resolutions of monitors? Of course if your company is completely standardized this would not be necessary (and I envy your utopian authoring environment).

Reducing the Size of Graphics

Graphics can really be a pain. One solution is to educate users that they don't need them (see Managing User Help later in this chapter). If a user gets tired of waiting for graphics, he can press Stop or he can turn graphics off completely. This will require your authors to use ALT text for the graphics and alternate navigation hypertext links for imagemaps. See Chapter 6 for an example of how to create pseudo buttons, which are not buttons at all, but tables that look like buttons. Pseudo buttons are preferable to graphic image buttons in two ways.

They do not take up as much bandwidth or slow down the load time. They also show visited and unvisited links.

Another way to reduce gratuitous graphic overload is to put thumbnail versions of graphics rather than their larger counterparts within documents. The thumbnails take a lot less time to load and may be sufficient so the user does not need to look at the larger version at all.

Reducing Bytes in Photoshop. The following steps were given to me by John Pendleton, who is a MacUser. If you work on Windows or UNIX perhaps you can translate these steps into your own platform language and find comparable applications. John reduced several graphic images for my Web site by about 60 percent. Here are John's directions:

1. Begin by opening the image in Photoshop.

2. Make sure the image is in RGB mode; if it isn't, just select RGB from the Mode menu.

3. Next change the image to Indexed mode using the same menu. You might get a dialog box asking if you want to flatten layers; click on OK. This process combines any stacked layers into a single unit, thereby reducing the file size somewhat. If this dialog box doesn't appear, don't worry about it. This simply means the image had only one layer.

4. Either way, a dialog box will now appear asking you to set Resolution (select 8 bits/pixel), Palette (select Adaptive), and Dither (select Diffusion). Click on OK.

5. Now go to the File menu and select Save As. A dialog box appears asking what name you want to give the file. Just to be on the safe side, limit the number of characters to 11, including a 3-letter suffix, which MUST be .gif in lowercase. Below the window where you typed in the name is a pull-down menu titled Format: that probably says CompuServe GIF. If this is the case, all is as it should be. Click on OK. If it says Photoshop 3.0 or some such nonsense, just select CompuServe GIF and click on OK. Be sure to note exactly where (to which directory or folder) you are saving the image, because you still have more to do.

6. Create a simple HTML page with only one feature, that being an image call (<IMG src="???">) with the name of your image

going in to replace `"???"`. Put this HTML page in the same folder as your image.

7. The next step assumes that you have an application called JPEGview by Aaron Giles. It is freeware, available at `http://www.fagg.uni-lj.si/cgi-bin/vsl-front`, which is the Virtual Shareware Library in Slovenia.

8. Open your HTML page with Netscape and (assuming that you have already preselected JPEG view as a helper application in Netscape's General Preferences) place your mouse cursor over your image and hold down the button without releasing it. A dialog box will appear. Select Save This Image As and give your image a new name. Save the image to the same folder as the old image and the HTML page. The reduction in size should be substantial.

9. Sometimes—not always—but once in a while, a further reduction in size can be achieved by using GIFConverter 2.3.7 by Kevin A. Mitchell (`http://www.wimmera.net.au/winhome/macgraphics.html`). Simply open the image in GIFConverter 2.3.7 and save as a JPEG (JFIF). Sometimes this works, sometimes not.

Retiring Old Documents

Many an "old" Web document merely gets replaced by a new one of the same name, and this keeps all its links working. Sometimes though a document becomes obsolete; it is valuable for historical information but you wouldn't want people to think it was new. For instance, you may have a preliminary requirements document that explains the rationale behind important choices that were made at the onset of a project. Within this document might be minimum hardware or software requirements that evolved as the year passed. You would not want users to skip to that section for the latest hardware and software requirements. A preliminary requirements document is not the ideal place to keep hardware and software requirements up-to-date. The best solution is to move these kinds of documents to a different part of your Intranet where they are still accessible but not so prominent. They should be filed in the online document management tool that best suits your Intranet needs. (For more about online document management tools, see Chapter 9.) Many of the document management tools have a Web interface. This means if you really wanted to, you could still give users the URL to the Document Management System, but when they browse the system they will get properties information that explains to them the value and limitations of the contents before they actually view them.

Another major problem with retiring old documents is broken links, the subject of the next section.

Finding Broken Links

There are basically three ways to find broken links:

1. Find them yourself through testing.
2. Wait for users to tell you by using feedback mechanisms you put in place.
3. Use software applications that seek them out.

Test test test. Every time you put up a page you need to test the links even if they worked locally. If you don't, and you think, "Oh it'll work," or you forget after you've moved them to the server to test them all, I promise, the second way to find broken links will become operative. It's so embarrassing. And, of course, when you have nothing else to do—like maybe you are lying awake at night wondering why you can't sleep—you might want to just go "play" with your Web site to see if all the links are still working. It's amazing how often you change something and you forget there's another page affected by the change.

User Feedback. Feedback forms and `mailto:'s` are your best assurance that you will have a lot of help keeping things managed. Users like to give you feedback because the Web is so "alive." How often have you read something on paper and wished you could say a little something to the author? (BTW, I would love to hear from you, joan@bannan.com.) Many times, when I receive broken link messages they are accompanied by other valuable feedback and often compliments. That's just one of the reasons being a Web site manager is a great job.

Software Applications. By the time this book goes to print you will probably have dozens of return hits if you search the Internet on "broken links." Every software application that can possibly get on the Internet/Intranet bandwagon will do so for a long time. As a Web site manager this is good news and bad news. The good news is that everyone is trying to help you do your job. The bad news is you don't have time to do your job, plus learn and evaluate every application that claims it can help you. That caveat aside, here's a URL worth checking out:

```
http://www.openmarket.com/omi/products/webreport.
html
```

You will get an automatic message that you found a broken link. The message is generated by their software, which, of course, you can purchase right there.

The other possibility that you might consider is a commercial solution to your entire Web site management that can do a lot more than find broken links.

Commercial solutions, such as Netscape's Live Wire, Cosmo Create, Adobe Pagemill, Sitemill, and Microsoft's Front Page all offer complete Web site management tools including authoring, posting, and sophisticated ways to view and test your links. I personally have only started to use two of these but of course I already have some opinions that I would like to share. I don't like the editors on the ones I tried because in their WYSIWYG way they detach me from the HTML code. I have little patience to learn another software program when I already know the coding. This may appeal to you, however, rather than keeping up with the HTML evolution and "browser wars." Another thing I didn't like about Web site management tools is that the two I tried needed to replicate my site somewhere else for me to use it. Then if I make a change to my site in my usual fix-it-on-the-fly-as-soon-as-possible style, I am a slave to go re-replicate or redo the action in the site manager. If you are building a brand-new site from scratch, however, you may love the way it graphically displays what you are building. The last thing I didn't like about one of the commercial solution site managers was the incredible amount of scary security warnings I encountered while installing the server extensions. So it's not that you shouldn't try these out, but if you are on a different platform than the site manager's default, plan to do your install on a day that you can focus on the warnings and instructions with a clear head and no interruptions.

Managing
User Help

No matter what size your company is, the more you help users understand your Internal Web, the easier it will be for you to manage it. One way to do this is to document everything you teach anybody, from neophyte Web site managers to end users. Give them as many standards, recommendations, expectations, instructions, and tips as you can.

Standards and Recommendations

One of your help sections should definitely be dedicated to helping authors create Internal Web documents. This is where you place templates, tips, and recommendations for setting up a Web site. You will want to include company standards for document properties (that is, "summary" or "META" information); posting these on your Web site will save you a lot of run-around-the-rabbit-trail time. For example, I got a feedback e-mail one day from a user who couldn't find something on a Web page that he found on a site linked to my site. He wanted information about something I knew nothing about. The other Web site had no feedback mechanism anywhere within five or six Web pages, but it had a link to a page on my site, so the frustrated user used my handy, dandy `mailto:` mechanism because it was the only one he could find. Fortunately one of the pages had a user ID in the META data that had been automatically placed there by one of the HTML editors or Web site management tools. I was able to track down the author, refer the user to him, and request that he proudly insert his own feedback `mailto:`.

Other standards may be to include META data keywords or descriptions as mentioned in the Company Discounts and Your Approved Product List du Jour section earlier in this chapter. The "author publishing help" Web pages could also include links to your internal security policies, which define restrictions on proprietary information and links to various places to find virus protection. Even if Netscape is not your browser of choice, you might appreciate their expert advice on "Creating Net Sites" at

```
http://home.netscape.com/assist/net_sites/
```

You might include the resource information for this book where you can find the resources (URLs) and glossary online at

```
http://www.bannan.com/Intranet-Doc-Mgt/Appendices
```

You can also add other company standards information, such as "How to configure your browser," which would include your use of proxy servers, and perhaps how to set the home page to be your Internal Web home. These help pages could also link to the browser's help pages. For instance, if your company's standard browser is Netscape, you might want to put a link to their very handy handbook at

```
http://home.netscape.com/eng/mozilla/3.0/handbook/
```

Expectations

Managing users' expectations might include a list of what to expect when they request hosting services on the Internal Web server. For instance, tell them what kinds of sites you are willing to host and any restrictions you have such as what size their site can be or scripts they can or cannot set up. You want an e-mail with certain information contained within. Tell them that within X amount of time they will receive their password from the Webmaster. Have a set of instructions on how to change their password and be sure to tell them about the help pages you have created to get them started publishing. Give them instructions on how to use existing server scripts such as feedback form scripts and then manage their expectations for how long it will take to implement them. Also tell them how to get their site linked to the high-level directories and tell them when their link will show up there. If you have automated any of these processes, you can instruct them how to test to see if their new Web site is now showing up in the "Organizations" alphabetical listing directory, or tell them when to expect it if the script is run once a day.

Instructions and Tips

You can give users tips on optimizing the performance of their browser. For instance, particularly if you have global users or not so global telecommuters, they may not be aware that they can turn off the pictures in the options box of Internet Explorer or uncheck the Auto Load Images in the Netscape Options menu. You can give them tips on how your Web site is organized to help them find stuff and direct them to search engines if the logic doesn't work for them. You could even set your help pages up with automatic fax back capability if your system and your server gurus have time.

Pushing Information to Users

If your Internal Web resembles even part of what this book suggests, your users will be pulled back for more. But you can push information in several ways. One way is to have moving entities that are hard to ignore. Some examples are the wonderfully obnoxious "blink" HTML tag, animated graphics that keep telling the user something as the page is loading, and JavaScript messages that keep trailing across the status bar at the bottom of your browser window. An example of using an animated GIF to push information can be found at

```
http://www.zdnet.com/anchordesk/story/
story_389.html
```

and an example of JavaScript at

```
http://home.highway.or.jp/syou-/hp/java-s1.htm
```

Another way to push information to users on your Internal Web is to integrate it with the rest of your Intranet. For example, when you set up user groups you can create a list service that e-mails each registered user. Each time a new comment, question, or flame is added to the user group, each user will get an e-mail message with its content.

Summary

Managing a Web site is, in my humble opinion, one of the most fun jobs in the world. There is so much you can do to help users get up-to-date information quickly that each time you make an improvement to your site you feel instant gratification. You can set up help documents that will save everyone time, especially you. There are tools that can help you manage your site—uploading tools, HTML editors, and commercial solutions for complete Web site management—but when it really gets down to it you need people to help you see what is broken, what needs to be done, and what they would like to see next.

8 *Using Scripts and Databases*

What You Can Do

The Web began as a vehicle to share findings among scientists at the CERN research facility in Switzerland. The roots of the Web, therefore, are in the field of data publishing. HTML, the lingua franca of the medium, is severely limited in that it only allows for static page presentation. Since research findings continually change as new data is accumulated, some means of allowing the presentation had to be found. The solution to this problem was the *Common Gateway Interface,* or CGI.

Definition *An* interface *is a standard means for interacting with a computer system or program. From a programming standpoint an interface (generally referred to as an Advanced Programmers Interface, or API) is a standard code base for developing on top of an existing application. From an end-point perspective, the inputs, menus, and dialog systems define the user interface.*

Definition *The* Common Gateway Interface (CGI) *is the standard mechanism for holding and manipulating variables in a Web application.*

The Common Gateway Interface allowed for a tremendous amount of innovation on the Web. It moved the Web from a static to a dynamic medium. Whereas HTML allows you to publish your personnel manuals on the Web, the CGI, bound to forms, scripts, and databases, allows you to publish time-sensitive or frequently updated information on the fly. Reports can have standardized formats per your company's

151

branding standard, yet contain data culled from your ongoing business operations, all without having to change the HTML that formats the content. This approach to dynamic page generation will help you keep your Intranet fresh, while helping you keep maintenance costs down.

What You Will Need

In this chapter we discuss basic ways to make dynamic Web pages using CGI scripts, HTML forms, and programming languages such as PERL. To create advanced Web applications you need specialized scripting languages such as Java and some sort of database interface. We turn first to CGI.

The CGI Foundation

The Common Gateway Interface comprises a series of standard variables that identify certain data elements about the client. Examples of data elements are the IP address and type of browser or agent making an HTTP request, the server software and version, as well as the requested document's content definitions. Perhaps the most important variable holds the *Query String.*

Definition A query *is a specific request for information from a data source.*

Definition A string *is a data definition that specifies that information being presented should be taken as is. While 2 + 2 would be represented as 4 when treated as a numerical data type, "2" + "2" in string form would be represented as "22."*

As a veteran Web surfer, you have undoubtedly seen this CGI Query String listed in the location field of your browser, the box where you usually type "http://www.navelgaze.com/" or the like. The odd combination of `lint?fuzzy=brown&outie=no` you may see tacked onto the end of that URL is actually the Query String variable being passed to some program via an HTML form's `Get` method. (To learn more about the range of variables accessible via the CGI, please consult *The CGI Book* published by New Riders Publishing.) You should think of the CGI as the tie that binds your application's front end (the user interface) to its back end (the program that knows what to do with the CGI information).

How to Use Scripts and Databases

Form Tags: The Basic User Interface

You already know from Chapter 5 that HTML is simply a series of specialized formatting tags that tell the browser how to display, hide, or link your content. The form tags allow your application to engage users by accepting their input data. For example, you might want your users to keep their own primary demographic information up-to-date. You could use the form tags to allow them to type in their name, address, and phone number.

As noted previously, two basic methods exist for passing data from one page through the CGI to a program able to process the data. A `Get` displays the information sent, along with the URL of the program it is being passed to, while a `Post` hides the information from the user's browser. Other significant differences between `Get` and `Post` include a 256-character limit for a `Get` and a multiple assignment limitation for a `Post`. While the selection of either method depends on the nature of your application, `Post` is generally the recommended method due to its lack of size limitation.

These form methods use a variety of input types. Free-form inputs, such as a name or description, are handled through the Textbox and

Textarea tags. Textboxes allow a single line of text input, while Text-areas allow users to enter multiple lines. When you want your users to select from a range of options, three tags allow you to guide their choices: Radio, Checkbox, and Select. Radio buttons force users to select one of several options, while Checkboxes present multiple options. When you have a larger list of options and want to avoid an unmanageable number of boxes to choose from, Selects are a better option. Select tags can be used to force single choices, or to allow for multiple choices. Hidden input tags can be used to quietly pass values such as the page origin or code-generated variables. Because your users are probably not perfect (and if they are, please contact me with the phone number of your Personnel Director at joan@bannan.com) one special input type is the Reset button. This tag, not surprisingly, sets all values back to their defaults, the default default being a blank or null value. The last standard tag is the Submit button, which sends the user inputs through the CGI to your application. One nonstandard tag developed by Netscape, and supported by most major browsers, allows for a File as an input.

Using our demographic example, the following HTML tags produce the form shown in Figure 8.1:

```
<HTML>
<HEAD><TITLE>Sample Form</TITLE></HEAD>
<BODY><CENTER>Personnel Update Form</CENTER>
<P><FORM METHOD="POST" ACTION="UPDATE.CGI"><BR>
Name: <INPUT NAME="NAME" TYPE="TEXTBOX"><BR>
Address: <INPUT NAME="STREET" TYPE="TEXTBOX"><BR>
City: <INPUT NAME="CITY" TYPE="TEXTBOX"><BR>
State:  <INPUT NAME="STATE" TYPE="RADIO">CA
        <INPUT NAME="STATE" TYPE="RADIO">OR
        <INPUT NAME="STATE" TYPE="RADIO">WA
Zip: <INPUT NAME="CITY" TYPE="TEXTBOX"><BR>
Reason for Change: <INPUT TYPE="TEXTAREA">
</FORM></BODY></HTML>
```

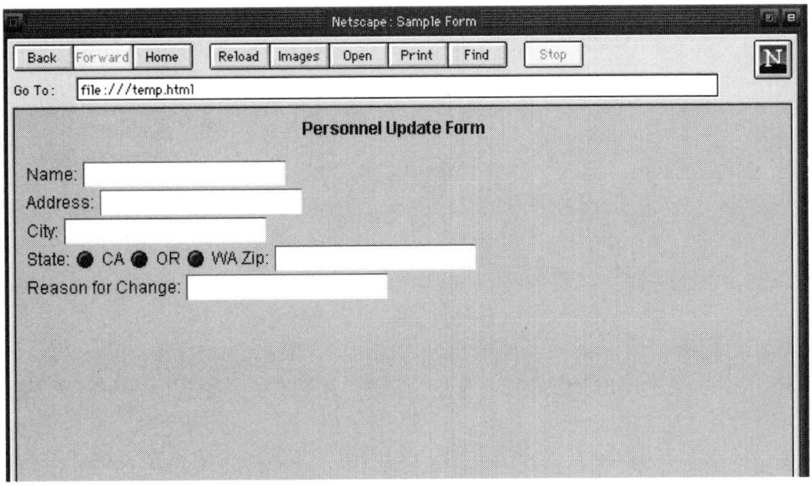

Figure 8.1

A simple HTML form

You may have noticed that the form tags in our example have special designations associated with them. The Name element for each of our input types exists to tell our application what piece of information is being referenced. Such name/value pairs help determine variable definitions and establish logical response paths within your application. The Action element used with the form tag dictates the program that will handle information gathered from this page.

Which brings us to the heart of the matter: your CGI program. Traditional programming incorporates the user interface, the data interchange, as well as the logic systems. In basic Web application programming, HTML tends to define the user interface, CGI handles the data interchange, leaving only the core logic systems. As you begin to examine which of your operations can be made more efficient by means of a distributed system, you need to consider that different programming languages are appropriate for different operations.

Programming Languages

Any major programming language can be used to process information, create dynamic displays, output HTML, and respond to user requests. Today's Web applications are being crafted in almost every language imaginable. Given that these systems range from old mainframe tongues like Rexx, to newer dialects such as Visual Basic, C++, and its object-oriented cousins, the Web is beginning to resemble the Tower of Babel. Not to worry, though, as a few well suited languages, namely *PERL* and *C,* have entered into the vernacular.

Definition   PERL (Practical Extraction and Reporting Language) *is an interpreted language. Interpreted languages always exist in source form and rely on an interpreter that handles the source at runtime.*

Definition   C *is a compiled procedural language. Compiled programs are turned into object code (not to be confused with object-oriented), linked to related* libraries, *and are then ready to run at any time.*

Definition   Libraries *are established code elements that can be linked to programs to perform specific tasks as needed.*

Definition   Object-oriented *programming means different things in different languages. Generally, objects are small reusable pieces of code that can be used interchangeably in a variety of ways (a concept known as polymorphism) and can take on properties of upper-level code elements (inheritance).*

Basic form response programs can be developed in simple shell or command-line scripts. UNIX, for example, has a variety of shells (for example, Bourne, Korn, and C shell scripts) and the Mac O/S has AppleScript. These low-level scripting languages, while they tend to be used for light administrative server tasks, can be pressed into service for simple Web applications. For example, UNIX systems administrators will use shell scripts to schedule backups or to launch Web servers at boot-time. A basic shell script could be built to take CGI inputs and turn them into a formatted electronic mail message. Having said this, use shell scripting if—and only if—you do not have any other language at your disposal because it opens significant security holes. (See Chapter 2 for details about security.) Fortunately, both PERL and C exist in robust and free forms and have been ported to most platforms.

As so many early Web applications were highly text oriented and built on UNIX platforms, Perl became a big favorite among developers.

As its full name implies, PERL exists to extract, report on, and handle strings. This is an especially important task when you are dealing with user inputs. In the UNIX environment, for example, you want to avoid the introduction of special "escape" characters along the lines of @/#%$* as they can be used to break systems. On an even more fundamental level, when handling the CGI Query String you will need to deal with the ?, &, and = characters passed along with the variable. Perl excels at taking these characters and *parsing* the string into distinct name/value pairs.

Definition   *To* parse *in programmatic terms is to divide and compartmentalize data.*

Part of the reason that PERL juggles strings so well on the UNIX platform is that it readily invokes two even more highly specialized languages called sed and awk. These two languages, without going into great detail, are perhaps the most powerful string search-and-replace languages on any platform. The best reference set for these UNIX utility languages is published by O'Reilly and Associates. Individual tomes are appropriately titled "Programming PERL" and "sed & awk." This string language triumvirate can be used for more than simply character replacement.

Say you want to create a program on your Intranet that new users access to select their passwords. You could build an application that would accept their password from an HTML form, pass it through the CGI, and then test it for letter-only combinations, or even against full dictionaries of words. You could further craft your script to switch between upper- and lowercase, reverse letter order, and the like. The script could then finish its program by either rejecting the password and notifying the user to try again, or notify them that the password was fine and dandy.

Other fine examples of scripting situations best handled with PERL are form validation and Bulletin-Board Systems, where text inputs need to be associated with earlier inputs and users might want to search through dozens or hundreds of messages for related information. We discuss this topic later in this chapter.

Perl has several major limitations. For one, it is not particularly well suited for heavy logic forking where a large number of variables need to be consulted to determine appropriate courses of digital action, nor does it deal efficiently with complex calculations. It also tends to be slow. PERL is an interpreted language, which means that each time a piece of code is called, the PERL interpreter needs to fire up, handle the code, and return the result. This adds up to lost seconds of productivity. This is not to say that PERL should be disregarded as a viable application language. Simply consider that PERL is very, very good for certain kinds of tasks and not very good for others.

Which leads us to the letter C. C is probably the most widely used development language in or outside of the Web. C is flexible, powerful, flexible, powerful, and flexible, not to mention powerful. The language earns these traits from its large number of data types and operations. C is also a compiled language, which means that the code is self-contained and ready to run on its own. This makes C a strong choice when your application requires sophisticated logic constructs and rapid computation. Another advantage of C is that it is available on every platform. You can develop your application on an NT platform and then recompile it on a Silicon Graphics machine or PowerPC. One more convenience of working in C is that most system integration products, including the majority of database packages, have a C language API. This allows you to bring a great deal of prebuilt functionality to your Intranet. There are literally hundreds of reference manuals available for C. One recommendation is *Workout C,* published by the Waite Group Press.

All right, say you want to create a page that not only generates a response, but gives the user different messages based on their input. Perhaps you want to do this in a registration screen where the second page displayed depends on the department the individual was hired into, and that this page brings up additional screens of questions based on the second page, and so on. This kind of dynamically created page could easily be handled by one relatively simple C program that splits through one fork, passes variables back to itself through the Hidden Form tag, calls itself, forks again, and so on until all appropriate questions have been answered.

The flip side to this flexibility is that C applications are more difficult to produce and debug. In comparison to PERL, C can do any string manipulation just as well. However, the code needed to accomplish these same maneuvers is much more complex and time-consuming to write in C.

One last note about C for those of you who may be asking if it is related to C++: The short answer is yes. C++ is a superset of the C language in a basic sense. The long answer is no, not really, as C++ is an object-oriented language, and much more complex. The learning curve on any object-oriented language is extremely steep, and where C is difficult to debug, C++ can be a nightmare. Still, if you have a good C++ hacker around, keep in mind that anything you can accomplish in C, you can accomplish in C++.

Higher, Stronger, Faster: Advanced Web Tools

Beyond the tried-and-true languages noted previously, several new ones have entered into the fray and hold much promise for the future. Java, developed by Sun Microsystems, is an object-oriented language that is beginning to push levels of interactivity to even greater heights. JavaScript, created by Netscape, is an object-oriented-lite language that can be extremely helpful in dealing with user interfaces and, more recently, is being positioned as an easy development language for database connectivity. Finally, Microsoft has most recently released ActiveX, a refined version of its existing *OLE* controls.

Definition   OLE (Object Linking and Embedding) *is a means for exchanging data such as charts, spreadsheets, and documents between Microsoft applications.*

Java is the language that is garnering the lion's share of hype in Web development. Java was originally created to be small, portable, and secure. It was also supposed to be an easier object-oriented environment relative to C++. C++ requires its developers to assign variables to certain areas in a computer's memory, and then to explicitly release that memory down the road. Given that object-oriented code tends to be black-boxish, finding all of that stray memory can be difficult, and that is one of the reasons that C++ is such a difficult language. Java solves this problem through an automatic garbage-collection mechanism that tracks down memory that is no longer being referenced. The other extremely powerful feature of Java is that it is platform-independent. That means that Java applications written on any platform can be run on any other. This innovation is made possible by Java's middle-of-the-road approach. Java code is compiled into a form known as byte-code. This code transfers well across the Web because compiling compresses it. It is then properly interpreted for the platform on which the browser sits.

This is one of Java's shortcomings, though. Java is slow for the exact same reason that PERL is slow: because the byte-code needs to be interpreted. And whereas PERL is interpreted on a server—usually a more powerful computer than your desktop model—Java is interpreted on the client. And when you take into account that most browsers are already memory hogs, waiting for a Java application to initialize can take an excruciatingly long time by Web standards. The other basic problem is that Java is a fairly young language. Although it was touted to be a secure environment, serious holes were identified within six months of its beta launch.

These shortfalls are being addressed, however. Just as PERL's interpreters get more efficient and speedy in each release of the language, so do Java's. And the security holes identified in release 1.0 of the Java Developer's Kit have been addressed in the 1.02 release made available in the late summer of 1996. Furthermore, the initial release of the Java Database Connectivity tool-set demonstrates that it is a significant addition to this already potent toolbox.

Java is almost ready for mission critical applications. In the meantime, it is a very powerful user interface tool. Its graphical and form elements are robust and allow for much more than your basic HTML form tags. Because Java is generating so much excitement, there exists a large body of free code for you to utilize. Java allows developers to build powerful multithreaded and networked applets. Be aware that multithreading is one of the most complex aspects of Java and, therefore, one of the most difficult elements to master.

How cool a tool is this: You have a networked whiteboard in one window, and a scrolling textbox chat-area in a separate window. Any number of users can log in from your Intranet and share, and you can set this application up for separate channels so that different departments or teams can access the basic application without messing up the work of another! This would allow you to take workgroups to an entirely new level. Java holds a tremendous amount of promise for the future, and any serious Intranet development will need to explore its possibilities. For a complete book about Java, see *Hooked on Java* by Arthur van Hoff, Sami Shaio, and Orca Starbuck, published by Addison-Wesley Developers Press.

JavaScript is a second-cousin once removed from Java. It is interpreted by certain browsers such as Netscape Navigator (2.0 and higher) and Microsoft Internet Explorer (3.0 and higher). Some of its syntax is drawn directly from Java, but JavaScript is an intentionally smaller language. JavaScript was developed by Netscape to allow the growing number of individuals coming into Web development from nontechnical backgrounds to move beyond HTML's inherent limitations. JavaScript allows for a greater degree of interactivity. For example, it makes it simple to provide messages to users in reaction to mouse activity. It also allows for more interesting user interfaces in the form of site navigation in small subsidiary windows, and reactions to user inputs. It is in this last area that JavaScript can be of great benefit to your Internal Web. If you are developing an Intranet system that asks users to interact with live data, you want to make certain that those user inputs make sense. This is known as data validation. For example, JavaScript can fire alert messages when users leave required fields blank, or can make sure that the answer to a yes/no question is not "14" or "Betsy Ross."

JavaScript's capabilities are also growing. Netscape is tying its SuiteSpot line of server tools to JavaScript. One such tool is LiveWire, which allows developers to connect to certain specific relational databases from Informix, Oracle, and Sybase. LiveWire also compiles the JavaScript applications so that they run on the server, rather than on the browser. While JavaScript is certainly not all things to all people, it is worth examining. Information and manuals for JavaScript exist online at Netscape's site at `http://www.netscape.com/ eng/mozilla/2.0/handbook/javascript.index.html`.

ActiveX is Microsoft's response to JavaScript. ActiveX is a beast of a different color, however, and is related to the OLE controls you may have unknowingly used if you've embedded an Excel spreadsheet in a Word document. If your organization has already invested time and money in Microsoft technologies, ActiveX will be of great use. You can, for example, display a Microsoft Word document in its native form using ActiveX. You can also create an Excel spreadsheet that contains a series of Web HTML links! ActiveX further brings a greater range of traditional Internet services (for example, FTP, Telnet, and the like) directly under browser control. This is only true, however, if you're using Windows NT or 95. ActiveX is a 32-bit application. If your organization relies on earlier versions of Windows, ActiveX in its current form will be of no help. Microsoft has also released its own scripting language called VBScript, which is to Visual Basic what JavaScript is to Java. It even has released its own version of JavaScript called Jscript. These relatively young technologies are not well established at this time, and the full breadth of their potential is only now being explored. Download more information on ActiveX and its related technologies directly from Microsoft at `http://www.microsoft.com/workshop/author/cpad`.

One cautionary note should be made about JavaScript, ActiveX, and VBScript. Despite claims to the contrary, none of these technologies is completely open. Internet Explorer, for example, chokes on certain aspects of JavaScript. And although an ActiveX plug-in has been developed for use with Navigator, it is in its infancy. While no claims are being made that these incompatibilities are intentional, they are at least suspect and irritating. These technologies are being released just as the browser war waxes from cold to hot. They represent interesting innovations, but also represent attempts to lock you into one of the two browsers. Most likely these two software giants will have to respond positively to each other's technologies. But there are no guarantees of goodwill in the software industry. Again, taking into consideration your embedded software base, make clear goals for your Intranet and select the technology most appropriate to the tasks at hand. Still other technologies on the drawing board, such as Java Beans, may become the glue that allows you to work between the two.

Data, Anyone?

We finish off this chapter back where we began, at play in the fields of the data. Web-centric applications are exactly the reason why anyone anywhere started referring to these systems as Intranets. Database tools have become commonplace in any sizable enterprise, so why not put that information online?

If your organization is using a database from Illustra, Informix, Oracle, Sybase, or any other SQL-compliant database, your data is nearly

Web-ready. Just about any *ODBC*-compliant database can be used on the Web. If you have, for example, Microsoft Access and an appropriate ODBC-compliant driver, you can have your programmers access existing data. This approach is not, however, recommended for any sizable organization since Access and other mid-level database tools do not have the speed to support more than a few hundred users over the network. Access is also limited in the size of each record and each table, whereas SQL Server, Microsoft's high-end counterpart to Access, is highly scaleable. Although some non-SQL databases have sprung up on the Web, such as FileMaker Pro, they generally are not up to handling the volume of activity that arises in most Web applications. A list of the most recommended database systems can be found in Table 8.1.

Table 8.1
Major SQL-
Compliant Databases

Vendor	Product	URL
Illustra	Web Datablade	http://www.illustra.com
Informix	Online Database	http://www.informix.com
Microsoft	SQL Server	http://www.microsoft.com
Oracle	PowerBuilder/Oracle DB	http://www.oracle.com
Sybase	Sybase Server	http://www.sybase.com

Definition   Relational Database Management Systems (RDBMS) *are databases that link internal tables via associated fields. Object-relational DBMS take this concept one step further, allowing for inherited elements and more flexible data relations.*

Definition   Structured Query Language (SQL, pronounced sequel) *is a standard data dialect used in most RDBMS and ORDBMS systems. The language basically allows developers to create/add/ modify/delete data from a certain source or sources under certain conditions in a certain order.*

Definition   *The* Open Database Connectivity (ODBC) *standard is a means for exchanging data between various database systems regardless of their internal mechanisms. For example, the Java Database Connectivity (JDBC) would-be standard has been created to allow Java applications to interact with a variety of data sources.*

Returning to our personnel update form, the example would be fairly worthless if there were no database back end. The assumption is that our UPDATE.CGI program performs some level of validation on the user inputs and then passes the information into our database, probably via a C language API.

As with any of the tools we have mentioned in this chapter, you should have a clear sense of what you want to accomplish and select the right tool for the job. The Illustra, Informix, Oracle, and Sybase databases are fast engines that offer very high counts of transactions per second (TPS) with Sybase at the low end at about 11,000 TPS and Informix at the high end at 16,000+ TPS. Microsoft SQL Server, on the other hand, will almost certainly receive some ActiveX integration.

The most powerful of these database tools are the Illustra Database and related Datablades, and the Oracle Database with PowerBuilder. These two databases are fast and powerful. Another major advantage to using either of these tools is that they are multimedia databases that can store and manipulate images, video, sounds, and the like. The other database tools can store these elements, but do not allow for querying off of the multimedia characteristics (for example, "Give me all images that contain puce"). Traditional databases hold these elements in a data type known as a Binary Large Object (BLOB), which is crude at best. Multimedia databases actually hold these elements in refined data types that are able to parse the image or video information. The other tremendous advantage to using PowerBuilder or the Illustra Web Datablade is that they tightly integrate with the Web server and bring special wrappers and pseudo-HTML tags into play that in many cases obviate the need for an API. For example, the Illustra Web Datablade has an inlined SQL tag that directly queries and updates the database, while showing the user only the appropriate outputs.

If your resources allow, the Illustra Database system is probably the best way to go. Of the tools listed, it is the only ORDBMS, the remainder being RDBMS. This is not to say that the others would be inadequate for the job. Rather, this is to say that Illustra offers the widest range of options. Illustra was acquired by Informix, and the new corporate entity is busy working on integrating the speed of the Informix engine with the advanced multimedia and ORDBMS aspects of Illustra. The new product, called the Universal Server, is due out in Spring 1997.

Database applications represent the highest level of Intranet functionality and dynamic paging. Smart systems will tie public Web sites to private Intranets. Let's say you have a distributed sales and support force. You could, with any of the databases listed, create a series of customer inquiry and feedback forms on your public site. Based upon user input, your central database is updated, and messages are directed to the appropriate individuals in your organization for action. Your employees can then log on to your Intranet to view past customer inquiries or a database of bug reports, fixes, and maintenance updates. As sales are made or problems are solved, your staff can again log on and keep the records of your customers up-to-date—all from anywhere in the world, anytime.

Summary

Dynamic paging, HTML forms, databases, scripts, scripts, and more scripts. A lot to consider, no doubt. Properly implemented, though, powerful Web-centric systems will allow for large productivity gains and will also open the door to new modes of teamwork and efficiency. One last word on basic Web development needs to be said. Well, perhaps a few words or even a sentence.

Even the simplest of applications requires some dedicated mental energy and planning time. Keep in mind that computers are only as smart as their programs; programs are only as strong as their coders; and coders without guidance and planning tend to play networked Doom in 3D. Some longtime developers will tell you that 75 percent of the development cycle should be spent in planning and organization.

Good conceptual models tend to save time and money. Pushing for deployment prior to proper testing and debugging will only lead to a full-blown cattywompus situation and a sharp rise of consumption from the analgesic and antacid food group. Proper planning, organization, and design will help ensure the success of your Intranet ventures.

9

Managing Large Collections of Documents

The best way to manage large collections of documents is with a Document Management System. This chapter describes basic concepts of document management, tries to convince you that you can't do business without it, and gives you an overview of the nitty-gritty tasks that you must do to successfully implement document management for your group or company.

What You Can Do

Why Do You Need Document Management?

Finally, you've gotten to the heart of this book—document management information a.k.a. document management content! You can put into place the most elegant, flashy Intranet possible, but if there's no meat, what's the purpose? Let's not lose sight of why we're doing all this in the first place. Sure, who doesn't like being the first on the block to know how to write HTML, create Java and CGI scripts, and it certainly doesn't hurt the résumé either. But let's get down to brass tacks; we're doing this to communicate information that is vital to the life of a company. Maybe this isn't the heart of the book, but, more accurately, it's the blood. Everything else, the e-mail, workflow, online meetings, the browser, and so forth, are the arteries and veins. Put all that in place, and you still have to transport good, healthy red blood—useful, accurate, current information—where and when it's needed.

167

Document management is how we can ensure that the blood, information/content, of a company is healthy because it's managed properly. Document management tools can assure us that we're working with healthy information and that it moves to where it's needed.

Information Byway to Highway History

Feel free to skip to "What is a Document Management System (DMS)?" if you don't want the history. But be forewarned that those who don't learn from history are doomed to repeat it.

Way back when, scribes were needed to write down information. Before information was scribed onto papyrus, a decision had to be made whether or not it was worth it. The entire process of recording information was acutely limited. It was laborious to share ideas, and only the privileged had access to written documents. There was great value placed on the written word. Throughout the ages, people worked to preserve written works and kept close track of what existed. Libraries and systematic filing and classification systems developed.

Many have said that the Internet is the epitome of intellectual freedom, and a strenuous battle wages to protect it from being censored. This freedom has furthered the movement of open and easy access to information. It has also accelerated the pace of change and placed us at the opposite end of the scribe/papyrus spectrum (see Figure 9.1). It is both easy to commit information to paper and/or electronic form and to access the information. The problem now is where is it? Available by search: Sure, "Here are the first 10 of 17,340 documents that match your search."

We have been accused of being a "throw-away" society. But not exactly. We are also very reluctant to dispose of unneeded items. Has anyone run out of hard disk space lately? How many ministorage depositories did you pass on your way to work today? This carries over to how we create and retain our work.

In the business world it is almost too easy to dash off a memo (e-mail of course) to a colleague. Now the question is does that memo have future value, and how can you tell if it has future value? When confronted with the thousands of written works created by a medium-to-large business in the course of one day, too often we lose track of

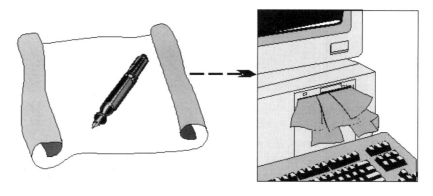

Figure 9.1

Progress: from highly prized documents to a plethora of electronic trash

critical information with future value. Lost because you can't find it but it's still around "somewhere." Or permanently lost/deleted in the fury of cleaning a full e-mail box, or lost when the only person who knew where it was leaves the company. Does the future usefulness of someone's work have to depend on the successor? No one ever fills someone else's shoes exactly. I know I have specialized in certain areas that my predecessor ignored and work in my specialized area was lost. And what about my successor, my successor's successor, and on down the line? Consider three case history examples.

Case History Number 1

One large consulting company admitted that they could locate only 20 percent of their electronic files for their company products. (We're not even talking about memos here.) This company produces millions of pages of information. Information is, in effect, one of their products. But they didn't treat it that way. Imagine having employees and management throw away 80 percent of their own product on a regular basis.

Case History Number 2

Another sorry sight was the large moving box filled with diskettes that someone pulled out and showed me. Somewhere, she explained, in a spreadsheet file on one of the disks was critical information from an expensive survey done about a year ago. The information was still useful, but there had been some turnover in the group, and now they couldn't find it. The numerous disks contained files with cryptic eight-character names. The only worse scenario would have been having the spreadsheet on paper only in invisible ink. They would have to redo the work.

Case History Number 3

In another company much time and effort was put into developing best practices for software development. Hundreds of templates from project management to user acceptance testing were developed and made available through the Internal Web. Software development teams faithfully used these templates and followed all the best practices. What was missing though was a best practice for where to put all the work-papers for sharing and future reference. Each team lost the opportunity to reuse and build on other teams' work.

Theses situations are neither unique nor new. What is new is that with the advent of online documentation, this pattern can be easily exacerbated or improved. Woe to the company that carries over its bad paper practices to online. What about freedom of speech and personal style? Does this mean I shouldn't create documents willy-nilly anymore? Not exactly, I'm asking that you better identify the valuable and useful information that you create. Take some credit for your good ideas that others can find and use. Document management isn't a new idea; this problem of creating and losing information wasn't as widespread when we had secretaries.

Secretaries preserved document management integrity. They were our helpers in creating, filing, and finding information. They set up systems for keeping track of information and conscientiously used them. Good secretaries also made judgments about what information had future usefulness. There were, and still are, classes in records management; it's a whole discipline for which degrees have been given and books have been written. When *WYSIWYG* word processors became available, everyone became a typist. Notice I said typist; I didn't say secretary.

Definition   WYSIWYG. What You See Is What You Get *is a revolutionary concept in word processing that gave content authors and subject matter experts the opportunity (or forced them) to be highly paid formatters.*

In fact, far too often no one replaces a secretary. Secretaries have become almost as obsolete as manual typewriters. Big mistake! We jumped too quickly on a new technology, ignoring the big picture.

Some companies have figured out that as they downsize and eliminate secretaries they need Document Management Systems as well as
word processing. But too often it is individual groups within a company that identify a need and solve it for themselves. The result is varying levels of document management and a heterogeneous environment
where multiple systems cannot talk to each other. Neither can they
search for documents company-wide. Individual groups doing their
own thing within a company are simply putting their finger in the dike
and holding at bay the onslaught of information.

It's hard to put something like this in place for a big company. (See
the Practical Strategy section later in this chapter.) It means gathering
information from each operational group, sharing this information between the groups, finding common ground or defining new common
ground, and filtering the new practices all the way to the top. It's true
reengineering. Just like having a secretary, for some it will seem limiting; for others it will be liberating.

What Is a Document Management System (DMS)?

Document management means different things to different people. We
tend to use the term *document management* loosely. It has been used to
describe anything from paper on a desk to files in a secured electronic
vault. For our purposes, document management is defined as a systematic method for storing, locating, and keeping track of information
that is valuable to a business. The key characteristics of a Document
Management System are the ability to manage information, to collaborate when creating information, to distribute the information, and to
allow secure access to the greatest number of people. Figure 9.2 shows
a user's desktop view of document management.

Definition   Document management *is a systematic method for storing, locating, and keeping track of information that is valuable to a
business.*

And what goes into these document management systems? Just
about anything. For ease here, I refer to *documents* as being in a Docu-

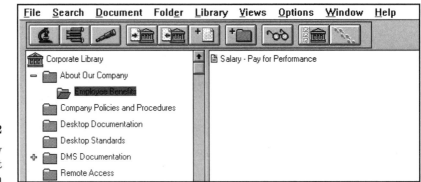

Figure 9.2

Typical user view
of a Document
Management System

ment Management System. But what is a document? A *document* can be a word processing file, a spreadsheet, a project management schedule, a graphics file, a CAD or engineering drawing, paper scanned as an image, a slideshow presentation, audio and even video, or any similar item that can be contained in an electronic file.

Definition   A document *is a word processing file, spreadsheet, project management schedule, graphics file, CAD or engineering drawing, paper scanned as an image, slideshow presentation, audio and even video, or any similar item (use your imagination) that can be contained in an electronic file.*

Some Document Management Systems allow you to manage external items that aren't electronic files. For example, you could manage and track a shared overhead projector or laptop computer, the physical copies of a book or magazine, and so forth, just by keeping meta-data on it.

I think of a Document Management System as a superefficient electronic secretary and librarian. Wouldn't we all love to have our own secretary? Remember the old movies where a secretary could make or break someone's career by her competence or incompetence? How freeing it would be to have an efficient secretary! You could concentrate on doing your job; you could build and improve on existing work; you wouldn't have to reinvent the wheel. Important papers would seldom be misplaced. Your worth would be obvious to the company. (You wouldn't be buried, literally and figuratively!) Is this a dream world? One key function a secretary provided was to figure out how to classify and file a document. In effect, he would attach to it key information that described the document. This could be information about who wrote it, was it regarding billing or sales, who is the client, and so forth. Today, this same type of information, or *meta-data*, needs to be associated with every document a company produces. Meta-data is data that describes data. One example of meta-data is the content of Summary Info or Properties dialog boxes in Microsoft Office applications. These dialog boxes, similar to the Summary Info dialog box shown in Figure 9.3, let the user add meta-data about the documents, presentations, or spreadsheets.

Definition   Meta-data *describes the data in a document, but it is not part of the text of the document. For instance, what is written on the tab of a manila file folder or on the tab of a hanging folder is meta-data. Another example of meta-data are the Summary Info or Properties dialog boxes in Microsoft Office applications.*

In some Document Management Systems, meta-data is referred to as *properties, attributes,* or *custom variables.* If the information de-

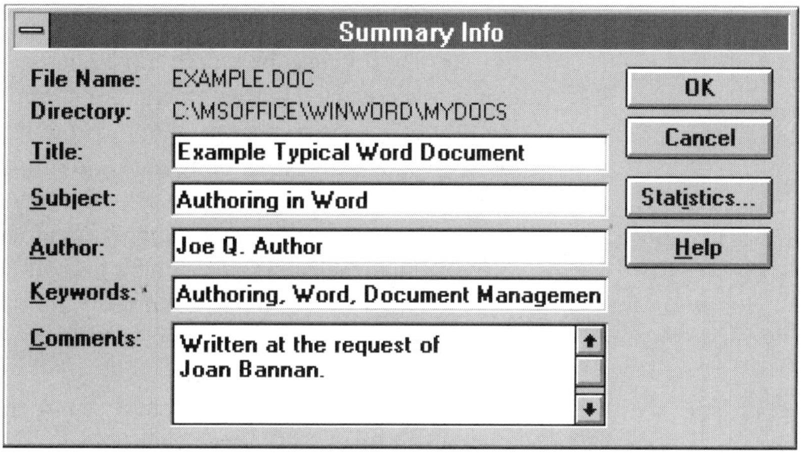

Figure 9.3

Microsoft Word
Summary Info
dialog box containing document
meta-data

scribes the document, then it is meta-data. A document management Properties dialog box is shown in Figure 9.4.

The importance of meta-data cannot be overemphasized. If meta-data is available for documents, it provides an easy way to search for

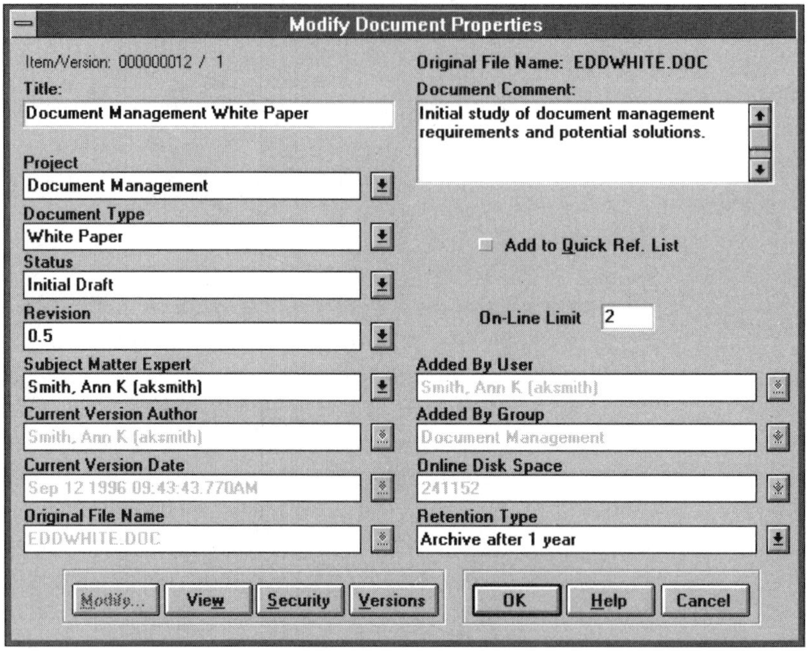

Figure 9.4

Sample meta-data in a Document Management System Properties dialog box

the document because the search can be narrowed down. Meta-data is the online way of classifying information, of putting documents into folders. But the best part is you don't have to make difficult choices: Should this go in my correspondence folder or my ABC Company folder? You can identify it both ways with meta-data because you're not limited to putting one piece of paper in one manila file folder.

Meta-data, however, has a potential problem of its own. If no corporate standards for meta-data exist, there might arise as many different approaches to classifying information as there are users. When groups share documents, basic standards will help users find information quickly. Allowing one leader to define meta-data for a group will keep things consistent.

What You Will Need

What you need in your Document Management System depends on your goals, which might include the following:

- sharing information throughout the company
- collaborating better and reusing existing work
- improving how technical writing professionals create and maintain documents

These goals aren't necessarily mutually exclusive, but may lead you to select one system over another because its strengths more closely match your goals. For example, a Document Management System that is very easy-to-use is better suited for sharing information than a sophisticated system designed for technical writers creating SGML documents.

The next section describes the basic functionality of a Document Management System. The High-Level Requirements Checklist later in this chapter gives a laundry list of all the different types of functionality to consider for a Document Management System.

What Types of Systems Are Out There?

If we take the basic functions of a Document Management System, we can compare various systems that provide these functions. You may be surprised to find that you probably already have and use some form of document management.

Basic Functions

From our definition we learned that we want to put in, take out, and keep versions; view status; keep secure, ensure accuracy, obtain approval; work together when scattered throughout an office or anywhere in the world; and distribute the information by sending it out or by letting people come in and get it. Those are the basic functions of a Document Management System.

Comparison Table

Table 9.1 classifies Document Management Systems into general categories. Names of actual products are listed at the end of the chapter to help you start your research for the products that will best suit the needs of your Intranet. Please be aware that these products are continually evolving with new features as existing applications come out with new versions and new products are frequently added to the software market.

Connecting with the Rest of the Intranet

Server-Side Document Management

So far this chapter has discussed Document Management Systems separate from the Intranet. Technically, because the system is tied in with the network, it is already part of the Intranet. But how does all this work with the Internal Web and the documents kept on Web servers? The answer is not simple. Please consider the following: As most Web site managers know, unless you are a UNIX super-user and use a sophisticated staging area to create your Web site, you probably created your documents locally, then copied local files using FTP to the Web server. As Table 9.1 shows, there is very little document management function in this scenario.

Newer Web server products such as Microsoft Front Page, Netscape LiveWire, and so forth, provide some limited document management functions. Web site management products have incorporated these document management functions because of the difficulties of trying to keep track of individual files and links to files that comprise even a small Web site. If you have a Document Management System used throughout the company, there will still be manual processes such as copying or FTP'ing documents from the Document Management System to the Web server. What merits close attention is any new market offerings that start to bring these together.

Web Access to Document Management Systems

An exciting new development is the ability to access the Document Management System through the Web. There are similar efforts that provide Web access to databases. In effect, the Web access becomes just

Basic Function	Local File Manager or Explorer	Shared Network Drive	E-Mail and Public Folders	Document Management System
Manage in/out and versions	Manually	Manually	Manually	Yes
Share files	Manually	Yes	Yes, but multiple copies are often created	Yes
Find it/search	Limited	Limited	Depends on the application	Yes
Add descriptive meta-data	Depends on application	Depends on application	Some built-in	Yes
English-like names	Yes, if Macintosh or Explorer or NT are used	Yes, if Macintosh or Explorer or NT are used	Yes, but depends on the application	Yes
Keep secure and limit access	Depends on individual security, password protection, and so forth	Limited, can password protect a file but can't prevent deletion or overwriting	Yes, but depends on the application	Yes
Distribute with work-flow	Manually	Manually	Yes, may be an add-on	Yes, may be an add-on
Collaborate and manage easily	Manually	Manually	Limited and depends on the application	Yes

Table 9.1

Comparing Document Management Systems and Functions

another client front-end into the document management system. Only a Web browser is needed to view the documents. This opens up a platform-independent interface for users to access documents and resources in the Intranet through one source, the user's browser, as shown in Figure 9.5. Document management features such as security and immediate access when checked in are available.

Suddenly, the author doesn't have to go through a Webmaster to make the document available, thus getting it out there faster. But, you ask, "What about converting it to HTML?" Conversion steps often

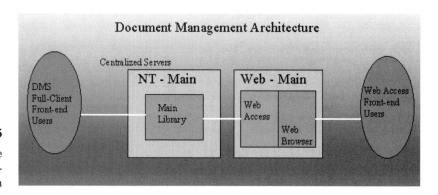

Figure 9.5

Web access to the Document Management System

prove to be a bottleneck in getting information out fast. Converting documents without a Document Management System actually increases the need for document management. Now there are multiple sources that need to be tracked. Assuming that the Webmaster provides HTML conversion services for documents created in the word processing application, there are three choices:

1. Configure your Document Management System to convert to HTML when the document is checked in. This requires that the author use styles that a conversion program can grab and assign HTML codes to.

2. Add a document viewer to your Web browser as a plug-in, thus negating the need for conversion to HTML. (See the list of plug-in viewer products at the end of this chapter.)

3. Have users configure their browsers with helper applications to launch documents in their native format. This requires that the user have the native application on their workstation or configured to execute the application from a shared location on a server.

These three options let you choose, depending on the document, whether it is best presented in HTML or in its native document format.

You can take this a step further and tie the meta-data in the Document Management System to Web crawlers and indexing. This is a true example of synergism—where the sum of the parts is greater than the individual benefits.

How to Manage Large Collections of Documents

Implement a Document Management System

The basic expectation for a Document Management System is that it will be a production-level system with trained client and server staff. There will be training, regular hardware and software upgrades, disaster planning, and service agreements mutually agreed upon by the client groups and the document management staff.

Get the Requirements

The most important step of implementing a Document Management System is to understand the company's or group's current work processes and needs. The usefulness and usability of the Document Management System is a direct result of the time spent gathering requirements and configuring the system to fit their work processes and needs. I would argue that if a company installs any one of the major Document Management Systems on the market today and no one willingly uses it, the fault lies with the configuration and implementation. Someone didn't do his or her homework before implementation. We're not talking about something as simple as installing a new word processing program or network connectivity. We are talking about changing the fundamental way each person works. You need to assess needs as well as obtain agreement and buy-in. The Checklists section later in this chapter includes a list of detailed requirements that can be used as a list of topics to understand the company's or group's current work processes. You would be wise to enlist the experience of vendor companies and third-party consultants to set up your initial pilot. I suggest that you design it, then try it out, get feedback, and redesign it before you begin widespread deployment.

Practical Strategy

One successful approach is the "build it and they will come" approach. Build a solid, scalable infrastructure and start small, maybe with a few departments. (All the while keep in mind the eventual widespread deployment plan.) This is sometimes the only way to implement a new system for a large company. Otherwise you get mired in bureaucracy. As for timing, you want to be somewhere between the extremes of "wait until document management is being cried for" and "shove it down their throats even if they don't want it."

Staffing

Implementing document management is similar to implementing e-mail in terms of the demands it will put on the support staff. Here are the functional areas that you'll need:

- The *product manager* manages and negotiates the contract, keeps abreast of market developments, and makes decisions about upgrades in product and changes in vendors.

- An *implementation analyst* gathers requirements and works to solve client groups' business needs, provides configuration information to the client-side and server-side specialists, and manages company-wide naming conventions.

- The *client group librarian* manages the logical organization of the library, maintains user IDs and passwords, communicates system information to users such as planned downtimes, upgrades, and so forth, and brings any new configuration requirements to the Implementation Analyst.

- A *client-side specialist* knows the client side of the application inside out, trains the training staff and/or provides training, installs client software in special cases, tests new client-side software, assists with bulk-loading of documents, and troubleshoots problems that can't be resolved by the Help Desk.

- A *server-side specialist* knows the server side of the application inside out, works with the implementation analyst and client-side specialist to configure the system for the client groups, assists with bulk-loading of documents, troubleshoots problems that can't be resolved by a client-side specialist, tests new server software on a test server, plans for and orchestrates capacity/volume testing to ensure work group and company-wide deployment feasibility, and selects, designs, documents, and tests logical system architecture for multiple servers.

- The *server administrator* maintains the hardware, operating system software, document management system software, installs and tests upgrades on a test server, performs backups, automates processes where possible, ensures that the system is available during all agreed-upon operating hours, integrates (where feasible) with any available company-support systems such as optical storage, juke boxes, and so forth, and selects, designs, and tests system architecture for physical archiving, and develops procedures for normal operations, failure, and disaster.

- Help *desk personnel* are fully trained and able to answer general user questions. They should use the system themselves for day-to-day work, and refer questions as needed to a client-side specialist.

- The *training staff* provide regular, ongoing training classes integrated with other company training classes, and create, maintain, and distribute quick reference cards.

Hardware and Network

You will need enough servers for the users and documents, as determined by the requirements analysis. In addition, you should have a development/test server that mirrors the production servers in use. Basic, typical network connections, such as TCP/IP are also necessary for all the servers and user workstations.

Sticky Issues in Document Management

There are a few issues that may arise. The answers to these questions depend on the complexity of your individual documents management situation and the document system you implement. You may need to consult with your document management vendor to find specific answers. I've listed some issues here:

- Compound documents are the electronic equivalent of binding together and photocopying and distributing. This is more difficult than it appears, so research carefully and have a plan.

- Know how to control and manage through the document's life cycle: draft release, revision, approval, rerelease, preview, staging, work-in-progress, production, and released document.

- Depending on how the document management system is integrated into other applications such as Word, the Help Desk may have difficulty troubleshooting and isolating some problems.

- Have a plan for pushing notification when new information has been released; don't depend on users reading a What's New.

- Know how to detect and clean up electronic littering. The documents are stored on the server and the users aren't running out of hard disk space, so they may not bother deleting obsolete documents.

Sample Project Plan

Implementing a Document Management System is similar to implementing a software development project. Too often, the standard development lifecycle (SDLC) or information systems best practices are skipped and deemed unnecessary because "we're just installing an off-the-shelf product." Because most of these systems are highly configurable, it is necessary to treat them in a systematic manner by obtaining requirements, trying them on a pilot group, testing, reconfiguring, and so forth. Next we look at the steps that a good project plan should include.

Prepare for Pilot Test

The following tasks (not necessarily in this order) should be completed before implementing a pilot test:

- Identify a project manager.
- Document the business needs to be met by the Document Management System.
- Identify users and documents.
- Gather the user requirements. (See the detailed checklists at the end of this chapter.)
- Resolve/plan the front end:

- which front end (if there are multiple choices)
- required or optional use of system
- Scope out any add-ons (for example, imaging software).
- Obtain commitments for
  - administrator/resource commitment
  - pilot group commitment
  - server in lab
  - user training
  - help desk support
  - vendor support
- Train staff.
- Ensure that the pilot group has met basic workstation requirements (for example, TCP/IP, network connectivity, and so forth).
- Identify technical tests (for example, network, memory issues, conflicts with other software, and so forth) and people to conduct technical tests.
- Identify user tests and people to conduct user tests.

Install

The installation should be completed in this order:

1. Install server(s).
2. Install users.
3. Load identified documents onto system.
4. Train users.
5. Conduct tests.

Conduct Pilot Test

You've laid the groundwork and are ready to conduct the pilot test. Here are the main points:

- Conduct identified technical tests.
- Conduct identified user tests.
- Use in daily work.

Evaluate Pilot Test

Now you must evaluate your system, based on feedback from the pilot group:

- Determine which requirements were met.
- Document results of tests.
- Decide to proceed or evaluate a different system.

Roll Out System

You're ready to roll:

- Incorporate pilot learnings into project rollout.
- Repeat the appropriate pilot steps but for rollout.

Checklists

List of Benefits

One of the benefits of using an electronic Document Management System is less time spent handling individual paper documents. The associated cost savings result from

- labor savings due to a reduced need for filing paper updates and changes to documentation
- reduced paper distribution and considerable related costs (reproduction, printing, manual distribution, and envelopes)

Another benefit is improved information availability:

- current and timely information (no lost opportunity cost)
- telecommuting and its associated benefits
- less retrieval time
- reuse of previous work instead of re-creating it
- reduced real estate for physical document storage
- better authoring and editing
- elimination of redundant, proprietary systems for accessing vendor documentation

High-Level Requirements Checklist

The checklist in the next section has even more nitty-gritty details of what to look for in a Document Management System. You can treat the following as a shopping list by filling in specific details for your own site:

- Be compatible with company and industry computer standards and scaleable over the entire company and its range of applications.

- Store document files in native formats (Word, Excel, PowerPoint, and so forth).
- Search, based on content or meta-data of the documents.
- Check out documents and start applications. Support integration with front-end applications. For example, opening a file through Word forces access through the Document Management System.
- View meta-data information.
- Check in documents.
- Provide revision control, legal and regulatory archiving, and automatic deletion as configured by clients.
- Send documents to archive. Support full range of electronic storage media (magnetic disk, read/write optical disk, WORM, CD-ROM, and tape).
- Be usable by all networked workgroup employees and be corporate licensed.
- Provide an optional multilevel hierarchical object management model (for example, library, room, cabinet, drawer, folder, document, and object).
- Provide security protection at many levels.
- Support connection to other applications, specifically index databases and document meta-data through application programming interfaces (APIs).
- Facilitate disaster recovery planning and data redundancy.

The Document Management System may include these interrelated systems, based on client requirements:

- view and annotation application
- workflow management system
- image management software
- forms processing
- scanning paper-only documents

The most effective Document Management Systems are thoroughly integrated with project management (create projects, members, tasks, and schedules) and workflow (view status, define routing, and approval processes).

Detailed Requirements Checklist

Again, all of these may or may not apply, but you can treat this as a shopping list by filling in specific details for your own site.

1. **Functionality of the Document Management System**

   1.1   Check-in/check-out capability:
   - identifies which users have checked in/out documents
   - works with off-line use

   1.2   Ownership and status information:
   - identifies who has write access to documents
   - identifies author of documents
   - displays date, time, file size, and current status of document

   1.3   Version control:
   - maintains multiple versions of document
   - convenient archiving and retrieval of multiple versions
   - audit trail of changes (marked up old copy with new changes)

   1.4   Archiving.

   1.5   Search for documents based on document attributes.

   1.6   Logically connects documents through life cycle (for example, Word drafts, Word final, HTML markup, and so forth).

   1.7   Documents workflow control and task routing, for instance; "if not reviewed by designated date, return to author for follow-up"

   1.8   Provides report routing and distribution.

   1.9   Handles all phases of the document life cycle (from creation to archiving).

   1.10   Review and annotation capabilities.

   1.11   Document library functions such as storing, defining, searching, retrieving, version control, and access control.

   1.12   Compound document management, which allows documents from various applications to be managed under one document profile (for example, related graphics files).

1.13 Interdocument dependencies (within each authoring environment) and notification to affected authors.

1.14 Intradocument dependencies.

1.15 Tracks the time spent on a document.

1.16 Aids in tracking the parts of a compound document; gives suggestions for which files need to be checked in or out.

1.17 Internal to a workgroup:

- allow free-form naming
- enforce workgroup naming conventions

1.18 Tie external name (based on corporate naming conventions) to internal workgroup names.

1.19 Can include all desired and required meta-data.

1.20 Can include cross-references.

1.21 Author approval (electronic signature verification).

1.22 Can store all types of documents: structured and non-structured data, word processing files, spreadsheets, graphics files, CAD or engineering drawings, paper scanned as an image, audio, video, and meta-data about external items.

1.23 Store an image and bring it back and use it in a native application; for example, identify the compression method used and know whether it's a proprietary graphic format.

1.24 Built-in security.

1.25 Import from desktop fax system.

1.26 Familiar interface with standard platform's look and feel, conventions, and styles.

1.27 Network efficiency, especially with graphics and images.

1.28 Has the flexibility to require or not to require its use.

1.29 Automatic, project-based, scheduled check-in.

1.30 Single file and batch methods of checking in and checking out documents.

1.31 Full-featured search ability (wildcard matching, Boolean, and so forth) on internal content and on meta-data.

1.32 Project milestones and project archiving.

1.33 Understandable labels for versions, such as "First Draft ABC Requirements."

1.34 Fully customizable version history and project reporting.

1.35 Wizardlike client installation and removal.

1.36 Remotely accessible.

1.37 Includes ability to add on scanning and image management.

1.38 Flexible and easy to integrate when groups with separate systems are organizationally merged together.

1.39 Gives warnings before deleting or overriding.

1.40 Documents can be viewed without launching application.

1.41 Most of processing is performed at server level.

1.42 Ease of exporting out of the Document Management System, especially compound documents with multiple files.

2. **Computer Environment**

The document management system should integrate with all parts of the standard platform, specifically

- standard desktop tools
- LAN services
- remote access
- Intranet (Web browser, e-mail, client/server systems, and so forth)

3. **Performance Requirements**

Here are the performance requirements:

3.1 Behaves responsibly as a typical personal computer application within the standard platform's environment.

3.2 Configured system supports a determined number of concurrent users performing varied operations.

3.3 Local client functions execute in less than three seconds whenever possible, but never take longer than ten seconds.

3.4 On a properly configured system and network, functions that require access to the server via network-based communication execute in less than five seconds wherever possible, but never take longer than twenty seconds.

4. Data Storage Requirement

There are two main considerations for storage capability:

- hardware, media, and limitations
- dynamic reconfiguration of storage real-time

5. Attributes

The system should have the following attributes:

5.1 System security and control:

- Adheres to the minimal security requirements specified in the corporate system security standards (for example, user passwords can be changed by users and must be changed every 30 days).
- Capable of multilevel security based on type of user (for example, manager, staff associate, database administrator, system administrator, author, and so forth) and type of access (read-only, read/write).
- Capable of security at both the application and data levels.
- Can limit security to only those authorized to use it and protect from unauthorized access.

5.2 Data integrity:

- Storage of information in the library does not cause any loss of data.
- Each user can have a concurrent, consistent view of the library at all times (that is, no out-of-sync documents or mismatched versions will be supported within the document repository).

5.3 Maintainability:

- Administrative and management tools are available to quickly and easily provide mechanisms for the ongoing maintenance and administration of the application.
- Tools are available to operate in a standard platform environment.

5.4 Transferability: operating environment supports portability from one environment to another.

5.5 Interoperability: does not limit ability to use other products.

5.6. Extensibility:

- Architecture permits addition of new document storage formats.
- New types of data elements and new interfaces are also supported.

5.7 Reliability: system reliability conforms to the corporation's standards relative to quality required for product release and production deployment.

5.8 Availability.

6. External Interface Requirements

6.1 User interface:

- Similar to other products that operate on the same platform.
- Different client front ends can be added for different client use. For example, an engineering/CAD front end can be added for an engineering group, a legal front end can be added for a legal group, and an SGML front end can be added for SGML authors.
- Help must be available at the menu bar level for all major functions and activities.
- Informational, warning, and error messages must be readily available and easy to understand to give users immediate feedback and suggest corrective actions where appropriate.

6.2 Documentation:

- in-depth user manuals on operating the application
- reference manuals (where appropriate) on using callable routines and utilities
- system administrators manual

6.3 Hardware environment can work with multiple servers.

6.4 Software interfaces:

- Meta-data information (author, abstract, catalog, and so forth) can be indexed by or sent to other systems.
- Is designed to fit with database-like repositories for common, reused parts of documents (for example, sections and paragraphs).

6.5 Communications interfaces.

7. System Administration

7.1 General administration tasks:

- tools to manage user access
- tools to back up, archive, and retrieve archived documents

7.2 Backup:

Provides

- a way to back up program/data files
- the ability to restore files easily and quickly
- real-time backup
- adherence to specified corporate system security standards

7.3 Recovery:

- echoing, system redundancy for duplicate documents, and profiles in case of network failure
- adheres to specified corporate system security standards
- volume load balancing for files stored on network

8. Site Adaptation Requirements

8.1   Packaging: tool and components must be distributed on a standard media based on the operating system used.

8.2   Software installation:

- The system uses ses a standard set of installation scripts for the software installation process.
- All prerequisite software and hardware are clearly explained in the installation documentation.
- The installation procedure for the software checks that all components of the system are present and at the appropriate revision levels, before installation can proceed.
- Default values for any parameters that could be set during the installation are provided, where appropriate.
- A procedure to test the success of the installation is provided. This procedure should act as an installation validation program and must be callable at any time.
- During installation, the user must be notified at meaningful intervals as to exactly what activity is currently being performed.
- Instructions or scripts should also be available for removing the software.

9. Support Services

9.1   Vendor provides technical support.

9.2   Complete training curriculum for the management, administration, and operation is available from the vendor.

Requirements/Implementation Checklist

All of these requirements may not apply to your system. You can treat this as a shopping list by filling in specific details for your own site.

1. Obtain user information.

2. Identify participants:

- How many will use the Document Management System?
- Who will use the Document Management System?

3. Customize or standardize the look and feel of the Document Management System.

Implement a standard desktop configuration—with the same menu bar, toolbar, and other items—for each group so the look and feel of the desktop is familiar and usable regardless of the user's location, group, or workstation. Ensure that required meta-data must be entered and can't be left blank. Meta-data could possibly be automatically linked and retrieved from summary information from the application, for example, the Summary Info or Properties dialog box in Microsoft Word.

For groups with a specific need, different client front ends can be set up. For example, an engineering/CAD front end could be set up for an engineering group or a legal front end could be set up for a legal group.

To increase usability:

  a. Customize the desktop for each group, and, if helpful, mirror the hierarchical structure of the Document Management System (that is, File Manager) that is being replaced or, it could also be organized logically.

  b. Give all items—libraries, folders, documents—on the desktop familiar and meaningful names so users can easily and efficiently locate their documents.

  c. Limit the number of libraries on the desktop to two or three. If a library is being shared by more than one group, give it a generic name such as "San Francisco Library 1." If a library is used for only one group, give it the name of the group, for example, "Corporate Accounting."

  d. Limit the number of top-level (parent) folders and sublevel (child) folders on the desktop.

  e. Load the desktop with work-relevant materials prior to installation on client workstations.

4. Set up defaults:

  • the access rights of users and groups
  • the defaults used when documents are added to the system

5. Determine custom document attributes and properties (that is, meta-data):

- Don't create too many.
- Make meta-data required so it can be used in searches.
- Make process as universal as possible throughout the company.

6. Obtain storage and retention requirements.

Assess the number, size, and type of files to be loaded and managed:

- total number of files
- predicted number over the next three years
- predicted versions per file
- average size of files (in bytes)
- average life of files
- storage requirements
- reporting requirements (legal and regulatory)
- number of external items to be referenced (items not contained in electronic files)
- performance expectations (time to retrieve documents)
- active use of information (when to move off-line)

Review governmental, regulatory, and retention policies pertaining to the documents:

- retention criteria by document type
- online storage categories
- off-line archive categories
- destruction procedures for versions and final documents

Consult departmental representatives regarding their current mode of storage and retention.

Develop specific departmental retention criteria for different documents.

Determine storage space requirements for the future Document Management System environment.

Create storage and archive categories that meet the users' and administrators' needs.

Identify retention assumptions, for example:

- Document owners will identify permanent versions.
- Document owners are responsible for unmarking or archiving permanent versions in the event more current documents are written to replace them.
- When the online document limit for the group is reached, prior versions of documents are automatically moved off-line and deleted unless users can provide a valid business reason for keeping these previous versions.
- Prior versions that are no longer needed or used, and that are not automatically moved off-line by the Document Management System, are manually moved off-line by the document's owner.

Describe when a printed copy will continue to be stored and whether the document management system will reference where these documents are physically located.

7. Configure and customize the document management system including

- desktop configuration
- preference settings
- system defaults
- integration with other (current and future) applications such as view and annotation applications, workflow management applications, Web browsers, image management applications, forms processing, scanning or handling of documents, and any others, as needed

8. Load legacy documents.

Gather the users' and groups' requirements in the following areas:

- amount to be preloaded
- type(s) of documents
- convert paper:
  - Find electronic source if possible.

- Scan documents (for example, external documents, legal, signed documents, marketing literature, and so forth).
- translation from one format to another
- bulk or manual loading required
- time-sensitive loading of documents

9. Determine accessibility requirements.

    Remote access:
    - number of telecommuters and users who work in the field
    - method of remote access
    - hours of business operation

    On-site (local) access:
    - frequency of access (by document type)
    - length and time of access by document type
    - most common type of access (to create, view, print, search for documents, and so forth)
    - performance expectations to retrieve documents
    - hours of business operation

10. Come up with user training and support requirements.

    - end user training
    - end user support
    - trouble flow procedures
    - communication plan (similar to trouble flow but better!)
    - system administrator training

11. Install the client-side Document Management System.

    Incorporate the system into company-wide systems for installing software.

12. Establish education/training services.

    - Complete training curriculum can be developed for the management, administration, and operation of the system.
    - Integrate with existing corporate training where necessary.

> • Set up ongoing training available from corporate training infrastructure.

13. Other considerations

     Incorporate into company-wide systems for administering servers (for example, backup and recovery strategies, physical security, and so forth).

Industry Resources

This is not an exhaustive list, and the software companies listed are not necessarily recommended. Just as with other software applications, the industry constantly evolves with new products and new features for existing products. But the material here will help you start somewhere with your comparisons.

Document Management Industry Groups

- DMA `http://www.aiim.org/dma/`
- ODMA
- SGML Open

Sample Document Management Products

- Arbortext
- Guide (InfoAccess)
- IBM product
- Interleaf
- Livelink Library
- Panorama
- PCDocs
- Saros (Saros Document Manager, Saros Mezzanine, and Saros @mezzanine)

Legacy Document Loading into DMS

- vendor companies
- third-party integrators

Legacy Document Conversion: One Format to Another

- Data Conversion Labs (DCL) `http://www.dclab.com`
- Systems Documentation, Inc. (SDI)
- Passage Systems (www.passage.com)
- search the Internet for data conversion services, especially in terms of SGML

Plug-in Viewers to Web Browsers

- Adobe File Utilities (Adobe)
- KEYview (FTP Software)
- Quick View Plus (INSO)
- Watermark Universal Viewer (FileNet)

Summary

Though there are multiple ways to set up document management on your Intranet, if it doesn't include a systematic method for storing, locating, and keeping track of information as a group effort, individual knowledge can be lost when individuals move. The key then is to implement a system that allows users to collaborate when creating information, to distribute the information, and to allow secure access to the greatest number of people.

10 Managing Large Documents

What You Can Do

Large documents present unique challenges with respect to their creation, management, and delivery. Standard Generalized Markup Language (SGML) is an excellent document management tool. In an SGML content management environment you can

- create enterprise-wide document format standards
- produce documents for multiple applications
- preserve information that has long-term value
- mandate conformance with an international, non proprietary standard
- automate document production
- create rigorously structured documents
- hyperlink information
- collaborate on document authoring
- manage information with a database-style approach.

What You Will Need

SGML is the Intranet designer's ultimate power tool. It takes some effort to master, but that effort is repaid by capability and potential cost savings that no other technology offers. Once you have a good understanding of SGML, you'll need:

199

- one or more document type definitions (DTD)
- an SGML authoring tool
- an SGML browser, or
- output from an SGML source tool or program

The well-stocked SGML shop would probably also have

- a DTD design tool
- SGML programming language
- an SGML-savvy programmer
- an SGML-capable search engine

Other possible goodies include

- an SGML-aware document management or database system
- SGML parser source code
- the HyTime SGML hypermedia processor
- an SGML consultant

How to Manage Large Documents

SGML

Every word processing application on the market has its own proprietary format for storing documents. You can't read a proprietary format created in one application with a different application, and it's quite impossible to read, for example, a Microsoft Word document in a text editor such as Notepad. It may be possible to tell your software to translate a foreign format, but usually something is "lost" in the translation. Yet most word processing applications do similar kinds of things, so do they all have to have different formats?

The surprising answer is no. It is entirely possible for all the vendors to agree on a common interchange format. But if they did, they wouldn't have you locked in to their software.

The information in your documents is as valuable as the data in your database, and like your database, you should not be restricted to having access to that information subject to software limitations. This was among the concerns that lead to the creation of SGML and its early adoption by organizations with huge quantities of information to manage such as the defense departments of the United States and other NATO countries. While it is true that five years ago SGML was an expensive and esoteric technology adopted primarily by big-budget organizations, the present availability of low-cost tools and a critical mass of users has brought it into the mainstream. The growth in the use of SGML has been greatly accelerated by the World Wide Web and Intranets, an environment where its advantages are keenly felt.

Features of SGML

The primary objective of this chapter is to help you determine whether an SGML solution might be appropriate for you, and to guide you in formulating your battle plan for implementing SGML on your Intranet. But before we can do that you'll need some SGML fundamentals. Bear with me, I'll make this as painless as possible!

SGML, ISO 8879 (International Standards Organization), is a language for describing languages that encode documents. This language can be read and understood by human beings, but it is also a formally specified language that can be processed by computer programs. While any number of languages can be designed with SGML, they all must obey the syntax rules of SGML. The common *syntax* of SGML languages enables well-designed *SGML applications* to read and process any SGML language.

An SGML language is defined in a *DTD* (Document Type Definition). The *SGML declaration* defines processing parameters such as the document's *character set*. A document that is encoded according to the low-level information in the declaration and the language definition in the DTD is called an *instance*. The fully annotated SGML standard is 664 pages long and contains many, many other precise terms for everything in SGML, only a few more of which we'll cover in this chapter.

An SGML document consists of the SGML declaration, the DTD, and an instance. The declaration is most often implicit; that is, there is one that your SGML program will use if you don't include your own. The DTD is not always included with the instance, but it must be at least explicitly referenced. An instance without a DTD is to the SGML application what a scrap of text in an unknown language would be to us. If the instance were also without a declaration it would be as if that language were in some sort of code where we could recognize neither individual letters nor word separations. Together the declaration and DTD give SGML the unique property of being *self-describing*.

The DTD defines which *elements* which can be used in the document and the possible relationships between those elements. An element is a container for each distinct thing in the document. It is up to the person who creates the DTD to decide exactly what "things" are; for example, paragraphs and headings. There are two kinds of relationships between elements: *parent-child* and *peer-to-peer*. In a parent-child relationship the child is contained by the parent. For example, a list might contain individual bulleted items. The entire list is a container that contains items. In SGML terms the list is the parent and the items are its children. The list item elements, in turn, could also be parents, containing, say, paragraph elements. In a peer-to-peer relationship, a group of elements have the same parent. For example, a memo header element could contain the peer elements to, from, date, and subject. The set of possible relationships between elements is fully described in the DTD.

Additionally, *attributes* may be declared for elements. An attribute is information that is attached to the element but not part of its content (that is, the text of the instance). Attributes are sometimes referred to as meta-data, meaning information about the data. For example, hyperlinks may be declared by attributes.

The names of elements and attributes are created by the DTD author. In the instance, elements are put directly into the text, surrounding the text that they are supposed to contain. An element marker is called a *tag,* and it is most often distinguished from the text itself by being surrounded by angle brackets. You are already familiar with tagging if you have viewed the HTML source code of a Web document. The start tag indicates the start of an element; for example, <PARA> for the paragraph element. The end tag has a backslash; for example, </PARA> Attributes are written after the element name within the angle brackets. SGML DTDs and instances can be read and written by human beings using any text editor, but they can also be processed by computer programs.

Definition   (ISO) International Organization for Standardization *is an international organization headquartered in Geneva, Switzerland concerned with the development of standards. Participation in ISO is through national standards organizations such as ANSI (American National Standards Institute). ISO standards are adopted by a vote of member national standards bodies and are reviewed and updated through ongoing processes specified by the ISO bylaws.*

Definition	Syntax *is the rules for putting together the parts of a language. Every language has syntax, whether natural (like English or Arabic) or constructed (like SGML or C++).*
Definition	An SGML application *is a computer program that understands SGML syntax and can process SGML documents.*
Definition	A character set *is the mapping of computer codes to a set of symbols such as letters and punctuation. Japanese and English, for example, use different character sets (although an attempt is underway to establish a single character set, known as Unicode, for all languages).*
Definition	A DTD (Document Type Definition) *is a formal statement of the encoding requirements for a particular class or type of SGML document.*
Definition	*The* SGML declaration *is a formal statement of the basic parameters of an SGML document such as its character set, the character sequences used to distinguish markup from the document content, and its utilization of optional SGML features.*
Definition	An instance *is the encoded text that conforms to a particular DTD and declaration.*
Definition	A self-describing document *contains the rules necessary for the interpretation of its content. The term* intelligent documents *is synonymous.*
Definition	An element *is a named container for a logical portion of a document. Examples of logical portions of documents include chapters, sections, tables, lists, paragraphs, and citations.*
Definition	A parent-child *relationship between elements means that the element known as the child is contained by the parent.*
Definition	A peer-to-peer *relationship between elements means that the elements are contained by the same parent.*

Definition Attributes *are information that may be provided about elements in addition to the element name and its content.*

Definition Meta-data *is a general term for the attributes of elements.*

Where to Learn More about SGML

If you survived the above, congratulations! You now know enough to read the rest of this chapter, which will help you identify the situations in which SGML is beneficial. You'll need to learn more as you go along, and following are some suggestions for various types of resources.

Online. You'll find one-stop shopping at `http://gopher.sil.org/sgml/sgml.html`, Robin Cover's *The SGML Web Page*. This is arguably the most comprehensive reference source and directory dedicated to a single subject on the Web. The Text Encoding Initiative's *A Gentle Introduction to SGML* is an acclaimed concise description of SGML available from the *The SGML Web Page* or at `http://etext.virginia.edu/etext/sgml.html`.

The primary Internet newsgroup for the discussion of SGML is comp.text.sgml. Currently this happens to be a very high quality newsgroup, with lots of useful advice and serious discussion, although perhaps a little intimidating for the beginner. On the other hand, there is a strong tradition of answering good questions from beginners (a "bad" question is one that you could have answered yourself with a reasonable effort). If you pose a good question, you may find that the person who responds is one of the world's leading authorities on the subject!

Classes. Professional training is available at various locations worldwide from the Graphics Communication Association (GCA). Contact them at 100 Daingerfield Rd., Alexandria, VA 22314-2888, (703) 519-8160 for course descriptions and a schedule. Many SGML software vendors also have training programs, and some universities and university extensions have begun to offer SGML classes including, recently, the University of Wisconsin, Cal Poly, U.C. Berkeley, and U.C. Santa Cruz.

User Groups. SGML user groups are active throughout the United States and in many other countries. You can find a current list at *The SGML Web Page*. The GCA should also be able to help direct you, or please feel free to e-mail me at joan@bannan.com.

Books. You should be able to find lots of books on SGML at any bookstore or library with a good selection of computer-related material. Sometimes it is difficult to know where to look: SGML is sometimes classed with computer languages, sometimes with the Web, and sometimes with desktop publishing. The actual SGML standard has been published with in-depth annotations by its inventor, Dr. Charles Goldfarb, as *The SGML Handbook.* (Oxford University Press, Inc.) You'll be universally recognized as an SGML super-geek when you can quote chapter and verse from this, the SGML bible. An easy introductory book for beginners is *README 1st: SGML for Writers and Editors* by Turner, Douglass, and Turner (Prentice Hall). *The SGML Implementation Guide* by Travis and Waldt (New York: Springer-Verlag, Inc.) and *ABCD . . . SGML* by Liora Alschuler (International Computer Press) are also appropriate for beginners. Both books focus on the overall system design perspective. An excellent intermediate level text, *Developing SGML DTDs: From Text to Model to Markup* by Eve Maler and Jeanne El Andaloussi (Prentice Hall), provides an exhaustive treatment of the subject of DTD design. A text dedicated to an in-depth exploration of SGML and Intranets entitled *Intranet Design with SGML* by Fuchs, Leventhal, and Lewis will be published by Prentice Hall in the fall of 1997.

Using SGML for Large Documents

SGML allows documents to be defined *hierarchically.* For an example of document hierarchy, consider that a Set contains Books; Books contain Front Matter, Body, and Back Matter; Body contains Chapters; Chapters contain Sections; Sections contain Subsections; and so forth. Contrast this to word processing documents and PDF, which do not permit any definition of document structure. It is possible to create a document delivery system that uses these hierarchical subdivisions as *retrieval* units. Either the user may select the information unit that makes the most sense, or the system may be set up to select a default retrieval unit that optimizes network traffic. For example, suppose that our online documents consist of repair manuals for automobiles (this is a popular example both because it is familiar to most people and because it is, in fact, a major real-world use of SGML). Such manuals usually are divided into chapters for each subsystem. Most of the time, however, the person doing the repairs only needs information on a specific component, for example, how to replace the fuel filter in the fuel system. So in this case it would be most efficient to design the system to retrieve small sections of component information by default.

Definition   *An SGML document contains a set of relationships between elements arranged in a* hierarchy. *SGML elements may be deeply nested; that is, children may be parents themselves ad infinitum (subject to user-specified limits).*

Definition   Retrieval *is fetching a document or portion of a document from the place where it is stored, for delivery to an application.*

On-demand *hierarchical retrieval* may use a table of contents interface to allow you to select the desired information unit, or it may isolate the desired information through a hierarchy-sensitive full-text search, or, often, it may do both. Shrink-wrapped Intranet software that enables hierarchical-based retrieval of SGML data includes products such as Open Text's LiveLink, Electronic Book Technologies' DynaWeb, and Information Atrium's LivePage. Some products offer the option of either translating SGML documents to HTML on the fly for delivery to any HTML browser or delivering SGML directly to a client equipped with SGML viewing software.

Definition   Hierarchial retrieval *is the retrieval of an element and its children from an SGML document. SGML retrieval systems are typically able to deliver elements from any level of an element hierarchy.*

Using SGML to Create Enterprise-wide Document Format Standards

HTML is the de facto standard for the delivery of information on the Internal Web portion of Intranets. Companies quickly find out that they need to promulgate some standards to ensure that all pages can be properly viewed by all users, that all related software will work properly (for example, searching, cataloging, and document management), and that there is some consistency among pages. Furthermore, these qualities must be preserved over time even with constant change in the technology. After all, an Intranet is a tool for streamlining business, not a playground for HTML hackers!

Many people know vaguely that HTML and SGML have something to do with each other. SGML is a language for defining other languages, and it is used, in fact, to define HTML. We learned in the previous section that SGML allows for the hierarchical definition of document structure and that HTML doesn't have that. The key word here is *allows;* SGML is a powerful, flexible tool that can be used for many different ends. The original HTML developers did not choose to use much of SGML's power to express hierarchy, but HTML still benefits from SGML's ability to unambiguously state what the rules are and to validate any document's adherence to those rules.

SGML provides clear standards for clean, supportable HTML. There are HTML DTDs that have been approved by *W3C,* the *World Wide Web Consortium,* and SGML conformity is the official policy of the W3C and of at least one major Intranet software vendor, Microsoft.

Definition The World Wide Web Consortium (W3C) *is an industry consortium, hosted by MIT, that has taken over most of the development and promotion of standards for the World Wide Web.*

HTML conformance to SGML is one side of the story. The other is that many organizations find that it is worthwhile to use an SGML application (other than HTML) to store their Intranet documents. Let me illustrate this with a real-world example. A company produced a large volume of documentation for an Intranet where the browsing technology was incapable of displaying tables. Although there was in fact a very large amount of tabular information, all tables were converted to a primitive tabbed representation. Within a year HTML tables began to appear, and the tabbed tables looked, and still look, ridiculous by current standards. Could this wasted effort have been avoided? Yes, easily! The key is to represent the data according to the organization of information in the documents, not according to the limitations of the current viewing technology. Complex tables can be readily represented in SGML. It would have been a fairly simple matter to translate SGML-encoded tables to the tabbed format required by the original browser and, without changing the source data at all, to change the output to HTML tables when that technology became available.

We recently saw HTML 3.0 being promulgated as the new "standard" only to see it withdrawn some time later. Now HTML 3.2 is supposed to take its place. Will it, or will HTML 3.5 be the next "standard"? If you are going to make HTML your corporate standard, you'd better think long and hard about which version of HTML that is going to be. For many organizations a more stable approach will be to create standards around SGML. Then you'll be set to ride whatever HTML wave comes along next.

Using SGML to Produce Documents for Multiple Applications

Most often, using multiple applications means that you want both publishing quality paper output and an online version. SGML is well suited for this task because it can represent documents in a truly application-independent way. Other approaches tend to favor the type of application they were designed for initially even if they are capable of doing some kind of translation. In general, the objectives and means of effectively communicating information on paper and online are profoundly different.

Multiple applications often mean other things as well, although those who are unfamiliar with SGML may have difficulty seeing possibilities that, to the SGML-initiated, are obvious. For example, a well-defined body of information might be reused in many different formats: say, a magazine article, an article in an encyclopedia, a Web page, an on-demand fax report, or a chapter in a book. While the information may be general purpose, it tends to get "locked in" to a particular use when created in a proprietary format.

Using SGML to Preserve Information of Long-Term Value

Document markup languages created with SGML can be specific to a particular task or they can be general. The objective of the former is lightness, a quick implementation and quick processing. The objective of the general markup system is reuse and preservation. Reuse means that the document is so chockful of meaningful elements and structure that we are readily able to formulate new uses for it. Preservation means that our documents retain their usefulness over time because, being so rich in structure and elements, they can be used with today's tools for today's needs and tomorrow's tools for tomorrow's needs. For example, most documents in the past were created without a formalized system for indicating that one piece of information was related to another piece of information either in the same or in a different document. Today we call that a hyperlink, and it is considered an essential part of an information system. SGML documents were created in that foggy past which did preserve such relationships even though the current set of display tools may not have supported hyperlinks. The language designers put it into the DTD because it was an intrinsic property of the information. Today those documents are readily translated into fully hyperlinked HTML. The information of long-term value was preserved; it survived into the next generation of tools.

Today, thousands of documents are being created in HTML that only support single, unidirectional hyperlinks. It is certain that browsers will eventually support a much richer set of relations between *information nodes.* There are SGML documents that encode the fact that one piece of information may be related to many other pieces of information. The SGML documents will preserve their information over the long term.

Definition   *An* information node *is a discrete piece of information, possibly connected to other discrete pieces of information.*

All SGML documents adhere to certain syntax rules. Any SGML document, irrespective of the particular application used to create it, can be read and processed by numerous SGML applications. This is because an SGML file is simply a marked-up text file. While it is nearly unthinkable to attempt to convert documents from a ten-year-old, obsolete typesetting or word processing format to something more current, ten-year-old SGML documents can be readily handled by more powerful tools than those that existed when they were created. It is also easier to modify SGML documents and add new information or structure to them since the SGML model allows complete control over the processing of the elements and the attributes of a document.

Using SGML to Mandate Conformance with an International, Nonproprietary Standard

Government procurements typically require adherence to applicable standards, and SGML is frequently the mandated standard for documentation. But would you use SGML without the incentive of a government contract? In fact, many industries have adopted standards for information delivery around SGML. Typically, suppliers are mandated to deliver documentation to the procuring organization in SGML encoded according to a DTD or DTDs that have been developed by industry consortiums. Often these initiatives are international in scope. For example, a great deal of work has been undertaken in aviation, automotive, and semiconductor industries. Electronic component manufacturers including Intel, National Semiconductor, Texas Instruments, Philips, IBM, Hewlett-Packard, and Hitachi have created an SGML standard for the creation and interchange of databook information. The newspaper industry has developed an SGML standard known as UTF (Universal Text Format), which is used for the delivery of information from news agencies to newspapers. SGML guarantees the long-term viability of the information delivered and does not lock the procurer into a particular vendor's documentation system. The DTD itself is a kind of subcontract that specifies to the supplier what information must be supplied and how that information must be organized. The supplier has the advantage of having clear, verifiable specifications, and the procurer has the advantage of being able to programmatically test conformance of the documents to the mandated DTD.

Using SGML to Automate Document Production

Organizations that produce a lot of documents typically seek to maintain high quality standards and consistency while reducing production costs. A simple form of automation is to impose standards for formatting and organization to reduce the amount of work required to go from raw input to a finished product. In addition to written guidelines, authors are often required to use word processing *style sheets* with a given set of styles. *Style* templates have the desirable side effect of causing authors to spent a lot less time wrestling with the word processing software and its formatting capabilities.

Definition   Styles *are named formatting characteristics used in word processing applications and other publishing software. Styles are similar to SGML elements in associating a name with parts of a document's text, but they do not define containers, are not hierarchical, and do not support meta-data. In word processing, using styles saves formatting instructions, making document preparation easier and more consistent.*

Definition Style sheets *are a collection of styles, often serving an analogous function to an SGML DTD in that the style sheet may define the set of legal objects in a particular document type. In SGML applications style sheets define a set of actions to be performed when processing a document. For example, a style sheet for display of an SGML document might define a set of formatting parameters that should be associated with a given element.*

SGML can be used for similar purposes and can be much more powerful than style sheets. Because SGML specifies the relationships between elements, *SGML editors* guide the author in structuring the document correctly. While it is rare for an author to produce a document that rigorously adheres to a style sheet, one can only produce an SGML document that doesn't follow the DTD by explicitly requesting that document *validation* be turned off. For example, a glossary entry is required to have a short reference title, a long title, one or more paragraphs of explanatory text in a special glossary style, and a final line with the words "See also" and references to other glossary entries. A word processing application style sheet will typically provide special styles for the short title, long title, glossary paragraphs, and "See also" references. It may or may not provide autotext for the words "See also." There is no guarantee that the author will use those styles, and if the author does use them, there is no guarantee that they will be used in the right sequence. The author may also insert unwanted additional spacing or formatting that looks okay on the screen but is inconsistent with the book style. An SGML editor, on the other hand, can require that the author create each of the required elements in the expected order. Moreover, SGML editors will typically insert any required elements, allowing the author to simply provide the text. The editor may also be able to check to see that the "See also" references point to actual glossary references.

Definition An SGML editor *is a computer program that allows an author to create SGML instances.*

> **Definition**   Validation *is the determination that an instance conforms to the DTD. SGML editors can validate documents as they are being created.*

Because SGML documents can, unlike word processed documents, be rather easily processed by computer programs, it is possible to automate document production in other ways, ways in which people who have only worked with word processors or desktop publishing tools will have difficulty imagining. It is very common to customize the generation of indexes, tables, lists, and glossaries, to validate hyperlinks or cross-references, to produce data for databases, and to add data from databases, just to name a few of the more common processes. I have seen publishing processes that took weeks of tedious, manual work reduced to a few keystrokes and a couple of minutes of computer time thanks to an hour's worth of SGML programming.

Using SGML to Rigorously Structure Documents

SGML is the only technology that exists for creating rigorously structured documents and validating them. You can think of SGML as a templating facility, similar to a database form or wizards found in some word processing software.

Using SGML for Richly Hyperlinked Information

SGML has a built-in facility for hyperlinking and also supports the creation of other hyperlinking systems. *HyTime,* a companion standard to SGML, includes very elaborate hyperlinking capabilities.

> **Definition**   HyTime, *ISO standard 10744, is a companion standard to SGML for hypermedia and time-based applications.*

SGML can express the fullest possible range of hyperlinking because SGML documents have a structure, and named elements and attributes. We can use these properties, in addition to the simple *source* and *destination* model, to express many different types of relationships between objects in a document. A hyperlink may be an SGML element itself and so can be typed, numbered, made conditional, or have other specific behaviors attached to it. Imagine, for example, that links are typed by areas of interest, say finance, marketing, and engineering. In order to reduce "link clutter" or simply to provide more information to the prospective user of a hyperlinked document, hyperlinks can be color-coded or perhaps only activated on the user's request. Or, as a way to address the problem of broken links we could have hyperlinks that only generally specify the type of destination they point to and that would be resolved when the user actually clicked on the link. Unlike a hard-coded URL, the destination could still be located if the address were changed or the link were moved.

Definition   *On the Web, the* source *is the place where you started, and the* destination *is the place you jumped to after clicking on the link.*

Even if the target output format is HTML and hyperlinks are translated into URLs, you may want to use some of SGML's expressive power for automatic generation of hyperlinks, validation of hyperlinks, and independence from continually evolving HTML hyperlinking standards. Any SGML element can be converted into a hyperlink source or destination, with unique identifiers generated automatically. You simply maintain the logical content of your documents and you get the management of hypertext at no extra charge.

Using SGML for Collaborative Authoring

SGML allows documents to be either physically or logically broken up into chunks, which can be parceled out among a group of authors. The SGML structure, as expressed in the DTD, ensures that the parts can be joined back together. This is the most primitive model for *collaborative authoring;* SGML permits a high degree of refinement of this concept. SGML-based software allows check-in/check-out and revision control on SGML elements. Examples of such products include Astoria from Chrystal (Xerox) and Information Manager from Texcel.

Definition   Collaborative authoring *is the creation of information by multiple authors working on a single document, possibly simultaneously.*

Using SGML for Database-Style Approaches to Information Management

In constructing a database management system (DBMS) the analyst develops a formal model of the information and the relationships between pieces of information. This approach and skill set carry over well to SGML system design. Often the strengths overlap and combine: DBMS for managing data and SGML for describing documents. A relational database management system (RDBMS) is a good fit with SGML when there is a large amount of meta-data associated with units of structured information, often consisting of dependencies that are identified by keywords or numbering systems. Object-oriented databases may work well with SGML in situations where the document components naturally fit the object paradigm. Such systems are characteristically organized around modules of information that are categorized by a natural model of a particular domain's knowledge base and may also be richer in multimedia content.

Document Type Definition (DTD)

Unless the use of a specific DTD or DTDs happens to have been predetermined by established interchange standards within a particular industry, the process of selection or development is complex, depending heavily on the objectives for your Intranet development and on your own environment. You have to decide whether to start from scratch or use one of the *public DTDs*. A general principle is to get as much as possible out of what others have already done; in the case of public DTDs this may be the equivalent of years of effort by some of the world's leading experts in document technologies. Among the most frequently used DTD for general purpose technical publishing is the DocBook DTD (`http://www.ora.com/davenport/README.html`).

Among the reasons for starting from scratch is the desire to construct a DTD that is rich in information specific to a given enterprise or industry and, on the other end of the scale, the desire to create extremely lightweight DTDs for very specific purposes. Even when starting from scratch, it is usual to borrow from existing DTDs; for example, most DTDs make use of the table model originally developed for the Department of Defense's *CALS* project.

Definition *A public DTD is a DTD that may be referenced using SGML's formal syntax for the standard DTDs. Less strictly, a public DTD is any DTD that has been placed in the public domain.*

Definition CALS (Continuous Acquisition and Life-cycle Support) *is a very large U.S. Department of Defense program to, among other things, use electronic information systems technology to reduce procurement and maintenance costs of weapons systems. SGML is one of the key components in the CALS initiative. CALS helped to stimulate the growth of the SGML industry and also supported the development of several key reference standards in such areas as technical publications, tables, and interactive electronic technical manuals.*

DTD design is considered a challenging and advanced undertaking. Part of the problem is that it involves not just the mechanics of creating a correct and robust encoding, but that it is intimately connected with the objectives of the Intranet, the specific knowledge base of the organization, the quantity and quality of existing documents, and even the corporate culture. *Document analysis* is the general term for taking all these things into account and coming up with DTDs. Many enterprises decide to work with an experienced analyst the first time through the process. See "SGML Consulting" for more discussion of this.

Definition Document analysis *is a branch of voodoo that has the development of DTDs as its primary objective.*

DTDs are text files that can be created with any editor or word processing application that can save a text file. Special DTD design tools are not essential, but they can be helpful, especially to those without any background in computer languages. Figure 10.1 shows a fragment of The DocBook DTD as a plaintext file. (A graphic view of the same fragment using the DTD tool Near & Far is shown in Figure 10.7.) The DocBook fragment shows element (!ELEMENT) and attribute (!ATTLIST) definitions for DocBook glossaries. Element definitions include the content model (in parenthesis); that is, the child elements that are permitted for each glossary element.

```
Glos.dtd - Notepad
File   Edit   Search   Help
<!-- =========================================================== -->
<!-- ########################################################### -->
<!-- =========================================================== -->

<!ELEMENT Glossary - - (DocInfo?, (Title, TitleAbbrev?)?, (%component.gp;)*,
                 (GlossDiv+ | GlossEntry+)) >
<!ATTLIST Glossary
                 %commonatts;
>

<!ELEMENT GlossDiv - - (Title, TitleAbbrev?, (%component.gp;)*,
                 GlossEntry+) >
<!ATTLIST GlossDiv
                 %commonatts;
>

<!ELEMENT GlossEntry - - (GlossTerm, Acronym?, Abbrev?, (GlossSee |
                 GlossDef+)) >
<!ATTLIST GlossEntry
                 %commonatts;
>

<!ELEMENT GlossTerm - - ((%inlineobj.gp;)+) >
<!ATTLIST GlossTerm
                 %commonatts;
>

<!ELEMENT GlossDef - - ((Comment | %para.gp; | %list.gp; | %object.gp;)+,
                 GlossSeeAlso*) >
<!ATTLIST GlossDef
                 %commonatts;
                 Subject     NMTOKENS #IMPLIED|
>

<!ELEMENT GlossSee - O (#PCDATA) >
<!ATTLIST GlossSee
                 %commonatts;
                 OtherTerm   IDREF     #CONREF
>

<!ELEMENT GlossSeeAlso - O (#PCDATA) >
<!ATTLIST GlossSeeAlso
                 %commonatts;
```

Figure 10.1

DocBook DTD fragment

SGML Authoring

There is a wide range of products to help create SGML documents. The bad news is that you cannot continue doing whatever you are doing and expect to get SGML out of it. The good news is that many of the tools with which your authors are already familiar offer SGML capabilities, although, that said, do not assume that the best choice for you will be the one that seems the most familiar.

Legacy Conversion

Legacy, as in the legal sense of the word, is what someone left you. However, *legacy documents* are the kind of legacies you don't want to get if you can help it. Typically, one is confronted with a mishmash of documents, in a mishmash of formats, that you somehow want to get into SGML all at once.

Definition   Legacy documents *are an existing body of documents that you may want to convert into SGML. SGML projects often begin with document analysis, the study of legacy documents to determine the logical components of the documents and their equivalent SGML representation. A major pitfall in this process is to base the DTDs exclusively on the legacy documents because these documents usually strongly reflect the limitations of the tools used to create them.*

This isn't an authoring job; it's a conversion problem requiring a computer program to do as much of the work as possible before handing the stuff over to some editorial grunts to do QA and clean-up. There are companies that specialize in this kind of work, and since it's a one-time thing it often makes sense to hire someone to do this. However, you should not expect miracles; it is difficult and sometimes impossible to go from documents that were created with little or no concept of structure to pristinely structured SGML documents. The legacy format may also impose limitations. This is all unfortunate since an enterprise may judge the value of an SGML system based on the results of an initial conversion of legacy data, determining that the technology is not cost-effective. I therefore recommend that when you prototype an SGML system be sure to include new material created from scratch as well as legacy data so that you get a balanced view of the eventual outcome.

Native SGML Editors

I'm afraid that the folks who should be reading this section have skipped it, having seen below that it is somehow possible to produce SGML using Microsoft Word. However, SGML editors, once they are set up properly, are easy to use; in fact, they are much easier than applications such as Microsoft Word. If you are footing the bill for your publications department, you'll be glad to know that if your writers don't kill you when you make them switch to an SGML editor, you'll see productivity increase in a fairly short time. And that isn't even the reason for using an SGML editor—the reason is that the quality of documents that comes out will be higher, and costs and problems at every step down the line will be decreased.

Not that there aren't downsides. Although prices are dropping rapidly, SGML editors remain mostly a premium-priced tool. It shouldn't be, but it always seems to be difficult to set up an SGML editor. You may have to understand terms like "Reference Concrete Syntax" and "Public Entity Catalog" within ten minutes of tearing off the shrinkwrap. There is no getting around the fact that you have to understand something about SGML to use one of these tools; for some authors it is unlike anything they have ever seen before. Finally, while I will hold to my contention that SGML editors are overall much simpler than Microsoft Word, Word is surely a widely used, robust, carefully designed product that cannot be matched in smoothness by the much smaller-scale efforts of the SGML vendors.

There are three categories of native SGML editors: high-end publishing systems, WYSIWYG or partially WYSIWYG editors that are roughly comparable to word processors, and non-WYSIWYG or structure-oriented editors.

Publishing Systems. These are the SGML cousins of desktop publishing tools such as Interleaf. They have extensive support for producing high-quality paper documents from the SGML source as well as other extended features for publishing automation. An example is the Adept Publisher from ArborText.

WYSIWYG or Partially WYSIWYG Editors. WYSIWYG (What you see is what you get) has slightly different meanings in the word processing and SGML worlds. In the former, it means that what you see on the screen is what you will see on paper, implying a process whose objective is to produce paper copy. SGML makes no assumptions about the output medium. SGML WYSIWYG editors use a style sheet to create on-screen formatting, so the structure of the document may be seen from the appearance of the text rather than just the tags. An example is Softquad's Author/Editor.

Structure Editors. Structure editors make no pretense of being WYSIWYG applications; on the contrary, they accentuate the fact that you have created a structured document in all its naked SGMLness. They could be as full-featured as the WYSIWYG editors but tend not to be, offering less support for paper output. They fall on the lower end of the price scale. InContext's editor, shown in Figure 10.2, is an example of this genre. InContext makes no bones about SGML structure, displaying the nested element view on the left-hand side and the content

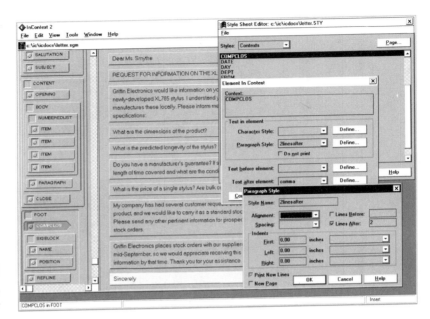

Figure 10.2

InContext SGML editor

of elements in boxes emphasizing the idea of containment. The upper right-hand window shows the style sheet editor, where we are creating a formatting association for the COMPCLOS element, which will be used in printing the document.

Hybrid Desktop Publishing and SGML

Desktop publishing (DTP) tool vendors had a leg up in the SGML business because their tools have always encouraged writers to think in a more structured way, and their internal markup languages have some strong similarities to SGML. It has therefore been possible to mutate their products to support SGML. One such product, Frame+SGML, maintains the document in an internal format that is extremely close to SGML. Although, unfortunately, "extremely close" still leaves a sometimes irritating gap, in most cases one can import and export pure SGML without difficulty. The author works in both WYSIWYG and structural modes, similar to that of the SGML WYSIWYG tools. The advantages of this genre of tools is that the full paper output capabilities of the original tool are preserved, as are the essential look and feel of the nonSGML product. To spring SGML on your unsuspecting writers, you could just remove their copy of Frame and swap in

Frame+SGML. Figure 10. 3 provides a look at the Frame+SGML interface, which provides a complete subset of the familiar capabilities of
the non-SGML FrameMaker product, but we see on the right-hand
side that SGML structure is simultaneously active. Here we are using
the glossary definitions from the DocBook DTD with the structure
view showing the element in use and the Elements showing what
elements may be added in the current context of a PARA inside a
GLOSDEF.

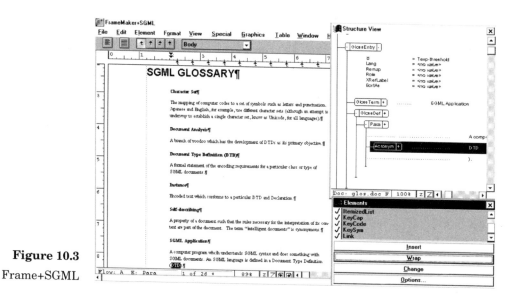

Figure 10.3

Frame+SGML

Word Processor-Based Environments

SGML editors may be integrated into a word processing application.
Examples include the Microsoft Word-based plug-in editors, Tag Wiz-
ard from Nice, and Near & Far Author from Microstar. These are low-
cost editors, but they do require that you have a copy of Word.

SGML Readers and Writers

This is the place you should have skipped to if you wanted to be told
that you can keep using Microsoft Word exactly the way you always
have, without changing a thing, and then hit the Save As SGML button
and have it all come out just right. Well, there is a product, from
Microsoft, SGML Author, that more or less does exactly that—down to

the Save As SGML button, but there's a catch, more than one. You have to use styles as if your life depended on it. Mess up and your SGML will be messed up. If your SGML does get messed up, you'll get a bunch of messages ten times more incomprehensible than you'd get from a vanilla SGML editor. This is because they are the messages from an SGML editor, which is buried somewhere beneath the Word interface you are using. Styles, unlike SGML, are not hierarchical, so you may find yourself having to simulate hierarchy by making dozens of style names such as second-paragraph-inside-first-bulletlistitem-inside-last-numberedlistitem.

And finally, the tool that actually converts Word to SGML is designed to be easy to use at the cost of not having enough flexibility to enable you to specify any and all mappings between the two formats. I can give three recommendations to increase your chances of success with this tool:

1. Ensure that you can tweak both your Word template and your SGML DTD in order to get around some of the weaknesses of the translator. You'll need as many degrees of freedom as possible!

2. Seriously consider converting to SGML in two steps. The first step would use SGML Author and have as its target a very simple DTD designed expressly to work with your Word template. The second step is to take the SGML from the first step and transform it into your real SGML using one of the power languages described in the section on SGML Programming.

3. Don't plan on foisting all of this on the authors without adequate support. Productivity will be higher if you have a document administrator who is thoroughly trained in SGML on hand to decipher error messages and debug conversion problems.

Text Editors

SGML can be edited very well, with any text editor (such as emacs or vi). So, while lots of slick tools exist to make the job easier, you can be sure that you will never find yourself unable to edit an SGML file for lack of a particular tool. For those who prefer to use emacs, for example, there is a major mode for SGML, psgml.

SGML Browsing

SGML documents can be viewed directly on Intranets with *SGML browsers,* or the SGML can be transformed into the specific format required by viewing applications that do not have general SGML capabilities, such as Web browsers. This section is concerned with the former situation, and the next with the latter.

Definition   *An* SGML browser *is a computer program that displays an SGML document based on any DTD. An* HTML browser *is a kind of SGML browser that displays only HTML.*

SGML browsers are able to display any SGML document. They require that a style sheet relating formatting information to SGML elements be prepared for each SGML application (DTD) used. The completeness, versatility, and ease of use of style sheets are important criteria to consider in evaluating SGML browsers.

SGML browsers typically have very similar capabilities to HTML browsers with respect to the way information is displayed, and support graphics, tables, lists, and multimedia. No SGML browser currently supports Java, Javascript, or ActiveX, although some of them have the capability to initiate local applications, some are OLE-capable, and some have interactive capabilities through private scripting languages. It is possible that the SGML browsers will add Java in the near future. Another tack is that SGML browsers will soon be appearing as plug-ins to the Web browsers.

SGML browsers have capabilities that HTML browsers do not have. The most common is that they use the document structure to automatically generate an expandable/collapsible hypertext table of contents. *Expandable* refers to the ability, when looking at a view that only shows higher-level headings, to click on a heading and see the subheading "beneath" it. *Collapsible* is the reverse process, the ability to click on an expanded view, causing the subheadings to be removed for easier viewing of the higher-level headings. The entire document itself may be expandable and collapsible. SGML browsers can reveal or hide SGML tags inline and often can display a tree view of the document structure using the tags. This can be especially useful when the documents contain hidden information in the element attributes. Some SGML browsers implement HyTime and other hyperlinking schemes, allowing for different types of hyperlinks unavailable in HTML such as *one-to-many* and *bidirectional* links and links that point to other links. Figures 10.4, 10.5, and 10.6 show the Panorama browser from Softquad. Figure 10.4 shows the expanding table of contents on the left-hand side. In Figure 10-5 we have changed modes to "Show tags" and can now see the underlying SGML structure and have also exposed the attributes for the PARA tag revealing the meta-data for that element. Figure 10.6 illustrates its one-to-many hyperlink capability. We have clicked on the CLINK text token, a one-to-many hyperlink, and are presented with three possible destinations.

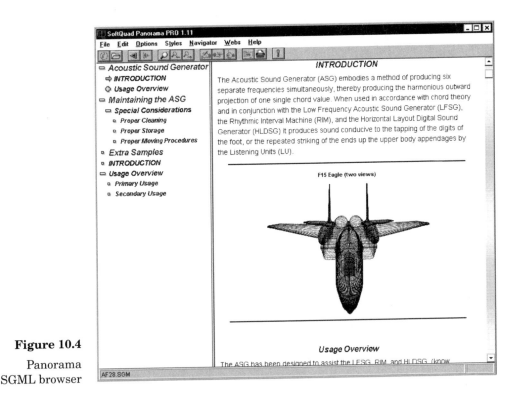

Figure 10.4

Panorama
SGML browser

Definition   A one-to-many hyperlink *is a hyperlink that has more than one destination.*

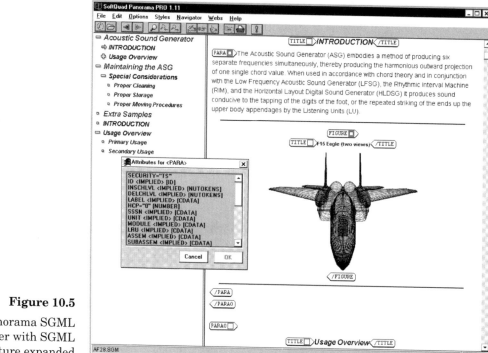

Figure 10.5

Panorama SGML
browser with SGML
structure expanded

Definition   A bidirectional hyperlink *is a hyperlink where both ends are both sources and destinations.*

Some browsers require that documents be converted from SGML to a binary format for more efficient *rendering* by the software. In general, this will be, at worst, an inconvenience for a fairly static collection of material, but it may be unacceptable if the data changes frequently or if documents are composed on the fly from SGML fragments.

Definition   Rendering *is the display of the document on the page, requiring the translation of the source data to a screen image.*

Basic HTML or SGML may be rendered very quickly, but complex data such as images or tables present a challenge. Typographical com-

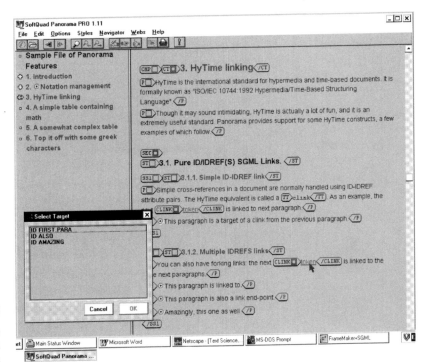

Figure 10.6

Panorama SGML
browser with
Hy-Time links

plexity also slows rendering, and aside from issues of screen resolution is among the reasons why a "paper look" may not be desirable for on-line documents.

Another important issue is the efficiency with which the browser works in a client/server environment. One of the advantages of SGML is its ability to deliver sections of documents based on the document architecture. However, this is only an advantage when the browser and the server software are capable of retrieving and delivering chunks.

HTTPD can be used on the server side to deliver SGML data to an SGML browser, but SGML-specific functions such as retrieving sections must be implemented by SGML-specific server-side software. Often such software may work with HTTPD through CGI or an equivalent extension.

The $64,000 question for many will be why should they consider an SGML browser when Netscape/Internet Explorer/HTML browsers have become ubiquitous and constitute a de facto standard. First, I'll have to strengthen, unfortunately, the argument against an SGML browser with the following consideration: although HTML is supposed to be an SGML language, SGML browsers cannot read the average HTML file as well as a browser designed specifically for HTML. As mentioned above, no SGML browser currently supports Java or JavaScript, and they do not support all possible HTML extensions. Nor do they support all the invalid HTML code that's out on the Web. So there isn't any question that you'll still need an HTML browser at least on the other side of the firewall. That granted, there are still reasons why you might want to consider an SGML browser in your Intranet environment:

- You want to maximize network performance by taking advantage of structure-based chunking of data between an SGML client (the browser) and server software.

- Your highly structured data or richly hyperlinked data is ideal for taking advantage of the special capabilities of an SGML browser, which HTML browsers do not support.

- You do not want to *down-translate* your SGML data to HTML (see the section Output from SGML Source) either for reasons of performance, or simply because the additional effort is not worthwhile.

- You intend to customize your browsing environment. Having SGML data on the client side allows for many interesting possibilities due to the high degree of compatibility of SGML with programming processes and the unlimited degree to which meta-information can be included in documents.

Definition   Down-translation: *The translation of documents from the structurally rich and generalized SGML format to an application-specific format such as HTML or PDF. Down-translation is usually quite easy, as the name implies, because you are merely releasing the potential energy packed into the SGML representation.*

Output from SGML Source

SGML is often used to encode information that will be delivered to the user in either non-SGML form or in an SGML encoding that is different from the encoding used to store the document. The most common scenario in Intranets is to translate the SGML, on the server, to HTML, which may be either SGML-compliant or *HTML du Jour*, as the non-standard variants of HTML are sometimes called. Of course, HTML is not the only possible output format: Word processor or desktop publishing formats, for printing and editing, are also common. We also see PostScript, PDF, proprietary formats used for CD-ROM production, proprietary typesetting languages, and multimedia/virtual reality scripting languages.

Translation from SGML to HTML may be performed on demand, that is, when the user requests a page, or it may be done off-line. The translation process is generally extremely simple and quick due to the similarity between HTML and other SGML languages, so on-demand translation is usually not unreasonable overhead for the server. The mapping between SGML and HTML may be accomplished through a style sheet or through a script written in either an SGML programming language or, with a little more effort, in any server-side programming language such as PERL or C.

Electronic Book Technologies' DynaWeb and Open Text's Live Link Server are two complete solutions to SGML delivery in HTML. They both translate to HTML on demand, using a style sheet mapping, and run off HTTPD. These products also offer automatic HTML table of contents generation from SGML, and SGML structure-sensitive search capabilities. Omnimark's Omnimark language (version 3.0) is a full-featured SGML programming language, which is also designed to run off HTTPD and can perform complex transformations as well as interface to a SQL database.

The primary advantages of performing SGML to HTML translation on demand are

- ability to deliver chunks of data based on SGML structure without deciding beforehand how to break down the document into HTML pages
- advantage of maintaining a single repository instead of parallel HTML and SGML, saving disk space and perhaps avoiding update problems
- dynamic composition of documents from SGML source and possibly out of, or with, data from databases

Off-line conversion of SGML to HTML has the advantage of not requiring any special server process, which may reduce cost as well as server load.

Conversion from SGML to other output formats can be accomplished with a variety of tools or by using a programming language. The latter possibility is discussed in the section SGML Programming Languages. Most of the WYSIWYG authoring tools discussed in the prior section have round-trip capabilities; that is, not only can you go from, say, Word to SGML, but you can also get from SGML to Word.

Many SGML translation products use style sheets to give the user a familiar way to specify some output mapping of SGML. Work that had been underway for a number of years to standardize this process has recently come to fruition in the passage of the *Document Style, Semantic, and Specification Language (DSSSL)*. A public domain reference application called Jade, which will output RTF (Rich Text Format) from an SGML style sheet, is in the advanced stages of preparation. You may wish to check *The SGML Web Page* (`http://gopher.sil.org/sgml/sgml.html`) for current status.

Definition   DSSSL (pronounced dis-ul, Document Style, Semantic, and Specification Language) *is a companion standard to SGML for the system-independent specification of formatting and general transformation of documents.*

DTD Design

DTD syntax is a tad complicated. There are quite a few statement types, each with its own syntax rules and many possible parameters. *Content models,* the notation used for expressing the arrangement of possible elements that may be contained by the parent element, are encoded using *regular expression* syntax from computer science. And that is the easy part. The hard part is forming all those DTD statements into a coherent, efficient, elegant, usable, maintainable, and extensible document architecture. The number of elements needed in a document architecture may be quite large; HTML, a "simple" SGML language, started out as "just a few tags" and has expanded—the latest HTML DTD is 60 pages long and still growing.

Definition   Regular expression *is a formal expression that describes a set of possible combinations or patterns.*

> **Definition**   *In an SGML element definition, the* content model *is the definition of possible content for that element including children and textual or nontextual (for example, graphic) data. The content model is based on regular expression syntax, which permits great flexibility and conciseness in stating all possible permissible combinations of child elements and data.*

Fortunately, there is at least one tool on the market that can be very helpful to the DTD designer, Microstar's Near & Far, a graphic design tool for constructing, manipulating, viewing, and documenting DTDs. Elements are presented as boxes that can be moved around on the screen and connected in expandable and collapsible tree structures to form parent and child relationships. Special types of connectors visually represent whether an element or element group is repeatable and/or optional. Attributes of elements may be viewed by clicking on element boxes. Near & Far allows the novice to create correct DTDs without mastering every detail of the syntax and gives any user the ability to understand the layout of the architecture at a glance. You will probably find this to be the case for the glossary fragment from the DocBook DTD shown in Figure 10.7 using Near & Far. Compare this presentation to the text version in Figure 10.1. Attributes are displayed for each element in a separate window on demand.

Near & Far is a sophisticated design tool that carries a not inconsequential price tag. There are less sophisticated and less expensive (including free) tools that provide a formatted view of the DTD. They are useful for understanding the document structure and perhaps also for documentation purposes. One pubic domain tool, DTD2HTML converts a DTD to a formatted view in HTML. See *The SGML Web Page* at `http://gopher.sil.org/sgml/sgml.html` for the current URL and information.

FRED, from OCLC, offers an alternate or perhaps complementary way to approach DTD design. FRED, available as a free online service at `http://www.oclc.org/fred`, will generate a DTD from marked-up documents. This could be very useful in creating a DTD for a legacy document set. You could take a representative sample of the documents, mark up all the elements and structures that occur in the whole set, and FRED will create a (probably rough) DTD sufficient to represent each type of document.

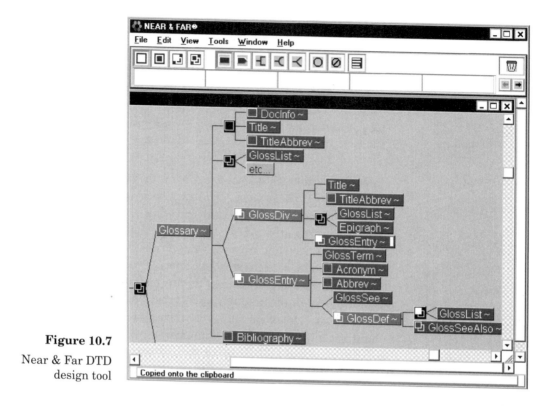

Figure 10.7

Near & Far DTD
design tool

SGML
Programming
Languages

I have mentioned lots of neat things you can do with a little programming and SGML. In fact, a big part of what SGML is about is combining the 4,000-year-old art of creating documents with the 50-year-old art of computing.

SGML programming languages are document manipulation languages. Each individual part of a document that is delimited by an element can be accessed by the programmer; and these parts can be changed, reordered, tested, and discarded according to the needs of whatever process has been defined. The programmer has complete access to the hierarchy of the document and the attributes of each element: for example, indent the first paragraph of a second bulleted item and italicize the second paragraph of a third bulleted item. Complex page-formatting commonly requires such fine-grained decisions, as well as much more complicated ones, and these can be done with SGML programming.

Among the SGML programming languages Omnimark is probably the most widely used. Other languages include Balise, Louise, and CoST, the latter being freeware.

SGML programming is occasionally done with general programming languages such as C, C++, and PERL. SGML programming languages have the advantage of already understanding SGML constructs such as elements and attributes, and are designed to efficiently process SGML documents. They are worth the cost, if there is any, and the effort to master them, because they save time, lots of programmers' time. General purpose languages may be suitable for tasks that can be performed without diving deep into the SGML, or if someone has already gone to the trouble of creating a set of SGML-specific routines. SGMLS.pm is one such public domain package.

In addition to manipulating documents by their SGML structure, it is often necessary to modify text in various ways. One may wish to substitute one phrase for another or find certain patterns. PERL happens to excel in these kinds of operations although all SGML programming languages provide this capability in one form or another. Figure 10.8 shows you a bit of the flavor of SGML programming, with a fragment of a down (to HTML) translation written in OmniMark. Omnimark programs define actions that take place each time an SGML element is encountered in the document being processed. The actions begin with the element statement, which is flush to the left margin in Figure 10.8. Processing can be conditional, based on the value of the elements' attributes, as shown by the statements that include the ATTRIBUTE keyword.

SGML Programmers

Managers of publication departments live in interesting times. The Internet, Intranets, and a whole caboodle of new tools and technologies have turned everything sideways and upside down. The good news is that documents are the hottest, most interesting, and most prominent

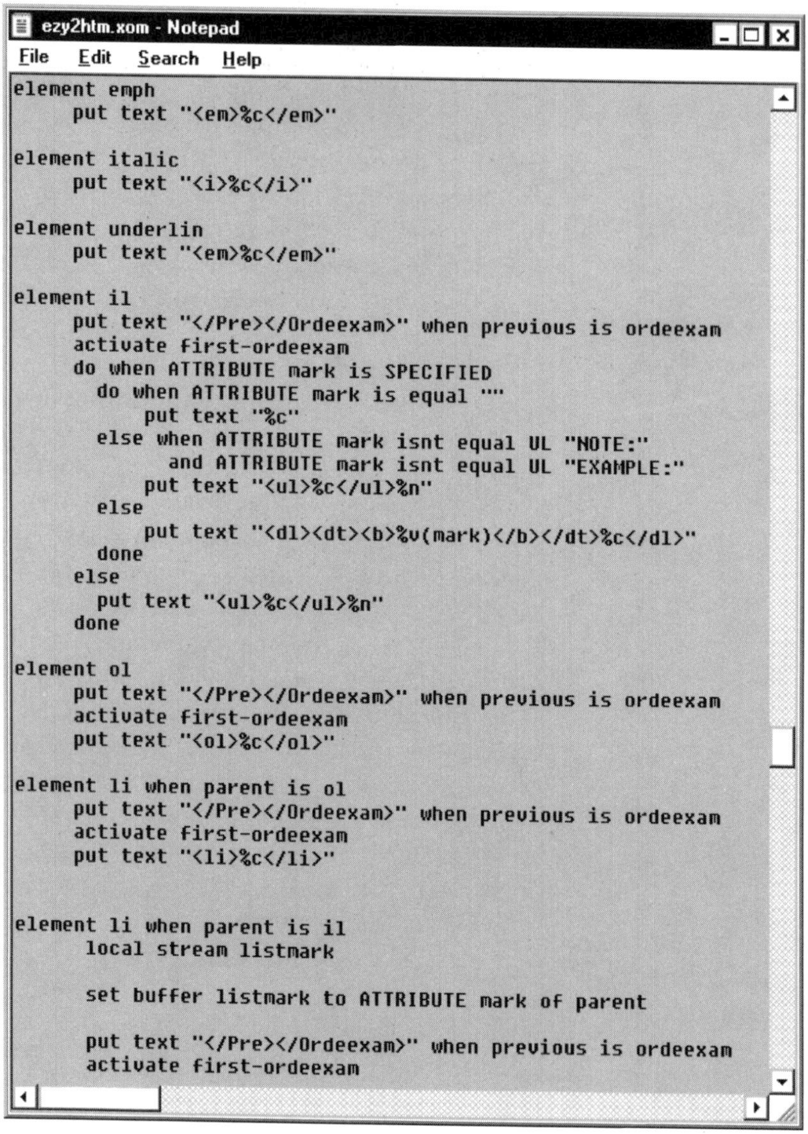

ezy2htm.xom - Notepad

File Edit Search Help

```
element emph
     put text "<em>%c</em>"

element italic
     put text "<i>%c</i>"

element underlin
     put text "<em>%c</em>"

element il
     put text "</Pre></Ordeexam>" when previous is ordeexam
     activate first-ordeexam
     do when ATTRIBUTE mark is SPECIFIED
       do when ATTRIBUTE mark is equal ""
           put text "%c"
       else when ATTRIBUTE mark isnt equal UL "NOTE:"
             and ATTRIBUTE mark isnt equal UL "EXAMPLE:"
           put text "<ul>%c</ul>%n"
       else
           put text "<dl><dt><b>%v(mark)</b></dt>%c</dl>"
       done
     else
       put text "<ul>%c</ul>%n"
     done

element ol
     put text "</Pre></Ordeexam>" when previous is ordeexam
     activate first-ordeexam
     put text "<ol>%c</ol>"

element li when parent is ol
     put text "</Pre></Ordeexam>" when previous is ordeexam
     activate first-ordeexam
     put text "<li>%c</li>"


element li when parent is il
      local stream listmark

      set buffer listmark to ATTRIBUTE mark of parent

      put text "</Pre></Ordeexam>" when previous is ordeexam
      activate first-ordeexam
```

Figure 10.8

Omnimark SGML programming language

focus of corporate activity today. Just to add to the manager's woes, it is quite likely that the potential introduced by SGML for cost reduction through automation and the addition of advanced capabilities will lead him or her to consider adding a programmer's talents to the department.

SGML specialists are not presently numerous, and it may be a better choice to give one's current staff a shot at it rather than attempting to hire someone with specific experience in this area.

Quite a few people coming from the authoring and document analysis side of the universe have become good SGML programmers. This would be the kind of person who has excelled at creating Word or Interleaf macros to perform all kinds of magic and has perhaps developed style sheet standards for the organization. In a UNIX environment they may be a whiz with awk and grep and may have picked up a little PERL. They have been doing SGML-like things for a long time without knowing it. The fortunate fact is that SGML programming with an SGML programming language is much easier than programming generally and should be a pleasant challenge for the technically competent generalist with an excellent grasp of SGML concepts.

Coming from a completely different direction, Internet/Intranet programmers can put their skills to good use in dealing with SGML. They may be more oriented toward programming than the document specialist is, but they'll also have to make more effort to unlearn bad habits. Knowledge of CGI will be helpful in setting up server-side *SGML transformation* and delivery. Unless direct delivery of SGML is part of your architecture, you will certainly have to do some of this. SGML is designed to be transformed, so this isn't hard as things go, but it doesn't happen magically and as easily as some people seem to assume. The transformation in the Intranet world these days is usually to HTML, although there are many other possibilities for print, CD-ROM, online, and database applications.

Knowledge of Java and the client side could be helpful in working with, customizing, or creating an SGML browser. Experience with HTML can be helpful as long as one is willing to see beyond HTML and the browsing environment and step up to SGML's broader and more structured view of the world of text.

Definition   SGML transformatio*n means changing SGML into something else.*

SGML Search Engines

SGML search engines are typically full-text search tools with the additional capability that they can restrict queries based on SGML structure. For example, suppose our documents contain the SGML element EMERGENCY PROCEDURE. We might find it useful to search for the word "sarin" in and only within the element EMERGENCY PROCEDURE if we were a member of a medical team responding to the gas attack on the Tokyo subway in 1995. Without the ability to narrow our search using context, our victims would probably all die before we had finished wading through 995 spurious "hits." SGML searches provide an additional way to add precision to search operations. An Intranet could present the ability to form ad hoc queries on arbitrary SGML elements if the users of the system are likely to know the element set or, more commonly, they may provide a preconfigured set of queries that take advantage of SGML structure but eliminate the need for the user to know anything about the encoding of the documents.

SGML search engines also often function as SGML fragment retrieval engines since they are able to isolate regions out of larger SGML documents in order to perform structure-based searches. An example of such a tool is Open Text's Live Link. Open Text also happens to be one of the popular general search engines on the Web, though the majority of its users are unaware of its SGML capabilities. Figure 10.9 shows Open Text's Power Search page on the Web with multiple within (container) fields for increasing precision. Open Text uses its SGML smarts to provide the ability to hone searches on the World Wide Web. On the right-hand side of the figure we see that we can restrict searches to summaries, titles, first headings, URLs, and any combination of any or all of these. Unfortunately, the usefulness of this feature is limited by the existence of tag salad. Intranets can really leverage this kind of capability by enforcing HTML standards and by using SGML.

Search engines can find matches among hundreds of thousands of documents quickly because they build indices where they can look up phrases. A simpler approach, for small document sets, is to go through each document one by one looking for matches. A public domain program, sgrep, does this and also has SGML structured search facilities (see *The SGML Web Page* at `http://gopher.sil.org/sgml/sgml.html`). It is possible to create a simple SGML search tool on Intranets by installing this program on the server and providing a CGI script to execute it on demand.

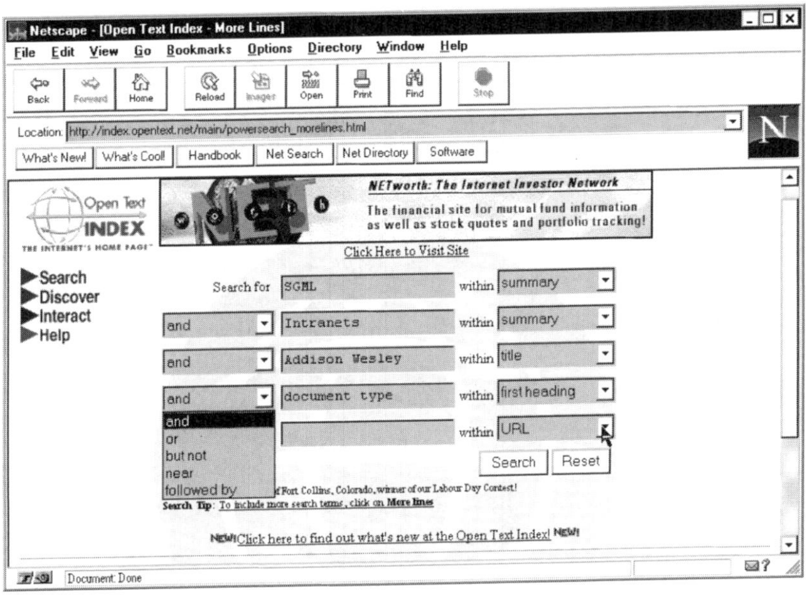

Figure 10.9

Open Text's SGML-
based search engine
on the Web

SGML
Document
Management
and Databases

Document management is usually some form of a database with special features designed expressly for the storage, modification, and retrieval of documents. Among the more common and important of such features are *check-in/check-out* and *revision control.* In the context of SGML, the difference between a Document Management System and a database is that the latter would have the possibility of handling fragments; that is, data at a finer level of granularity than the document. For more about Document Management Systems, see Chapter 9.

Definition   Document management *software allows documents to be stored centrally; retrieved using keyword, full-text search, and navigational criteria; and updated, archived, and written collaboratively, to mention a few of the possibilities. Document*

Management Systems are almost always a database application. SGML documents can be stored in a Document Management System, but SGML-savvy Document Management Systems can manage the components of SGML documents and make use of SGML meta-data.

Definition   Check-in/check out *enables collaborative authoring by allowing only one person at a time to work on a document (check-out). When a document is checked in, the repository is updated and the document may be checked out by another author. In an SGML system check-in / check-out is implemented at the document component level, so it is possible for authors to work on different parts of the same document.*

Definition   Revision control *maintains multiple versions (revisions) of a document, making it possible to recover older versions. Each time a document is checked in a new version is created, made current, and the older version is archived. An SGML system would maintain version information at the component level.*

SGML document management and database systems have been implemented in most flavors of database technology: relational, object-relational, and object-oriented. RDBMS products may get you some mileage out of your investment in current database technology. Object-oriented databases seem to be the wave of the future, especially as database technology coalesces with distributed object standards (a technique for putting services or programs on the network in the same way HTML pages are currently distributed) in Web/Intranet environments. SGML can fit in well with object-oriented concepts, and it would be quite plausible to put a CORBA (a standard for distributed objects) wrapper around intelligent text objects based on SGML.

SGML Parsers

An SGML parser is a computer program that can process a document instance using the DTD and SGML declaration. Parsers are used standalone to find errors in the encoding of a document or DTD, and to produce a fully expanded version of a document for easier postprocessing with utility programs. Parsers are also often at the core of SGML tools including editors, browsers, programming languages, converters, and SGML databases. The parser solves the problem of how to get at all the parts of an SGML document so the application designer can get on with the interesting things to be done with those parts.

Both commercial and public domain parsers are available. The most recent and complete parser, SP, is written in C++ and was expressly designed by its author, James Clark, to be readily integrated into applications. Its source code has been placed in the public domain. Information may be found at `http://www.jclark.com/sp/index.htm`. Nsgmls is an older parser, also maintained and enhanced by James Clark, and also available as source code in the public domain, written in C. Its source is available at `ftp://ftp.jclark.com/pub/sgmls`. Both parsers are available in binary format for many different platforms.

With these parsers it is possible (not just theoretically, it has been done) to set up a zero-cost SGML production shop. While tools are nice to have, DTDs and SGML instances can be created with any editor. The correctness of the encoding can be verified with a parser, and the parser output can be used with a free programming language such as PERL to produce any output desired. The repository of documents can be searched with sgrep. While in a corporate Intranet setting the availability of a zero-cost setup may not be of great direct importance, it is still important as it is one of the major conditions necessary to ensure that the technology will continue to evolve in universities and among small developers.

HyTime

SGML is quite good at providing a syntax for document encoding, but it has nothing to say about what the encoding might be used for. To do that, you need a specific language such as HTML. It was discovered that people were continually reinventing the wheel: creating SGML languages that do the same thing but calling them by different names. This has been at least in part the impetus behind HyTime, a companion international standard to SGML, which codifies a set of common behaviors having to do with hypermedia. HyTime preserves the ability of the language creator to create his or her own element names, but provides a mechanism for indicating that a particular element or attribute conforms to one of the codified common behaviors. For example, HyTime provides several different types of hyperlinks including aggregate, bidirectional, and indirect links and provides markup-based methods for referencing objects by temporal and spatial position.

Parts of HyTime have been implemented in some SGML browsers, databases, and other SGML applications. A HyTime engine is a processor that can interpret SGML documents with HyTime behaviors, providing the set of services defined in the HyTime standard. A commercial HyTime engine has been implemented by TechnoTeacher (`http://www.techno.com`). HyTime is a modular standard. It may be of interest to those constructing Intranets who simply want to support a richer hypertext paradigm. On the other end of the scale, HyTime can be used to implement the state of the art in hypertextual, hypermedia, interactive, dynamic Intranets.

There are a number of companion standards to HyTime that further specify the application domain to which HyTime may be applied. For example, Topic Mapping uses HyTime's link behaviors to define a standard way to support arbitrary, typed relations (mappings) between pieces of information in a repository. Topic Mapping provides a way to say why one piece of information is linked to another.

SGML Consultants

The demand for technical professionals with a background in SGML currently greatly exceeds the supply. Many companies choose to quickly ramp up their SGML projects by bringing in consultants. This can be a successful approach as long as you are careful to ensure that part of what you buy is knowledge transfer. SGML is kind of complicated, and efforts to implement it and reap its benefits over the long run do not come to fruition unless understanding seeps down deep.

Services typically offered by consultants include one or more of the following: general architecting of an SGML-based Intranet strategy, development of DTDs, conversion of legacy documentation, programming SGML input and output filters, integration of tools, development of custom SGML tools, and training. There are no agreed upon standards for what training or experience an SGML consultant should have, and no certification. As with many other things, one's main criterion has to be whether or not the consultant has obtained satisfactory results on similar projects. It may be helpful if the consultant has a broader view of Intranets and information management because an SGML consultant should be able to identify lots of possibilities for automation and effective information delivery.

Summary

Huge documents present challenging problems in balancing network load, authoring well-organized and consistent documents, and in providing readers with efficient ways to find the information they need. This chapter discussed how to tackle these challenges by using SGML as the binding agent in a document-centered high performance Intranet architecture. A range of solutions were proposed for various scenarios, and the application of a large number of off-the-shelf SGML tools and SGML resources was described.

Controlling the Chaos

What You Can Do

By now you have the idea that establishing an Intranet will encompass a variety of technologies and the cooperation of many people. Intranets are, despite their digital components, organic creatures—they tend to grow in unforeseen and unexpected ways.

Definition Chaos *is a state of apparent cattywompus. Chaotic systems are not really random, but are sufficiently complex as to appear so. Most chaotic systems have their own rhyme and reason, which may seem inscrutable.*

Intranets can even mutate uncontrollably. This chapter will help you select the right mix of seeds, plan your garden, pick your gardeners, and keep back those pesky weeds and root rot. This lesson in functional horticulture will include some factors in information modeling:

- sources
- lenses
- destinations
- permanence
- centralization

Drawing on the following topics, we will then discuss how to make your model an Intranet plan:

- architects
- services

- architectures
- a centralized model (case one)
- a decentralized model (case two)

What You Will Need

Deconstructing Your Environment

Before we launch into some specifics on *modeling* your information environment, let's examine why it's important. A growing host of writers and pundits have trumpeted the arrival of the "Information Age." While many agree that there is something to this notion, there is a great deal of disagreement as to what this something really is.

All but the most core user technologies (for example, FTP and Telnet) are quite new and anything but immutable. To make matters more chaotic, and to quote from an old pop song, "we've only just begun." Despite this confusion, a few things are expressly clear. First, individuals and organizations are beginning to think of information as a primary resource, if not the primary resource, in their everyday life. Just as plastics are found in almost every nonedible product, information permeates every unit of every organization. Second, in a sense, information is "alive." Information moves, and when it flows properly, the organism, er, organization survives. If it doesn't, limbs atrophy and die. Information has a life span, sometimes long, often short. Finally, each instance of an informational element has a distinct context that affects its shape and scope. Whether you view a graphic, read someone's scribblings, or hear a piece of music, information is being transmitted from some source to you, and that context (graphical, textual, or aural) affects how you interpret and use it. Marshall MacLuhan captured this in his proclamation: "the medium is the message."

Lest these ideas seem pretentious, be apprised that (counting the likes of Microsoft, Netscape, Sun Microsystems, SGI, Oracle, Informix, and every specialized company listed in this book) the folks building the tools for your Intranet accept them as fact. Your Intranet cannot help but be affected by these principles.

Definition   A model *is an abstracted description of a system. Modeling is used in many design and engineering functions to demystify complex systems. An information model looks at the form and flow of focused and specific data sets.*

Given, then, that participation in the Information Age means that information can be viewed as a ubiquitous, organic, and contextual resource, let's begin building some conceptual tools of our own.

Model One: Informational Physics

Every piece of information in your company has a source. That source in this model takes one of three forms: an individual, a group, or everybody. Furthermore, every piece of information in your company should have a destination, which will take one of those same three forms. Finally, information will be refocused in some way, perhaps multiple times, between its source and destination.

Take, for example, e-mail, which invariably has a single source. E-mail mechanisms act as lenses for general interpersonal communications, focusing the flow of communication. Messages may be redirected through a mail list to a larger, perhaps global audience. More often than not they will go to another individual.

As you begin to examine the information needs of your organization, track how patterns of relationships are mimicked throughout. This information can influence your plans in several ways. Not surprisingly, the services controlled almost completely by the individual, such as e-mail, will cascade with greater chaos than those controlled by a large group. Some chaos is a good thing, as new, more natural lines of information flow are established. Other services are best managed on a few-to-few, or few-to-many basis. Each service you provide creates a specific focus, or lens, for the information. This affects, if nothing else, the scope of the audience. Some lenses, such as Web database applications, actually act as prisms, spraying information in more fluid, yet distinct patterns. Each service can also be seen to affect how the information is focused by virtue of its context, partially as a result of the implied permanence of the medium. By permanence I mean how long the information has value for its intended audience. For instance, if information is sent as an unformatted e-mail message, the receiver might assume that it is disposable information, to be read and discarded. If the information is sent by e-mail but the main content of the information is sent in a formatted attachment, the receiver would probably assume they are supposed to do something with the information; save, review, edit, or pass it on. If the information comes in an e-mail and links to a URL in a document management library or the Web, this information is intended to be kept for future reference and reuse.

Model Two: It's About Time

All information has a finite life span. Some information needs to live only briefly, while other information may need to last for years, if not decades. Most of your information will be impermanent. This, again, should be considered in light of your organization's needs with standards set to classify the permanence of various categories and classes of information.

E-mail is a great form of impermanent to semipermanent communication. It is generally terrible for organizing information for the long haul. It can be pressed into greater service, however, if your system includes a Document Management System (DMS) that can hold e-mail for messages of greater permanence (for example, agreements, workgroup proceedings, and archives).

Some information will be so time-sensitive that you'll reference it primarily by date. Database data, policy updates, code iterations, planning documents, and the like will all need special dating consideration. For example, preliminary requirements documents quickly lose their content relevance as the requirements of a project inevitably evolve, but they retain significance as a model for future preliminary requirements documents. A good DMS allows you to set the properties so documents automatically archive.

Model Three: Close to Home or Far and Away?

Information can be managed centrally or decentrally. To return to the issue of your tools, many applications you'll use in your Intranet are client/server based. This leads to the atomization of your environment as users have greater control over what they say, see, and hear. Many of the Web-page creation tools allow for a direct link to a live server. Many of the Web-server tools allow for source code control, access control, and revision dating and logging. The expectation is that you will release greater control of your information to individuals. Time and again these very enabling technologies excite the urge to publish individual ideas, team activities, to share information between departments, and so on. You have to decide how much distributed information management your organization can reasonably handle.

Centralization in this context means that your servers, whether dedicated to services or not, are managed by a small number of IT gatekeepers. It also means that the form and function of your Intranet is generally determined top-down and directed by a relatively focused group. Your model will probably include a mix of central and distributed services. The smaller the information foundation your organization already has, the more centralized you'll want to be at first. Devolution away from the center is likely over time and should be planned for when possible.

How to Control the Chaos

The Importance of Metaphor

Before we apply these models to your environment, we will examine one subtext contained in this book: the power of metaphor. Information can be understood as both a noun (a distinct data set) and a verb (the transference of data and meaning). Because Intranet systems are so complex, finding the right metaphor for your organization's Intranet can greatly aid in the education of your users.

Your information environment may now seem more complex or rich than it once appeared. You'll find that as you grow your Intranet new patterns of managing it will evolve. At first, however, recognize that no matter which tools you use, you're expecting your employees to learn entirely new systems. You can make use of metaphor by having your Intranet client access look and feel like the applications they're already used to. Many Web integration companies emphasize the process of internal branding, whereby your external corporate image is matched by your Intranet systems. Just as in advertising, impressions, impressions, impressions help link an abstract concept to a concrete product or service. The system you are creating will be adopted more readily by your users if, in your training programs and systems, you provide a metaphor that fits your current corporate culture, or the culture you want to foster in your organism, er, organization.

In the Beginning . . .

The first part of the process is an examination of your company's existing information model. How much is your organization tied to paper? How about word processing and spreadsheets? You probably already have e-mail and file sharing. How extensively are these resources used? About the only way to gather this view of your existing environment is through discussion with, or survey of, department or group heads. At the same time, you should commit a certain number of individuals to the task of analyzing the data and creating a service plan.

This group should look at all of the options relevant to your corporation. First, plan for services that best fit your existing management strategies and workflow needs, but even the first rollout of the system should contain examples of as many future services as possible.

Once the services plan is ready, implementation plans and actions should be made by a larger number of even more specialized teams. These teams should always move forward in as coordinated a direction as possible, but a large group of services will not allow for complete concurrence. Still, use as many overlapping services as possible.

We'll take each of these steps in turn and examine how they can apply to two specific situations.

Architects

In reading this book you are taking the step of educating yourself on the possible elements of your systems and, by taking advantage of the resources listed in each chapter, the pros and cons of different brands of client/server system software. Even in a small organization you will need a team of internal experts to really get a hold on your current and future needs.

How you define the word *expert* will almost certainly change as you progress. On the one hand you want organizational specialists, people who know the day-to-day processes of your various groups and departments. These people know the reality of your existing communication and information patterns. On the other hand you will probably want technical specialists, too. Members of your IT staff, especially managerial representatives, can appreciate the hardware and software infrastructure needs as they are identified. You will probably want the involvement of your communications staff, perhaps in the form of a technical or copywriter. A human resources representative could be helpful because this department already deals with categorization and flow of larger volumes of information. Also, graphic and interface designers can help shape the look and feel of your systems.

An important trait in these people is their willingness to explore new technologies. You want people who are capable of self-education. You're looking for a team of "fiddlers" who have well-developed problem-solving skills. They will, either by enforcement of corporate standards or as educators and advisors, make your Intranet succeed or fail. Although absolute consensus may be impossible, the goal throughout the process is to establish a universally appropriate service base.

Finally, a few members of your team should be true generalists. Every Web has its own weft and weave, and generalists, or those who can see across a narrow set of functions and systems to find synergy, can help you integrate your systems in dynamic and cost-saving ways.

Services

It's easy to see how the word *Web* came into its contemporary usage. Each service can be seen as an information nexus with links. Some services encircle others in increasingly larger and more comprehensive spheres, while others simply bind information nodes in one or more ways.

E-Mail

E-mail, as seen in our previous examples, is at the heart of almost any Intranet. E-mail still contributes a large chunk of the packets transmitted on any network because it is so flexible and easy to use. It is great for short, directed, unformatted messages. Groups can be small or large in scope depending on the universality of the subject at hand. Lists can be set up decentrally (for example, majordomo or other subscription-based lists) or centrally (administered lists). One or more e-mail lists can be used immediately to aid communication between your Intranet team members and, if possible, the extracts of the group's work held for posterity or public review. E-mail tends to be fired off more frequently than any other form of messaging. As volume builds most people will lose track of, or simply delete, most messages. Consequently, e-mail should not be relied upon for institutional memory, and it's crucial to implement advanced e-mail filtering, list-archiving, or a flexible DMS with easy importing capabilities.

Newsgroups

Newsgroups represent an equally chaotic but useful one-to-many tool for unformatted documents. You can have your group find existing USENET newsgroups that contain information useful to your company, and you can have them establish new groups to facilitate communication for your Intranet team in the planning stages and beyond. The utility of USENET can degrade over time for the same reasons as FTP, namely that the larger the volume, the more difficult it is for users to find the answers they want. As mentioned previously, some chaos can be a good way of identifying new synergy, so access to newsgroups generally adds value for little cost.

FTP

FTP is another quick win for your Intranet. FTP works best as a few-to-many tool, and its utility decreases if it becomes a many-to-many environment (although a good search engine will help larger collections hold their value). FTP services should be as organized as possible. This encompasses hardware considerations (how much disk space will your company afford to the task, and where will such space be located); file compartmentalization (what kind of hierarchies will you use, and who will monitor and grow them), and usage guidelines (will they include personal space, and what kinds of files are appropriate). You may decide to make some things available via FTP, such as standards, architectural guidelines, policies regarding security and usage, and your image base and branding requirements. Even if another service (such as the traditional Web) becomes the central clearinghouse, an instructional README file should always be placed in your FTP directories to demonstrate the form and function of this common space to the wider audience. Client tools and utilities can also be efficiently distributed with this service.

Telnet

Telnet only works well as a one-to-few resource. It is a direct command-line access to other machines, whether they be clients or, more likely, servers. If your enterprise has a sizable IT staff, Telnet is probably, along with FTP and e-mail, already being used by your technical staff. There may be some utility for nontechnical gatekeepers to have Telnet access depending upon your usage of *staging areas* or scripts in your Intranet architecture. For example, it may the best way for Web site managers to change passwords, but too much Telnet access is both a chore to administrate, a security risk, and a disproportional expense as a means of tying together services.

Definition   Staging areas *are places where users can put files for review and editing prior to making them available to a larger audience.*

Document Management Systems (DMS)

Document pools handled via DMS are a great way to manage larger volumes of information that require a longer period of permanence. This will be especially true for larger groups that are already entrenched in electronic information production. Word processing documents, spreadsheets, CAD plans, and many more forms of digital data can be organized efficiently and tracked with revision dating and control. Access can be granted along functional, departmental, or project lines. Using a DMS, however, requires greater organizational commitments than do other services. One commitment is financial. The cost of a truly powerful DMS is higher than that of other services. The other cost is personnel. You need people to learn the ins and outs of configuration and administration. This usually means that a small group will filter documents through the DMS to a larger audience. For really huge collections, multiple dedicated servers and a large staff are probably required, which will allow for a many-to-many model.

SGML

SGML is well positioned as a few-to-few, centralized power tool or service. SGML editors are getting more user friendly, but creating a DTD is still a complex task. For example, specialized teams can make technical manuals more permanent by allowing information to be distributed in its native, flexible SGML form to equally specialized end users, or patterned off to its smaller nephew HTML for distribution to a larger audience. Because SGML is an international standard it may be the prescribed way documents are distributed between vendors. The costs of SGML editors and browsers, not to mention the need for its own specialists, make it a more viable solution for small- to mid-size collections that need specific, consistent formatting, and that have a significant legacy value.

Simple Webs

Web technologies get more and more powerful all the time and represent one of the best balances between low cost and high gain for a large group of people. Browsers are cheap or free and usually encompass access to other universal services such as e-mail, FTP, and USENET. More and more client/server packages allow for revision control and logging. As entry-level servers decrease in price, it is increasingly feasible to use the Web for decentralized publishing. In contrast, high-end servers are generally flexible and powerful enough to allow for centralization. The other advantage to basic Web serving is the ease of HTML production. Whether WYSIWYG or not, publishing tools are easy to learn, and you'll probably find that people will rapidly push expansion of the document base. Again, your Intranet group will want to publish standards and policies as soon as your Web is launched. Web publishing is generally used for information of short to medium shelf life. The medium is not particularly well suited for more permanent data because HTML changes rapidly and tends to outmode itself quickly. Also the Web acquires layers that can make documents more difficult to find as time passes, a problem addressed by using search engines.

Web Applications

Web applications usually take one of two forms: mechanisms (usually scripts) that assist in the maintenance of a larger Web site, or closely focused systems that tap into other services, such as forms that become e-mail or faxes. In most cases Web applications work best in a few-to-few arrangement, where smaller groups act as gatekeepers, but they can work in a many-to-few arrangement, where a larger number of sources funnel information to a smaller audience. An example of this is a series of Web forms that allow your entire enterprise to request supplies from a central or departmental purchasing staff. Some basic applications, such as scripts that take form entries and generate e-mail, can be written with enough flexibility and simplicity to allow less technical users to apply them. Web applications are often less flexible and more costly (although not always tremendously so) than traditional HTML because they require the assistance of one or more programmers. They also tend to be more centralized, with their focus defined by a control group.

Web Database Applications

Database applications help you manage the flow of larger sets of information to larger audiences. Information from many sources is immediately made accessible to a variety of destinations. The destination can change page by page, depending on the needs of the audience. While costs are decreasing, adoption of these technologies is still the most expensive if your enterprise does not have any existing Web-ready databases. Legacy databases, however, can be made Web-ready for about the same cost as more simple Web applications because your organization already has some information model to draw on. Data is impermanent because more data is accumulated all the time, and permanent because tools abound for data archiving and mining. Costs issues will almost certainly place this service in a centralized mode.

Meta-Services

There is also a class of services, perhaps even meta-services, that are at once more broad in their conceptual model, but more precise in their application within any of the aforementioned services. While these meta-services have been examined in some detail in earlier chapters, let's take a look at three special kinds: search engines, revision control, and log files.

Search Engines Intranets usually grow into information magnets. E-mail already has widespread use; shared file systems will accumulate a greater number and class of files; Webs will accrete layers of organization as well as pages; and data keeps on keepin' on. Of primary importance for many of these services is a search engine meta-service. Search engines can take a variety of forms. A few are limited to creating indexes of files by type. Document Management Systems and some lower-level file tracking systems allow for this kind of search. One of the great facilities found in more powerful DMS tools is the ability to narrow the search by meta-information, and some even allow you to search for documents that contain the information your users are looking for. Most database applications can be built with broad search capabilities, although global search capabilities will be difficult to provide as data has different meaning in different contexts. Providing search tools to your users will help as your Intranet grows in breadth and depth.

A great number of content-based search tools exist for static Web pages, and these tools can help make larger collections of HTML documents easier to manage. Web-based search engines, such as Lycos, generally work by having specialized programs (known as agents, crawlers, or spiders) prowl across sites and create a database of links. This database is the source that is actually searched. Additionally, most search engines allow you to submit URLs in the event the spider hasn't found it yet. Table 11.1 contains some valuable search engine resources to help you start exploring these capabilities.

Another Web-based solution is a catalog-based search tool. The best example of this is Yahoo. Yahoo gives you a table of contents view where you can drill down in a category, find subcategories to define your interest, and likely find a manageable set of sites and pages to meet your needs. Typically, cataloging engines require a fair amount of labor-intensive work, as people are required to categorize and validate the sites. However, you could make use of invisible comments in your HTML or use meta tags to have your authors self-categorize their sites.

URL	What You Will Find There
http://www.lycos.com	Lycos
http://www.hamline.edu/library/ links/search.html	Comparative analysis of search engines
http://www.digitalcafe.com/ ~webmaster/set01.html	Reference for system integration of search tools
http://www.excite.com/?bam/	Excite
http://www.yahoo.com	Yahoo

Table 11.1

Search Engines

Then your Web searching spider could build a catalog database along with your searching database; smart, eh?

Revision control Revision control is another great meta-service. Even if your basic approach is to keep things centrally managed, a great many people will impact a large number of documents and chunks of information. Source Code Control Systems (SCCS) can be used with almost every one of your services, with basic FTP being a definitive exception. E-mail and newsgroups come somewhat version-controlled as each message has a nearly unique imprimatur (that is, FROM, TO, and DATE tags). Higher-level services will benefit from more rigid version control. Most major Web servers, or at least those being positioned for heavy Intranet use, have built-in Source Control filters. Database Management Systems also tend to have built-in control systems. DTDs can be built with author and date tracking elements. Any code your IT or programming staff creates should be held in an SCCS. Even if you adopt a very decentralized approach and have few person-based gatekeepers, Source Code Control Systems will help everyone by tracking the movement and growth of particular nodes in your Web, and protecting against problems of overwritten or overlooked (outdated) information.

The Log File One last meta-service worth noting is our old friend, the log file. Each service will probably have its own logging facilities. Some high-end hardware servers can take advantage of log files to balance loads, and scripts can be written to notify appropriate individuals of certain activities tracked in a log file. More often than not, though, log files will need to be reviewed, either in native or summary form, by members of your Intranet team to help you identify which of your servers, as well as your services, are being used more or less frequently. Statistics applications, discussed in Chapter 7, access log files to deliver valuable information to help you evolve your Web to best meet your Intranet document management needs.

Table 11.2 summarizes the characteristics of each service we've discussed.

Service	Source	Destination	Permanence	Centralization
E-mail*	One	One	Impermanent	Decentralized
E-mail Lists	One	Few/many	Impermanent	Centralized
Majordomo	One	Few/many	Impermanent	Decentralized
Newsgroups	One	Few/many	Impermanent	Either
FTP	Few/many	Few/many	Impermanent	Centralized
Telnet	Few	Few	Impermanent	Centralized
DMS	Few/many	Few/many	Permanent	Centralized
SGML	Few	Few/many	Permanent	Either
Web	Few/many	Many	Impermanent	Either
Web Apps	Few/many	Few	Permanent	Centralized
Web dB	Many	Many	Permanent	Centralized

Table 11.2

Services in an Information Model

*E-mail can be made more permanent with tight integration with other services.

Architecture

Now that your Intranet team has examined the range of possible services, they are prepared to implement a plan. This assumes that you've already developed your basic information model and have identified the physical infrastructure and equipment needs for your system.

Definition *The word* architecture *in Intranet terms includes your information model, equipment arrangement, range of services, and the means, whether human or digital, of getting information in and out of those services.*

The next step is to see where you can combine some of the services you've selected. As noted previously, the more powerful Web browsers now allow for client access to e-mail and FTP, as well as older services such as gopher. This is an example of the kind of synergy your team might identify. Others might include SGML to HTML, HTML to SGML, HTML to DMS, existing TCP/IP applications on the Web, and so on. Much of this will depend on the specific tools you select from specific vendors.

As you may have inferred from this book, you will want to select one of your services as the core of your system. Generally speaking this will be your Web, by virtue of its simple publishing facilities, low cost of entry, ability to leverage information out on the big "I" (Internet), be the platform-independent interface to Document Management Systems, plug in universal viewers, and its simplicity for users. Make sure it contains all of your structural documents, technical or branding standards, usage rules, help files, and communication pipes to appropriate advisors and experts. This way everyone in your enterprise will know exactly where to go to find answers to their most fundamental questions.

The next step is to implement the most basic of your services. This will probably be some combination of e-mail, USENET, FTP, and a small Web. These basic services will help your core Intranet team learn the ins and outs of the technologies, communicate more readily about the shape and direction of your efforts, and demonstrate your organizational commitment to future technologies. Again, this initial release should contain all of your architectural documents, in progress or otherwise. This first launch will help your team test the assumptions made in the model, fix any incongruities, and plan for the more advanced (and costly) systems.

This initial release will also help you plan how general users will transmit their information. Will you have Web interfaces for information? Will you use staging areas where people can examine their work before its release to the world? Will you use FTP as a dumping ground for information? What kinds of scripts and macros can your team build to help less technical users? Who, if anyone, will review these materials?

Of particular note at this point is the issue of staging areas and site mirroring. Again, a staging area is a system where your users have the opportunity to preview and change any work prior to public release. You can help control access by giving users write privileges in staging areas and only your gatekeepers write privileges in public areas. Likewise, you can assign passwords to staging areas so a selected few can view incomplete documents before they become "prime time." Again, this shows how your security policies dovetail with your usage policies. This is one form of site-mirroring. For a Web site, this means running two servers for each public site, one for staging and testing, the other for public access.

A *mirrored site* is a separate server (usually, but not always, on a separate computer), including both hardware and software, located in a different location than the primary server. Site mirroring can have benefits beyond error and spell checking. If your organization is larger and has offices in different locations, having your public sites mirrored locally will improve general performance, so users can go to the least busy server (usually the server closest in geography). If you go this route, you can create scripts to propagate the basic site to your mirror sites as things are updated.

Definition   A mirrored site *is a separate server, including both hardware and software, located in a different location than the primary server.*

A test release will help you identify archival needs for your system. How much disk space is required? How often will backups take place? Will archival space be available to some, many, or will it simply sit as a backup? Will any database data be extracted and taken out of rotation? Who decides when information is outdated, and what criteria exist for determining legacy value? These are key questions your team should address prior to a global release point and are again relevant to either management mode.

Next, you should release your initial system to a wider audience and begin implementing the higher-end services (which services depends on those you select based upon your revised model). Again, you should have your core team (which may now be several teams working on specific elements) test each system independent of any others, and then look for synergy.

Finally, release the more powerful systems to your enterprise. Then start anew. Each step, from modeling, to team building, to review, release, integration, and so on, should be repeated for each phase. Both centrally and decentrally managed systems will need this process, with the only difference being the number and focus of the teams involved and how enterprise-wide standards will be agreed to and enforced. This summary has not emphasized the need for training. Keep in mind, however, the distinct opportunities and pitfalls of each service as described in other chapters and plan for extensive training of every individual who will come into contact with your Intranet.

Case One: A Centralized Model

One West Coast transportation think tank has decided upon a very centralized model. They have one service that handles all of their e-mail, FTP, HTML, and Web applications, and this server is managed by a contract Web development company. They decided to handle things this way to save costs on the server administration and infrastructure.

The core of their system is their Web application environment. They have online forms that funnel most requests straight into the published Web. Other, more data-intensive information is handled through an off-line database. Only 7.5 percent of the people in this organization have the authority to tag most information for publication (with representatives from corporate relations and media services being these primary gatekeepers). This information is transmitted via e-mail or FTP to the developers, who then filter it through more than 50 PERL and C scripts. The filtering process generates a global-search capability for all of their content. They have one decentralized component to their system that allows nonemployee members of the group to update their profiles, with these additions and changes still filtered through the developer.

This model works and is somewhat cost-efficient. Greater efficiencies could be gained if their database technologies were upgraded for direct publishing. Other efficiencies might be gained from a DMS because the amount of paper generated is large and changes fairly regularly.

Case Two: A Decentralized Model

A more open approach comes to us from Silicon Graphics, Inc., a well-known case history appropriately touted by publications for their Web-technical innovation. The core system is known as "Silicon Junction," again an HTML Web where data is sliced in a variety of formats based on user function, division affiliation, date, and other categories. The interface allows users to customize their views based upon the kind of information they generally need. This junction also includes daily corporate communications, hot items, top art, and is refreshed several times a day.

At first SGI was completely decentralized, where almost every workstation was a server. As the number of URLs increased to nearly 500,000 (!!!) the volunteer system started to break down, and the utility of their system decreased. The solution was to put extremely powerful search engines and cataloging agents in place.

SGI also has distributed e-mail lists (both subscription and not), distributed FTP areas, Web dB tools, and much, much more. The synergy that has developed from this system has far outweighed any cost issues stemming from their commitment to ongoing equipment upgrades and training.

Eyes on the Road Ahead

As has been stated in almost every chapter in this book, these technologies change often. Your team should always be on the lookout for new technologies and how they can help get information out to your entire organization. We're not too far away, for example, from point-and-click dB application builders. Java-based tools, such as those being developed by the likes of Marimba (`http://www.marimba.com`), will help organizations notify users when content or code has changed and automatically update their views and tools. And you never know when one of your organization's tools might be useful to the Intranet world at large and your services become products!

Summary

How your organization views information in any form will affect the structure and usability of your Intranet, not to mention its costs and its returns. Spend the time to devise a clear model, develop specific goals and a timeline, leave room to grow, and charge a team of people with the task of asking, "What next?" Look for ways in which the flow of the right piece of information at the right time in the right manner will enhance the efficiency of your operations, and lower the likelihood that you will be reduced to herding cats.

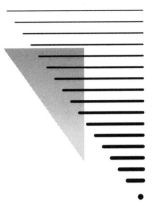

APPENDIX A
Resource Listings

Introduction

URL	What You Can Find There
http://www.sun.com/	Sun hardware
http://www.hp.com/	HP hardware
http://www.ncsa.uiuc.edu/SDG/ SDGFlier/SDGHowToObtain.html	NCSA software
http://home.netscape.com/	Netscape software
http://www.apache.org/	Apache software
http://www.sgi.com/	SGI hardware

Chapter 2

URL	What You Can Find There
http://www.datawatch.com	Virex Disinfectant, widely distributed freeware, Mac O/S
http://www.microsoft.com	Microsoft AntiVirus Windows 3.11/ 95/NT
http://www.symantec.com	Norton AntiVirus Windows 3.11/ 95/NT
http://www.drsolomon.com	Dr. Solomon's ToolKit Virus Scan, widely distributed freeware, OS/2
http://www.cyber.com	Vfind, UNIX (most variants)

http://www.cert.org	Computer Emergency Response Team (CERT)
http://www.ncsa.com	National Computer Security Association
http://www.genome.wi.mit.edu	Strong body of content regarding O/S-specific security issues
http://www.cerf.net/~paulp/cgi	More information on specific language vulnerabilities
http://www.microsoft.com	Some basic firewall programs for Mac O/S, Windows 95/NT, Catapult Proxy Server
http://www.raptor.com	Some basic firewall programs for Windows 95/NT HP-UX BSD Unix Eagle
http://www.checkpoint.com	Some basic firewall programs for Solaris SunScreen SPF-100 Firewall 1
http://www.zeuros.co.uk/firewall	Firewall software programs; detailed summary of available packages
http://www.verisign.com http://www.rsa.com	Two of the largest and most trusted certification authorities in the United States

Chapter 3—URLs

URL	What You Can Find There
http://www.cs.columbia.edu/~hauben/ papers/nwg.txt	"Behind the Net: The Untold History of the ARPANET," Michael Hauben
http://www.columbia.edu/~rh120/ ch106.x07	"Behind the Net: The Untold History of the ARPANET" and "Computer Science," another chapter by Michael Hauben on the same subject (but these are not linked)

http://www.columbia.edu/~rh120/ch106.x03	"The Social Forces Behind the Development of USENET," another chapter by Michael Hauben
http://www.cs.unca.edu/~davidson/history.html	"History of the Internet," by Bruce Sterling
http://www.qualcomm.com/	Eudora
http://home.netscape.com/	Netscape
http://www.roma2.infn.it/infn/ftp-interface.html	List of anonymous FTP sites
http://www.ipswitch.com/	Order WS FTP
http://www.apache.org	Apache
http://www.oracle.com/	Oracle WebServer
http://home.netscape.com/	Netscape Enterprise Server
http://home.netscape.com/	Netscape Fast Track Server
http://www.microsoft.com/	Microsoft Internet Information Server
http://java.sun.com/	Jeeves
http://home.netscape.com/	Netscape Navigator
http://home.netscape.com/	Netscape Navigator Gold
http://www.microsoft.com/	Microsoft Internet Explorer
http://www.sun.com/	HotJava

Chapter 3—Recommended Books

Book	Topic
Douglas E. Comer and David L. Steven, *Internetworking with TCP/IP*, vols. 1–3, Prentice Hall	TCP/IP
W. Richard Stevens and Gary R. Wright, *TCP/IP Illustrated*, vols. 1 and 2, Addison-Wesley	TCP/IP
Craig Hunt, *TCP/IP Network Administration*, O'Reilly & Associates, Inc.	TCP/IP

Bryan Costales, with Eric Allman and Neil Rickert,   SMTP
sendmail, O'Reilly & Associates, Inc.

Cricket Liu, Jerry Peek, Russ Jones, Bryan Buus,   HTTP, FTP, List Servers, Gopher
and Adrian Nye, *Managing Information Services*,
O'Reilly & Associates, Inc.

Susan Estrada, *Connecting to the Internet*,   Internet connections
O'Reilly & Associates, Inc.

Peter van der Linden, *Just Java*, Prentice Hall   Java

Chapter 3—RFC Protocol Table

RFC number	Title
768	User Datagram Protocol
791	The Internet Protocol
793	Transmission Control Protocol
821	Simple Mail Transport Protocol
959	File Transfer Protocol
1460	Post Office Protocol, Version 3

Chapter 3—Newsnet Categories and Topics

Category	Topic
comp	Computers and computer science
sci	Sciences other than computer science
news	The Newsnet itself or general interest
rec	Recreation activities
soc	Social topics
talk	Subjects that promote debate (politics and religion
misc	Subject that do not fit into other categories

Chapter 4

URL	What You Can Find There
www.collaborate.com/intranet.html	Analysis by Collaboration Strategies of how major corporations are leveraging networks and collaborative software for competitive advantage
http://www.internetdatabase.com	The Internet Resources Database guide to information, including shareware, available on the Internet

Chapter 5

URL	What You Can Find There
http://www.ncsa.uiuc.edu/General/Internet/WWW/HTMLPrimer.html	"A Beginner's Guide to HTML"
http://www.pcweek.com/eamonn/crash_course.html	Crash course on writing documents for the Web
http://werbach.com/barebones	"The Barebones Guide to HTML"
http://www.hwg.org	The HTML Writers Guild
http://www.bannan.com	MAILTO:joan@bannan.com
http://www.irs.ustreas.gov/prod/	IRS home page
http://www.pearson-plc.com	Pearson—Addison Wesley Longman's parent company
http://www.brooknorth.com/htmlpro2.html	HTML Assistant Pro
http://www.sausage.com	Hot Dog
http://204.91.49.11/hteds.html	Public HTML editors
http://www.columbia.edu/~rk35/www/editors.html	Suggested editors
HTTP://www.infoaccess.com	HTML Transit
http://rs712b.gsfc.nasa.gov/704/dgd/xl2html.html	Tips on converting graphic images

Chapter 6

URL	What You Can Find There
http://www.w3.orgas	World Wide Web Consortium
http://home.netscape.com/assist/net_sites/frame_syntax.html	Netscape's help pages Frames tutorial
http://www.newbie.net/frames/index.html	"The Netscape Frames Tutorial" by Charlton Douglas Rose
http://www.physics.iastate.edu/numaps/96/days/04/frames2.html	Sample code from FRAMES AND ANCHORS - NUMAPS96
http://ucunix.san.uc.edu/~solkode/w3guide/frames.html	"All about Frames" by Dave Solko
http://www.websight.com/current/usecool/usecool.html	Two opinions about frames. One says no the other says "Cool."
http://www.sgi.com/	Cosmo Color Web page
http://wwwvoice.com/hatefrm.html	I Hate Frames Club
http://www.ummed.edu:8000/pub/i/ijosh/frames/	Why frames suck
http://www.xmission.com/~mgm/gif	"Great GIF licensing controversy"
http://boutell.com/boutell/png	The PNG effort is an open standard, created by research efforts and critiqued openly in the Internet Engineering Task Force (IETF).
http://www.matisse.net/files/formats.html	A great list of general information about all file formats found on the Internet
http://www.stars.com/Vlib/Providers/Images_and_Icons.html	Resources for Web development including a library of graphic images
http://www.pixelsite.com/	Pixelsite offers a myriad of images and clip art and the ability to modify your images on the fly
http://innovate.sgi.com/listings/summarysearch.CGI/gif	Innovate Online! - another great Silicon Graphics site, creates a virtual Web development environment; also has a place to exchange tools, content, and documentation with other members
http://www.sesd.stsci.edu/latex2html/manual/node29.html	Good definition and step-by-step how-to about image maps

http://www.w3.org/pub/WWW/Daemon/User/CGI/HTImageDoc.html	W3C HTTPD clickable image support for image maps
http://hoohoo.ncsa.uiuc.edu/docs/tutorials/imagemapping.html	NCSA Imagemap Tutorial
http://www.ecaetc.ohio state.edu/tc/nit/	MAP THIS home page for image maps
http://www.ncsa.uiuc.edu/Edu/MMM/MacMapMaker.html#CanDo	Instructions for MacUsers for image maps
http://netware.novell.co.jp/img4.htm	Image map scripts test page
http://www.magi.com/~kk//tbi.html	Creating transparent background images, freeware
http://members.aol.com/htmlguru/transparent_images.html	FREE WEB TOOLS Transparent Background Images
http://www.best.com/~adamb/GIFpage.html	The Transparent/Interlaced GIF Resource Page
http://www.mit.edu:8001/people/nocturne/transparent.html	"Transparency, What Is It?" About making the background of your GIF transparent with the GIF89 file extension.
http://www.globalx.net/kerry/tbi.html	Step-by-step how-to for transparent images
http://www.mccannas.com/	A beautiful, free art Web site, with excellent Photoshop tips to boot
http://www.webdiner.com/annexc/gif89/snowstpl.htm	Animated GIFs
http://www.philips.com/	Slow-loading graphics workaround example
http://www.gamelan.com	More about Java and JavaScript and resources
http://www.cybes.com/expsign.html	Time dissolving "new" GIF
http://members.aol.com/sportfan69/Helpme.html	Example of most of the gimmicks discussed in this chapter
http://www.brailler.com/	Links for visually impaired

Chapter 7

URL	What You Can Find There
http://www.cbu.edu/~ewelch/Unixhelp/tasks_ftp2.html#ftp2	Transferring files using FTP
http://www.cbu.edu/~ewelch/Unixhelp/tasks_ftp2.1.1.html	List of FTP commands
http://www.dee.uc.pt/UnixHelp/tasks_ftp2.1.3.html	List of useful FTP commands
http://www.csra.net/junodj/ws_ftp32.htm	Download WS_FTP
http://freenet.vcu.edu/help/file_maint/ftp.html	FTP commands and tutorial
http://www.bazaarsuite.com/	Bazaar Analyzer: Java-based platform independent; Stats Collection Application
http://www.webtrends.com/	Web Trends is compatible with any Web server that supports the Common or Combined Log Format; Stats Collection Application
http://www.marketwave.com/	Hit list: Designed for UNIX and NT servers
http://www.CQMInc.com/webtrack/webtrack.htm	Web Tracker: Looks like it only does NT, not sure if it does UNIX. Stats Collection Application
http://www.fagg.uni-lj.si/cgi-bin/vsl-front	"JPEGview" in the Virtual Shareware Library in Slovenia
http://www.openmarket.com/omi/products/webreport.html	Broken link finding tool
http://home.netscape.com/assist/net_sites/	Expert advice on "Creating Net Sites"
http://www.bannan.com/Intranet-Doc-Mgt/Appendices/Resource.htm	Authors/Web publishers online glossary
http://home.netscape.com/eng/mozilla/3.0/handbook/	Netscape handbook
http://www.zdnet.com/anchordesk/story/story_389.html	Example of an animated GIF
http://home.highway.or.jp/syou-/hp/java-s1.htm	JavaScript pushing information

Chapter 7—Very Common Web-head FTP Commands and Their Purpose

FTP Command	What It Does
cd (change directory)	Change to whatever directory you would like to send files to
lcd (local change directory)	Change to the directory on your local host where all the cool HTML and GIF files you have created and tested are anxiously waiting for their public appearance
binary	Send the next files in binary exchange. I want to put up graphics that often get the hiccups on the way if they are sent in the default format, ASCII, and come out a mere portion of their original form when they reach the server
ASCII	Send the next files in ASCII format. The best way to send HTML files is in ASCII format. The FTP client I use defaults to ASCII when it opens.
put	Followed by the filename
Get	The reverse of put

Chapter 8

URL	What You Can Find There
http://www.netscape.com/eng/mozilla/2.0/handbook/javascript.index.html	Information and manuals for JavaScript
http://www.illustra.com	Illustra Web Datablade (major SQL compliant Database)
http://www.informix.com	Informix Online Database Datablade (major SQL compliant database)
http://www.microsoft.com	Microsoft SQL Server Datablade (major SQL compliant database)

http://www.oracle.com	Oracle PowerBuilder/Oracle DB Datablade (major SQL compliant database)
http://www.sybase.com	Sybase Server Datablade (major SQL compliant database)

Chapter 9

URL	**What You Can Find There**
http://www.aiim.org/dma/	Document Management Industry Groups
http://www.dclab.com	Data Conversion Labs (DCL)

Chapter 10

URL	**What You Can Find There**
http://gopher.sil.org/sgml/sgml.html	Robin Cover's *The SGML Web Page*
http://etext.virginia.edu/etext/sgml.html	Text Encoding Initiative's *A Gentle Introduction to SGML*
http://www.ora.com/davenport/README.html	DocBook—among the most frequently used DTDs for general purpose technical publishing
http://gopher.sil.org/sgml/sgml.html	A public domain reference application called Jade, which will output RTF (Microsoft Word format) from an SGML style sheet
http://www.oclc.org/fred	FRED, from OCLC, offers an alternate or perhaps complementary way to approach DTD design
http://gopher.sil.org/sgml/sgml.html	A public domain program, sgrep, does this and also has SGML-structured search facilities
http://www.jclark.com/sp/index.htm	The most recent and complete parser, SP, is written in C++ and was expressly designed by its author, James Clark, to be readily integrated into applications.

| http://www.techno.com | A commercial HyTime engine implemented by TechnoTeacher |

Chapter 11

URL	What You Can Find There
http://www.lycos.com	Lycos
http://www.hamline.edu/library/links/ search.html	Comparative analysis of search engines
http://www.digitalcafe.com/ ~webmaster/set01.html	Reference for system integration of search tools
http://www.excite.com/?bam/	Excite
http://www.yahoo.com	Yahoo
http://www.marimba.com	Marimba—Java-based tool, point-and-click application, and dB application builders

APPENDIX B
Glossary

ACK. An acknowledgment packet telling the source computer that the destination computer has received the message packet.

Alias. A duplicate hostname for a computer.

Animated GIFs. A bunch of standard gifs, grouped together in a single file with some instructions on time delay, looping, and so forth. Think of it as single-cell animation for the Web. The end result is that your users experience a short animation.

Architecture. In Intranet terms, includes your information model, equipment arrangement, range of services, and your means, whether human or digital, of getting information in and out of those services.

Asynchronous Transfer Mode (ATM). Another high performance network system approach that allows packets to be sent via disparate lines at disparate times. Each packet can then attempt to find the most efficient route at any given moment in time.

ASCII (American Standard Code for Information Interchange).

Attributes. Information that may be provided about elements in addition to the element name and its content.

Bandwidth. The available amount of network fiber. Effective bandwidth is the measure of how much is available.

Bidirectional hyperlink. A hyperlink where both ends are both sources and destinations.

Binary. The basic numbering system for calculations, codes, and data in all computers, consisting only of the digits 0 and 1, in contrast to the 10-digit decimal system.

Bounced. An e-mail message that is returned to you if it cannot be delivered for some reason. This is one reason why having a correct return address is important.

BTW (by the way). A common Internet acronym.

C. Compiled procedural language. Compiled programs are turned into object code (not to be confused with object-oriented), linked to related libraries, and are then ready to run at any time.

Cache. A designated area of hard-disk or memory which holds commonly referenced information.

CALS (Continuous Acquisition and Life Cycle Support). A large U.S. Department of Defense program to, among other things, use electronic information systems technology to reduce procurement and maintenance costs of weapons systems. SGML is one of the key components in the CALS initiative. CALS helped to stimulate the growth of the SGML industry and also supported the development of several key reference standards in areas such as technical publications, tables, and interactive electronic technical manuals.

Chaos. A state of apparent cattywompus. Choatic systems are not really random, but are sufficiently complex as to appear so. Most chaotic systems have their own rhyme and reason, which may seem inscrutable.

Character set. The mapping of computer codes to a set of symbols such as letters and punctuation. Japanese and English, for example, use different character sets, although an attempt is underway to establish a single character set, known as Unicode, for all languages.

Check-in/check out. Enables collaborative authoring by allowing only one person at a time to work on a document (check-out). When a document is checked in, the repository is updated and the document may be checked out by another author. In an SGML system check-in/ check-out is implemented at the document component level, so it is possible for authors to work on different parts of the same document.

Checksum. A mathematical method to ensure that data that has been transmitted has not been changed by the transmission.

Chunking. Breaking a document into smaller documents. This is a bandwidth-friendly, not to mention user-friendly, way to present information.

Client. A system that accesses data from another primary system.

Collaborative authoring. The creation of information collaboratively; multiple authors working on a single document, possibly simultaneously.

Common Gateway Interface (CGI). Standard mechanism for holding and manipulating variables in a Web application.

Content model. In an SGML element definition, the content for that element including children and textual or nontextual (for example, graphical) data. The content model is based on regular expression syntax, which permits great flexibility and conciseness in stating all possible permissible combinations of child elements and data.

Digital Certification. The process of trusted third-party electronic verification of an organization's identity.

Distribution lists. Electronic version of traditional mailing lists.

DNS (Domain Name Service). A client/server process for acquiring the IP address that belongs to a hostname.

Document. A word processing file, spreadsheet, project management schedule, graphics file, CAD or engineering drawing, paper scanned as an image, slideshow presentation, audio, video, or any similar item (use your imagination) that can be contained in an electronic file.

Document analysis. A branch of voodoo that has the development of DTDs as its primary objective.

Document management. A systematic method for storing, locating, and keeping track of information. Key characteristics are the ability to manage information, to collaborate when creating information, to distribute the information, and to allow secure access to the greatest number of people.

Document Type Definition (DTD). A formal statement of the encoding requirements for a particular class or type of SGML documents.

Down-translation. Translation of documents from structurally rich and generalized SGML format to an application-specific format such as HTML or PDF.

DSSSL (pronounced *dis-ul*, Document Style, Semantic, and Specification Language). A companion standard to SGML for the system-independent specification of formatting and general transformation of documents.

Dumb terminal. Interfaces that access mainframes and consist of a monitor and keyboard only, without any local storage or processing power.

Element. A named container for a logical portion of a document (for example, chapters, sections, tables, lists, and paragraphs).

E-mail (electronic mail). A method of sending mail to someone over the Internet.

Encryption. The masking of information, usually through sophisticated mathematical algorithms.

Ethernet. A particular physical network system that combines high-bandwidth fiber optics (from 1.45 to 100 megabytes per second) with special send and receive hardware. Ethernet is used in a variety of network topologies.

Firewalls. Software- and/or hardware-based systems that allow for a high degree of access control and logging of network activity.

FPT (File Transfer Protocol). Allows users to send and receive certain files from one computer to another on the Internet. (See also TCP/IP.)

GIF (Graphic Interchange Format). Graphics file format originally created by the CompuServe Online Service.

Hierarchical retrieval. Retrieval of an element and its children from an SGML document. SGML retrieval systems are typically able to deliver elements from any level of an element hierarchy.

Hierarchy. The set of relationships between elements in an SGML document. SGML elements may be deeply nested; that is, children may be parents themselves ad infinitum (subject to user-specified limits).

Home page. The main document or top page in a collection of organized information on a Web.

Hostname. Alphanumeric representation of a computer's IP address, which can be converted by the DNS protocol.

HTML (HyperText Markup Language). Document coding language of the Web.

HTTP (HyperText Transport Protocol). The protocol of the WWW.

Hypertext Transport Protocol Daemon (httpd). A type of information server that uses HTTP.

HyTime. ISO standard 10744, a companion standard to SGML for hypermedia and time-based applications.

Image map. Visual navigation item, usually a single image with different "hot spots" corresponding to URLs.

Information node. A discrete piece of information, possibly connected to other discrete pieces of information.

Instance. Encoded text that conforms to a particular DTD and declaration.

Interface. Standard means for interacting with a computer system or program. From a programming standpoint, an interface (generally referred to as an Advanced Programmers Interface, or API) is a standard code base for developing on top of an existing application. From an end-point perspective, the inputs, menus, and dialog systems define the user interface.

International Standards Organization (ISO). An international organization headquartered in Geneva, Switzerland, concerned with the development of standards. Participation in ISO is through national standards organizations such as ANSI (American National Standards Institute). ISO standards are adopted by a vote of member national standards bodies and are reviewed and updated through ongoing processes specified by the ISO bylaws.

IP (Internet Protocol). Standard numbering convention for computers attached to the Internet. It is a best-effort delivery system that takes data and tries to get it from one computer to another over a network. No promises are given that the data will arrive error-free or even arrive at all. (See also TCP/IP.)

IP Packet. An IP packet is the collection of the necessary information needed to move a chunk of data from one computer to another using the IP protocol. This information includes the data itself, the source computer's IP address, and the destination computer's IP address.

JPEG. (Joint Photographic Experts Group). Graphics file format that handles 24-bit color (or 16.7 million colors) and is one of the smallest image file sizes (on disk).

Legacy documents. An existing body of documents you may want to convert into SGML.

Libraries. Established code elements that can be linked to programs to perform specific tasks as needed.

Mailbox. Temporary storage place for e-mail until the user gets around to reading it.

Mainframe. Large monolithic computers that dominated the computing industry in the recent past. These systems were accessed via dumb terminals and were often warehouses of an organization's computing power.

Meta-data. Data that describes data in a document but is not part of the document's contents, for example, the Summary Info or Properties dialog boxes in Microsoft Office applications, which let users add information about the documents, presentations, or spreadsheets.

Mirrored site. Separate server, including both hardware and software, located in a different location than the primary server.

Model. An abstracted description of a system, used in many design and engineering functions to demystify complex systems. An information model looks at the form and flow of focused and specific data sets.

Multicast Protocol. A protocol that drastically reduces the amount of bandwidth needed for certain specific types of applications such as live audio and/or video broadcasts.

Object-oriented programming. Generally, objects are small reusable pieces of code that can be used interchangeably in a variety of ways (a concept known as polymorphism), and can take on properties of upper-level code elements (inheritance).

OLE (Object Linking and Embedding). A means for exchanging data (for example, charts, spreadsheets, and documents) between Microsoft applications.

One-to-many hyperlink. A hyperlink with more than one destination.

Online meetings. An alternative virtual space in which to conduct a meeting.

Open Database Connectivity (ODBC). Standard means for exchanging data between various database systems regardless of their internal mechanisms. Database Connectivity (JDBC) would-be-standard has been created to allow Java applications to interact with a variety of data sources.

Packets. Small blocks of information that contain requests for network services, computer addresses, and data.

Parent-Child. A relationship between two elements such that the element known as the child is contained by the parent.

Parse. In programmatic terms: to divide and compartmentalize data.

Peer-to-peer. A relationship between elements such that the elements are contained by the same parent.

PERL (Practical Extraction and Reporting Language). PERL is an interpreted language. Interpreted languages always exist in source form. They rely on an interpreter that handles the source at runtime.

Personal Address Book. An individual user's address book housed within the e-mail system where one may set up individual entries or distribution lists to facilitate mailings quickly and efficiently. It is essentially an online "Rolodex," with additional options.

PNG (Portable Network Graphic). A new format, currently supported by plug-ins in the Netscape and Microsoft Internet Explorer browsers. PNG combines the quality and size of JPEG with the viewing speed of GIF, producing quality results.

Ports. Defined locations in memory that dictate the path of information transfer between a CPU and its peripherals.

Port number. Another number that helps a computer selectively refine its search for another machine on the Internet to the right service after it finds the right computer using the IP address.

Pretty Good Privacy (PGP). A publicly available program developed by Phil Zimmerman that encrypts data via an electronic key. This freeware is so good the government attempted to ban its use.

Protocols. Sets of rules (communications convention or standard) that enable everyone to understand how something is supposed to work. Protocols exist everywhere in our world and are the basics of our standards.

Public DTD. Strictly, a DTD that may be referenced using SGML's formal syntax for the standard DTDs. Less strictly, any of the DTDs that have been placed in the public domain.

Query. A specific request for information from a data source.

Regular Expression. A formal expression that describes a set of possible combinations or patterns.

Relational Database Management Systems (RDBMSs). Databases that link internal tables via associated fields. Object-Relational DBMSs take this concept one step further, allowing for inherited elements and more flexible data relations.

Rendering. The display of the document on the page, requiring the translation of the source data to a screen image. Basic HTML or SGML may be rendered very quickly, but complex data, such as images or tables, present a more challenging problem. Typographical complexity also slows rendering and, aside from issues of screen resolution, is among the reasons why a "paper" look may not be desirable for online documents.

Retrieval. The "fetching" of a document or portion of a document from the place where it is stored for delivery to an application.

Revision Control. Maintains multiple versions (revisions) of a document, making it possible to recover older versions. Each time a document is checked in, a new version is created and the older version is archived. An SGML system would maintain version information at the component level.

RFP (Request for Proposal). Companies often write up desired specifications and requirements for a particular service or product, then submit it to vendors. Vendors who wish to compete for the contract write a proposal detailing how they can meet those specifications and requirements.

Router. A device connected to two or more independent networks that chooses which network to forward the IP packet onto based on the destination IP address, network bandwidth, and load-balancing algorithms.

Secure Hypertext Transfer Protocol (S-HTTP). Encrypts the transmission of WWW information in the application layer of the network hierarchy.

Secure Socket Layer (SSL). A system of WWW information encryption that occurs between the application and transmission layer in the network hierarchy.

Self-describing. A property of a document such that the rules necessary for the interpretation of its content are part of the document. The term *intelligent documents* is synonymous.

Server. A system that responds to clients' requests with information.

SGML (Standard Generalized Markup Language). An international standard for defining markup languages to encode documents in a way that describes the content and the appearance of document objects.

SGML application. A program that understands SGML syntax and processes SGML documents.

SGML browser. A program that displays an SGML document. (An HTML browser is an SGML browser that displays only HTML.)

SGML declaration. Formal statement of the basic parameters of an SGML document such as its character set, the character sequences used to distinguish markup from the document content, and its utilization of optional SGML features.

SGML editor. Software used to create SGML instances.

SGML transformation. Changing SGML into something else, usually HTML.

Snail mail. The jargon among e-mail users to describe the usual ole way to send mail on paper by post or one of the numerous competing couriers.

Source and destination. On the Web, the source is the place where you started, and the destination is the place you jumped to after clicking on the link.

Staging areas. Servers where users can put files for review and editing prior to making them publicly available.

String. Data definition that specifies that information being presented should be taken as is. For example, while 2 + 2 would be represented as 4 when treated as a numerical data type, "2" + "2" in string form would be represented as "22."

Structured Query Language (SQL, pronounced *sequel*). Standard data dialect used in most RDBMS and ORDBMS systems, it allows developers to create, add, modify, and delete data from a certain source or sources under certain conditions in a certain order.

Styles. A saved set of formatting characteristics for a paragraph or characters that have a name. Styles not only help with conversion but they make the author's job easier. For example, making a title big, bold, and blue will take only one step when applying the style as opposed to three steps without the style.

Style sheets. Collection of styles, often serving an analogous function to an SGML DTD in that the style sheet may define the set of legal objects in a particular document type.

Syntax. The rules for putting together the parts of every language, whether natural (like English or Arabic) or constructed (like SGML or C++).

TCP (Transmission Control Protocol). A protocol that allows computers to have error-free bidirectional communication together over a network. Utilizes IP for routing and delivery with sequencing, error detection, recovery, demultiplexing of services, and guaranteed delivery added to allow error-free communication.

TCP/IP. Combined protocol standard that generally determines how computers send and receive data over the Internet.

Telnet. A network service that allows users to connect to a shell or command-line interface on a host machine.

Transparent GIFs. GIFs with a single color (Red Green Blue value) invisible, allowing images to appear in shapes other than square on your Web page.

Trojan horses. Insidious programs designed to give outside users access to data, individual computers, and, by extension, whole systems.

UDP (User Datagram Protocol). Protocol that allows computers to have error detection and unidirectional communication over a network. Utilizes IP for routing and delivery with sequencing, error detection, recovery, and demultiplexing of services.

UNIX-to-UNIX copy (UUCP). A file, directory, and disk copy mechanism particular to the UNIX Operating System.

URL (Universal Resource Locator). It's that sometimes very long string of characters at the top of your browser that starts with HTTP:// and often includes "WWW." If you put an address there then press Enter, it "tells" the browser what page to open in the World Wide Web or, once your browser opens the address you entered, the URL indicates what page is already open. For more about URLs, particularly about "Relative URLs," see Chapter 5.

Validation. The determination that an instance conforms to the DTD. SGML editors can validate documents as they are being created.

Viruses. Computer programs designed to destroy data on a computer, so named as they tend to replicate in the host system.

Web glut. Sites full of hype, nonsense, trivia, and/or gaudy and poorly executed and designed Web applications.

Workflow. Uses computer networking technology to route work processes in a manner that models the path taken to carry the process from start to finish.

World Wide Web Consortium (W3C). An industry consortium, hosted by MIT, that has taken over most of the development and promotion of standards for the World Wide Web.

WWW (World Wide Web).

WYSIWYG (What You See Is What You Get). The monitor view of documents and files on most word processing and desktop publishing software, and now on some Web authoring tools that displays how the printed page will look.

Index

285

Addison-Wesley Developers Press

Addison-Wesley Developers Press publishes high-quality, practical books and software for programmers, developers, and system administrators.

Here are some additional titles from A-W Developers Press that might interest you. If you'd like to order any of these books, please visit your local bookstore or:

 FAX us at 800-367-7198 (24 hours a day)

 CALL us at 800-822-6339 (8:30 AM to 6:00 PM eastern time, Monday-Friday)

 WRITE to us at Addison-Wesley Developers Press
One Jacob Way
Reading, MA 01867

REACH us online at http://www.aw.com/devpress/

International orders, contact one of the following Addison-Wesley subsidiaries or call 617-944-3700 x5190:

Australia/New Zealand
Addison-Wesley Publishing Co.
6 Byfield Street
North Ryde, N.S.W. 2113
Australia
Tel: 61 2 878 5411
Fax: 61 2 878 5830

Latin America
Addison-Wesley Iberoamericana S.A.
Blvd. de las Cataratas #3
Col. Jardines del Pedregal
01900 Mexico D.F., Mexico
Tel: (52 5) 568-36-18
Fax: (52 5) 568-53-32
e-mail: ordenes@ibero.aw.com
   or: informacion@ibero.aw.com

United Kingdom and Africa
Addison Wesley Longman Group
Limited
P.O. Box 77
Harlow, Essex CM 19 5BQ
United Kingdom
Tel: 44 1279 623 923
Fax: 44 1279 453 450

Southeast Asia
Addison-Wesley
(Singapore) Pte. Ltd.
11 Cantonment Road
Singapore 089736
Tel: 65 223 8155
Fax: 65 223 7155

Europe and the Middle East
Addison-Wesley Publishers B.V.
Concertgebouwplein 25
1071 LM Amsterdam
The Netherlands
Tel: 31 20 671 7296
Fax: 31 20 675 2141

All other countries:
Addison-Wesley Publishing Co.
Attn: International Order Dept.
One Jacob Way
Reading, MA 01867 U.S.A.
Tel: (617) 944-3700 x5190
Fax: (617) 942-2829

If you would like a free copy of our Developers Press catalog, contact us at elizabs@aw.com

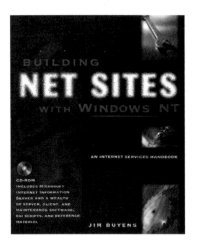

Building Net Sites with Windows NT™

Jim Buyens
ISBN 0-201-47949-4, $39.95 w/CD-ROM

Building Net Sites with Windows NT™ provides the essential tools
and information to build a full Internet site offering Web pages,
e-mail, FTP and more on Windows NT. It covers site planning,
security, site maintenance, and Microsoft's Internet Information
Server. It also explores advanced Web techniques including click-
able image maps, CGI programs, Server Side Includes, Java,
database interfaces, and more. A CD-ROM contains server,
client, and utility software.

CGI Programming in C & Perl

Thomas Boutell
ISBN 0-201-42219-0, $34.95 w/CD-ROM

This book shows you how to create interactive, dynamically-
generated Web pages with CGI programming in two practical
languages: C, which has distinct performance advances, and
Perl, one of the most popular choices for CGI today. You'll learn
how to generate HTML pages and images on the fly, parse form
submissions directly, and much more. The CD-ROM contains a
complete range of CGI software libraries in both C and Perl,
ready to plug into your Web site.

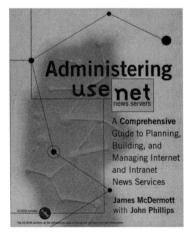

Administering Usenet News Servers

James McDermott and John Phillips
ISBN 0-201-41967-X, $39.95 w/CD-ROM

Administering Usenet News Servers is an indispensable guide to
planning, building, and administering a UNIX news server. The
netnews applications INN and DNEWS are both thoroughly
covered as well as such leading-edge concepts as high-speed
news routers, dynamic sucking feeds, and streaming. It contains
useful background information to help educate USENET new-
comers and to demystify a topic that has to date been shrouded
in Internet folklore. The CD-ROM includes all application
software, utilities, scripts, and URLs necessary to implement
an INN or DNEWS server and keep it running smoothly.

| DATABASED ADVISOR |

The pioneer database magazine

now brings you client-server and Internet/Intranet solutions

✓Intranet ✓Data Warehouse ✓Java ✓ActiveX ✓OLE Automation

Anniversary Issue: Guiding Information Systems Professionals for 13 Years

DATABASED ADVISOR

Which Internet Middleware Works Best?

6 Reporting Tools Turn Data Into Information

How ActiveX Expands Your Web Capabilities

Case Studies:
■ Mainframe-to-PC Data Warehouse is a Hit
■ Just Say "No" to Paper Faxing

ProtoView InterAct:
ActiveX Gives You Hot Graphics

Symantec Café:
Cook Up Java Applets

Oberon Prospero:
Read Data from Any Source

Bluestone Sapphire/Web:
Connect Corporate Databases to the Web

www.advisor.com

WHAT'S ON THE DISK:

Companion Resource Disk

• Source code
• Compiled routines
• Support files
• Extended examples
• Sample applications
• Programming utilities
• Add-on product samples

SAVE TIME:
FAX (619)279-4728
or
CALL 800-336-6060

Advisor Publications Inc.
P.O. Box 429002
San Diego, CA 92142-9002

Since 1983, DATABASED ADVISOR has been a leading provider of real-world advice on developing and managing database systems using state-of-the-art technology. Today, DATABASED ADVISOR remains at the forefront by helping IS professionals select and use distributed Internet/Intranet and client-server database architectures, products, and techniques.

DATABASED ADVISOR SHOWS YOU HOW TO:

• Develop and deploy Internet/Intranet databases
• Design and manage data warehouses
• Manage database development
• Integrate database applications
• Choose the right add-on product
• Manage client-server environments
• Choose and use classes and object programming
• Optimize database servers
• Implement multi-tier and middleware solutions

Subscribe Now & Save $20.00

❑ **MAGAZINE ONLY:** 12 issues just $39.* I'll save $20.00 off the annual newsstand price—that's like getting 4 issues FREE!

❑ **MAGAZINE + COMPANION RESOURCE DISK:** 12 issues + 12 disks for just $129.**
   ❑ Payment enclosed   ❑ Bill me

Name _____

Company _____

Address _____

City _____ State _____

ZIP/Postal Code _____ Country _____

E-mail _____

* Canada add $20; other countries add $40. ** CA residents add $6.97 sales tax. Canada add $40; other countries add $70. U.S. funds from U.S. banks only. Annual U.S. newsstand price $59.88   25031